S. Weir Mitchell

S. WEIR MITCHELL

Novelist and Physician

❧ ❧

by

ERNEST EARNEST

Philadelphia

UNIVERSITY OF PENNSYLVANIA PRESS

1950

Foreword

SILAS WEIR MITCHELL was almost a genius. His contemporaries believed that he was one, an opinion Mitchell came to share. The reasons for this belief were impressive: his book on *Gunshot Wounds and Other Injuries of the Nerves* (1864) was still in use by the French in World War I; his "rest cure" for nervous diseases was famous throughout Europe and America; his discovery of the nature of rattlesnake venom was the foundation stone for later research in the fields of toxicology and immunology; his *Hugh Wynne* was compared to *Henry Esmond*, his *Ode on a Lycian Tomb* to *Lycidas*.

He translated a fourteenth-century poem, *The Pearl*, into modern verse; he wrote a scholarly and controversial biography of Washington, a children's story (*Kris-Kringle*) which went through twelve editions, and an excellent tragic novel about a neurotic woman. These are only highlights: he also wrote thousands of letters, published hundreds of medical papers, several volumes of verse, numerous short stories, two popular books on medicine, and a dozen novels—all this in addition to a medical practice which brought him nearly $70,000 in a peak year. He was equally in demand as a speaker at banquets and before learned societies. Among scores of friends he numbered Oliver Wendell Holmes, Phillips Brooks, Sir William Osler, Andrew Carnegie, William James, Augustus Saint-Gaudens, James Russell Lowell, and George Meredith. He was the patron of such different persons as Hideyo Noguchi and Walt Whitman. He sat on the boards of trust companies, of charitable institutions, and of learned societies. His Saturday evenings at home became famous for good wine and conversation. No wonder he was regarded as the most versatile American since Franklin.

As so often happens, the generation following a man's death tends to forget or undervalue him. This is especially true of persons whose reputations were over-inflated by their contemporaries. For various reasons this process has been particularly operative upon Mitchell. His rest cure is outmoded; his novels are little read. Yet, as the foregoing list of some of his achievements shows, he was important in a number of fields. For two or three decades he was probably the leading psychiatrist in America, and there are few better American novelists between 1885 and 1905. It is time for a revaluation of the man.

No full-length study of Mitchell has appeared since Anna Robeson Burr's *Weir Mitchell, His Life and Letters* in 1929. Although badly arranged, it is useful as a source because it contains the only published form of parts of Mitchell's Autobiography and of numerous letters.

Mitchell papers and letters are widely scattered. In the possession of the family are diaries from 1894 to 1912, the manuscript Autobiography, family letters from Mitchell's student days in Paris, letters to his sons, and the Sarah Butler Wister correspondence. The Mitchell family has permitted me to use all of these.

The following collections have also proved valuable: correspondence with Lowell, Holmes, Henry and William James in the Houghton Library, Harvard; correspondence with John Shaw Billings, New York Public Library; correspondence with Howells, Gilder, James Whitcomb Riley, and Henry Charles Lea, University of Pennsylvania; pamphlets and manuscripts, Philadelphia College of Physicians. In addition I have been permitted to use two extensive private collections of Mitchell papers: that of Dr. Clements C. Fry at the

Yale School of Medicine, and that of the late Dr. Josiah Trent at Duke University.

I am much indebted to the owners and custodians of these various collections. In addition, the reference librarians of Temple University have been most helpful in finding elusive items. *The American Scholar* has permitted me to quote from my article, "Weir Mitchell as Novelist." Among those who have given of their time are Dr. S. Weir Newmeyer, Dr. W. B. Cadwalader, Mr. Homer Saint-Gaudens, and Mitchell's granddaughters: Mrs. William Gammel, Mrs. Vinton Freedley, and especially Mrs. Mitchell Macdonough. Finally, my thanks to Temple University for the grant from the Committee on Research and Publication which made possible the necessary travel and secretarial expenses in the preparation of this work.

E. E.

Gladwyne, Pennsylvania
June 1949

Contents

Illustrations

Philadelphia Boyhood

1829 - 1851

"Fair seed-time had my soul."
—WORDSWORTH, *The Prelude*

WEIR MITCHELL was a Philadelphian. That is perhaps the most important single fact about him. Boston may be a state of mind, but Philadelphia is a way of life. That was especially true before the motor car made possible the exodus of Mitchell's class to the Main Line. The word "class" is important, for Mitchell never forgot that he was a member of a class. His manner of life and his works are products of the most nearly British society in America.

There is no American word for this class. It was not quite an aristocracy, for as a rule it did not hold the highest positions in church and state. It was not the plutocracy of the Vanderbilts and the Astors; it did not own yachts or baronial estates. Nor was it the upper middle class of trade and commerce. "Gentry" most nearly describes it. But it was not identical with the British gentry. It had almost the same sense of family, of living according to a code, but it was not in the nineteenth century a country-estate class. Nor did it look down on earning a living. Its members were executives of banks and insurance companies, the lawyers for estates and corporations; they were editors, and scholars, and clergymen (especially Episcopal) and physicians.

In Philadelphia from the eighteenth century on, the physician has held a high social position—far higher than his British counterpart. M.D. was a title Weir Mitchell always wore proudly. He was contemptuous when told that he could be received into European society if he would drop it from his card. For in Philadelphia medicine had a proud history with names like Thomas and Phineas Bond, Caspar Wistar, Benjamin Rush. In the mid-nineteenth century the city became the medical capital of the country, drawing to its institutions such men as Osler and Billings and producing Pepper, Weir Mitchell, W. W. Keen, and de Schweinitz.

Silas Weir Mitchell was born into this class. His father, John Kearsley Mitchell, was a successful Philadelphia physician, who entertained at his home various notables including Edgar Allan Poe, Bayard Taylor, and Oliver Wendell Holmes. Dr. Mitchell in some respects foreshadowed the career of his more famous son.

In addition to the practice of medicine Dr. John Mitchell held the Chair of Chemistry, first at the Philadelphia Medical Institute and later at the Franklin Institute. Subsequently he held the chair of Medical Practice at Jefferson College. At a time when there was little medical research in America, he published various medical papers, among them one "On the Cryptogamous Origin of Malarious and Epidemical Fevers," one of the most famous monographs in the history of American medicine. This presented the theory that infectious diseases might be caused by minute fungi, a theory which was widely held until the later discoveries of bacteria. Dr. Holmes wrote, saying that he had long thought that "life, growth, germs, swarms" rather than meteorological changes were the agents in contagious diseases, but until he read Mitchell's paper he had not realized how complete an argument could be advanced for such theories.

Dr. J. K. Mitchell was the first in Philadelphia to use ether in childbirth. At medical school young Weir attended a lecture

in which Professor Charles Meigs undertook to demonstrate
the peril of the elder Mitchell's method. This was the same
Dr. Meigs who, in a debate with Holmes, denied the value of
asepsis. A billy goat was etherized until pronounced dead. The
corpse was moved to an adjoining anteroom. As the class
trooped out after the lecture, the goat, very drunk, charged
into the mass of delighted students. Dr. John never tired of
inquiring of his colleague about the patient's health.

Also foreshadowing his son in another field, Dr. Mitchell
dabbled in poetry. His little volume, *Indecision and Other
Poems*, contained a song which became popular in drawing
rooms from Boston to Washington. Its nature is illustrated
by the refrain:

> Oh, fly to the Prairie, sweet maiden with me
> 'Tis as green and as wild and as wide as the sea.

This, despite Dr. John's taste for Dryden and Pope, indicates
that he knew his Tom Moore.

In still other respects the father foreshadowed the son. Physically active, he made great efforts to establish cricket as an
American game. He was fond of social life and became a
member of all sorts of literary societies, including the American Whig Society for the Promotion of Literature, Friendship, and Morality. He set the pattern of extensive entertaining
and dining out which his son was to follow after he could
afford to. "At dinner we had a saddle-of-mutton, soup, fish,
turkey, ham, oyster pie, pies and puddings, jellies, blanc-
mange, whips, fruit, confections in great profusion," Dr. John
wrote home during a visit to Richmond.

The elder Mitchell was, in fact, a Virginian by birth. He
was born at Shepherdstown, May 17, 1793, the son of a
physician, Dr. Alexander Mitchell, who had migrated from
Ayrshire, Scotland. John's mother, Elizabeth Kearsley, died
four years after the boy was born. Two years later Alexander

Mitchell also died. The orphan was sent to live with his maternal grandmother and, at her death, to his father's people in Scotland. He attended the academy at Ayr, where he won prizes in French, Greek, Latin, mathematics, philosophy, and bookkeeping—the last a subject which seems to have helped him little. During the war years 1812-14 he attended the University of Edinburgh. On one occasion on a stage coach, he met and was invited to visit Sir Walter Scott. After some wandering through Scotland, sometimes in company with James Hogg, the Ettrick shepherd, he tried the study of law.

Then, with the end of the war, he returned to America. Although his only estate was two Negro slaves, he set them free. Their rent had paid his fees at Edinburgh. However, when he decided to study medicine, a Kearsley relative provided some of the necessary funds, so that by 1815 John was studying at the University of Pennsylvania. He received further aid from Mr. John Lisle and Dr. Chapman, two men for whom he retained a loyal affection. In fact, he later named a son Chapman. As a further means of paying expenses he interrupted his studies to go as a ship's doctor on a voyage to China. He later made a second voyage. On one of these the ship stopped at St. Helena, where Napoleon was then imprisoned. Mitchell was given a lock of Napoleon's hair and made some verses upon St. Helena. On shipboard he amused himself by making a dictionary of quotations based on Johnson's edition of the British poets.

On his return from the first of these journeys, he resumed the study of medicine and graduated in 1819. As was the custom, he then entered the office of a physician, Dr. Griffiths.

In Philadelphia he fell in love with Sarah Matilda Henry, the daughter of a prosperous merchant. At first her father opposed a match with an impecunious physician. Medicine, for all its high standing in Philadelphia, was not business. In that city a professional man had to establish social position by making money. Since the close of the eighteenth century mere scholars, scientists, and authors have ceased to be important. There has been little of the Bostonian respect for the professor or the scholar as such.

Thus the young man, forbidden to see or correspond with his beloved, made a second journey to China as a way of making money. For a time the young people managed a clandestine correspondence, then, with the relaxing of the parental ban, an open one. In a stilted, condescending manner, Dr. Mitchell advised Miss Henry about her reading:

I hope my dear Matilda will not deem it obtrusive in me to accompany the list of books, made at her request, with a few observations upon the best method of deriving advantage from reading. . . . Now as all English literature is a field wide enough to occupy all the leisure hours of a woman who does not neglect her domestic concerns, and is also the more valuable as it affords conversation suited to the great mass of one's acquaintance; I do not think that your time can be better employed than in acquiring as thorough a knowledge as possible of the best authors of your own language, and by a familiar intercourse with the greatest minds both of your own and preceding ages, to fix and establish your opinions upon the great points of morality and religion.

. . . During your scriptural reading you will become acquainted with a part of the history of the ancient world, and in the interesting work of Rollin you will find the best account of the remainder. I feel much at a loss to direct you to a good author for an account of the decline and fall of the great Roman Empire. The otherwise delightful work of Gibbon, does not appear to me to be favorable to the religion we profess, and I dread to expose you to the insidious innuendoes of apparent impartiality and affected candour. But, with these cautions and the firm hold which I hope religion will have upon your mind, you may venture to glance over the pages of Gibbon . . .

He further advised a reading of Shakespeare as the best means of obtaining a knowledge of human nature "without exposure." Then, after pointing out the importance of reasoning carefully about her opinions, and not, like some women, judging on the basis of external decoration, he closed with what he apparently regarded as a passionate note:

For my part I have again resumed my studies with a determination to distinguish myself that I may the sooner claim the promise of your father, and lead my Matilda to the blessed ordinance which will unite us forever. I cannot forbear at times to murmur at the sentence of separation; but hope still holds her golden visions up to check despondency and to point to happier hours. They are all associated with your image . . . I feel as if I were entering upon forbidden ground and to secure myself from all hazard of breaking my promise, let me assure you that I am
                                        Entirely yours,

The young lady was more colloquial:

Mary is very anxious to know how many sets of ruffles you have soiled and rumpled for the Chinese ladies.

Their meetings at first were also clandestine. On his return he wrote Matilda, saying that after dark he would be between Eighth and Ninth on Chestnut on the north side. She was to let no one know of their plans.

Somehow the parental objections were overcome, and in 1822 John married Matilda. They took a house at 119 South Fifth Street. Here the first three of their nine children were born: Alexander Henry in 1823, Elizabeth in 1825, and on February 15, 1829, Silas Weir.

Until his death in 1858, Dr. John had a great influence on his third child. The father was no longer the rather stilted person of his letter of 1819. In his son's memory he lived as "a model of manly beauty, of perfect courtesy, quick to resent the least imputation upon his honor, believing there was only one way to settle serious difficulties among gentlemen." A strongly built man, six feet tall, he was an excellent shot, skillful at all games, a gay and resourceful companion. Much handsomer than his son, Dr. Mitchell had a florid oval face, clear blue eyes, and wavy chestnut hair which never turned gray. Never had he need of a dentist.

His extrovert, sanguine personality seems to have dominated the home. Whatever worrying had to be done was left for his wife, who, as the family multiplied, seems to have become a bit anxious and querulous. Dr. Mitchell found Philadelphia rather slow; he wished he had settled in New York with its faster pace and more lavish style of living. He noted that whereas in Philadelphia no one spent more than ten thousand a year, New Yorkers spent twenty or thirty, kept handsome carriages, and entertained much more. A physician in New York might make sixteen thousand dollars a year.

Not that Dr. Mitchell was unhappy in Philadelphia. From Richmond he wrote his wife:

How favorably I am situated as to country! My family came from *Scotland*, where I was educated. I was born and raised in *Virginia* and I reside in *Philadelphia*. . . . What wonderful favor God has shown me! Appearance, health, mind, enterprise, industry, education, elocution, birth, residence, unmerited reputation, affectionate friends, the kindest and best of wives, good, warmhearted, healthy children, influential and devoted relations, etc.

Beside such a man the frail, imaginative Weir felt hesitant and inept. Into later life the boy carried the memory of passionate love for his mother and veneration for his father. The boys learned from Dr. John the Virginia code of honor, something Weir carried throughout life and made a recurring theme in his novels. Once at dinner the twelve-year-old Weir told how he had fought a larger boy in a stable. To equalize matters the larger boy had his left hand tied behind his back. Dr. John ordered the boy from the table. "If, sir, you fight and must fight, you must do it like a gentleman." Over fifty years later Mitchell put some of his boyhood memories into the picture of the lads in *All the Woods Are Green*. In it a

father's most crushing reprimand to a naughty son is, "Off
with you—you are not fit to associate with gentlemen."

For many boys, life in the Mitchell family would have been
ideal. Weir remembered the pranks, the fights, the constant
scrapes, the skating on a pond at Broad and Walnut, the pig-
sticking with pins set in a stick. His younger brother Walsh
reveled in war. And it was Walsh who in his teens was the
hero of an adventure on the Schuylkill. Dr. John, then fifty-
six, and his sons Chapman, Ned, and Walsh were skating
above the Fairmount dam, a place where Philadelphians have
managed to drown themselves for a hundred and fifty years.
On this occasion the ice with several hundred persons on it
started over the dam. Dr. John and Ned became separated
from the two boys, Chapman and Walsh. In the vast confusion Chapman became frozen with panic. As the ice went
over the dam, Wally shouted to his brother to jump. Chapman
sat down on the ice. "Get up. If you don't jump on my back,
sir, I'll hit you." With Chapman on his back, Walsh managed
to reach the summer house below the dam. The boys were
taken to the tavern and rolled in blankets.

Weir could admire the courage of his younger brother and
become involved in his escapades, but he was of a different
mold. He was troubled by religious doubts, fearful that the
Holy Ghost would appear to him at night. He carried into
adulthood a memory of hated Sunday school and incomprehensible church. "It was too sober a life for an imaginative
child," he wrote many years later. At seven he told his mother
of seeing a golden chariot with horses and trappings. For this
he was scolded, and on another occasion sent to bed with
bread and water for twenty-four hours for insisting he had
seen a pink elephant on Chestnut Street. Weir never forgot
these incidents. Throughout his professional life he warned
parents not to mistake "richness of imagination for poverty of
moral sense."

On visits to his aunt, Weir was required to learn a daily Bible text and to attend church twice on Sundays. He managed to make the service less boring by smuggling in a copy of *Midshipman Easy*, which he read in a dark corner of the pew. At home because of his mother's Presbyterian training there was an atmosphere of puritanism, which gradually relaxed. Cards were forbidden in the early years. On Sunday there were cold roast beef and cold rice pudding. No games at all were permitted.

Weir's younger sister Sarah had similar recollections of their father. It was to Dr. John rather than to her mother that Sarah took her childish joys and sorrows. Long afterward she wrote, "To my father's care and teaching, and perhaps inherited from him, we owe whatever of courage, patience or endurance we may have." He had the gift of interesting his children, of keeping them in order with an even-handed justice, and of making them believe in themselves. A lie was punished, but truth and honesty were not rewarded; they were taken for granted. Dr. John took Sarah driving with him on his visits to patients, talking to her as if she were an adult. Thus when she asked if the story of the Flood was true, he answered, "It does not matter, but I think not." It was Mrs. Mitchell who insisted that the children daily read three chapters of the Bible and five on Sundays. It was Dr. John who burst into uproarious laughter at the sight of a nurse whose hair Sarah had cut off on one side. He meted out a punishment, but it was his laughter she remembered.

There were games and countless childish pranks. On Halloween they bobbed for apples and burnt their faces with a candle on the end of a revolving stick whose other end held an apple with money in it. Weir once set a table on fire and burned his hand in an attempt to cast lead bullets. On another occasion he saved Sarah's life by beating out the flames when she set her apron on fire. At times they played in their father's office, terrified by the nearness of "the French lady," a skeleton. Once just before his father's lecture to some students, Weir stuck a lump of bread in the lady's mouth.

Weir remembered sitting on the knee of Francis Scott Key and hearing him recite the "Star Spangled Banner." On another occasion when the boy told Dr. Holmes how much he liked "Old Ironsides," Holmes wrote out the verses, a treasure Weir kept throughout life. Other memorable visitors were General Scott and Robert E. Lee.

Young Weir's chief delight was reading. One of his first books was *Robinson Crusoe*. This was stolen by a servant, only to turn up years afterward on a bookstall, where Mitchell bought it for his grandson. His favorite was the *Arabian Nights*, which he read aloud to the other children. Because none of them would do lessons while Weir read, their mother burned the book amid great lamentation. However, on a day that Weir remembered with joy, his father took him in his gig to the Library Company on Fifth Street. The boy first took out Captain Cook's *Voyages*. From this he went on to a huge folio on Peru by Garcilaso de la Vega, and then the *Conquest of Mexico* by Vernal Diaz del Castillo. The boy spent much of his spare time within the gloom of the library's monastic alcoves. It was not the sort of library which would normally attract a child. Around him were yellowed busts of ancient worthies, and at the tables or moving sedately about the room, gray-haired men almost as marble-like. The books were such as to attract the historian and the bibliophile rather than the general reader. Here young Weir developed that taste for history which remained throughout his life and led him to write both history and historical novels.

At home he would take his latest treasure up to his room, where he would sprawl on his stomach and read for hours. There was also a library of two thousand volumes in the dining room at home. The children were taught how to use encyclopedias, encouraged to read aloud, and to discuss their reading. As they got older, mealtime became the occasion for heated literary arguments. Dr. John loved this sort of thing as much as did the older children. Often someone would jump up from the table to find a book which would refute an adversary. The young people liked to tease their father about his taste for eighteenth-century poetry. They would quote some new verse to trap him into an admission that there had been poets since Byron. Thus one New Year's Eve, Weir read aloud Tennyson's *Ring Out Wild Bells*.

It is hard to understand why Weir should remember of his childhood a mood "over and above all, of wearisome ennui." Only in adult life was he free of this. Possibly it had a physical cause. Weir was a frail, bookish boy in the midst of a household of active, vigorous people. He may even then have been tuberculous, for at sixteen he spat blood and was advised to spend as much time as possible outdoors. The long hours of reading and browsing in the library suggest a lack of physical vitality.

Another reason may have been that he found little besides reading to challenge his active, creative imagination. He was not good at cricket, his father's favorite game. Instead, he found one of his greatest joys in going to hear Dr. John lecture on chemistry at the laboratory at Locust Street west of Eleventh. For the boy this was a fairyland. At times he was allowed to take home chemicals, and on one or two occasions succeeded in mildly blowing himself up. His father had an even more heroic adventure. While lecturing he broke a vial of hydrocyanic acid, cutting his hand badly. To the class he said, "Leave the room. It is deadly." Then he plunged his head and shoulders into a tank of water. He called an assistant to open windows and throw water over him, then fell unconscious. As a result he was blind for several days. But this realm of adventure was closed to Weir with his father's resignation due to a growing practice. Sadly Dr. Mitchell burned a drawer full of notes for further research.

Weir's school life was not a challenging experience. His later friend, Talcott Williams, says Mitchell believed that he had been ill taught. There was good reason for this belief. While the Mitchells lived at Eighth Street, the children went to school to the Misses Donnaldson in Blackberry Alley. Later, apparently after the move to 1100 Walnut Street, Weir was sent to a boys' school under the Rev. Joseph Engls, then to one under a cleric named Shaw, who thrashed brutally. Next he went to a school under Enoch Wines at Eighth and Chestnut. Wines he described as an unpleasant humbug, easily seen through by keen-sighted boys. As this was supposed to be a model school, the queer boys and the bad ones were sent there along with the bright ones. Here Mitchell began a life-long friendship with Henry Wharton, "beautiful as a young Apollo." It is possible that Wharton is the painter's model for Jack Warder, "the girl boy" of *Hugh Wynne*.

At about thirteen he went to the University grammar school at Fourth and Arch. This was presided over by another sadistic clergyman, the Rev. Samuel Crawford. "I thank heaven schools are better now," Mitchell wrote many years later. Crawford sat on a raised chair in the center of a large room. Over his head he kept a supply of rattans, four of which were in a tin box to preserve their pliancy. Armed with these "Tobies," as he called them, Crawford marched about the room, distributing stout whacks on the shoulders of the boys. "Now, sir, Toby has a good memory." If he struck a boy by mistake, it would be, "Well, that will do for the times when you deserved it and Toby forgot you; ah, Toby knows the bad boys." The more serious thrashings were given after school. Although Dr. John had asked that Weir be spared the whippings, such an atmosphere must have been a strain on a sensitive boy. Certainly Crawford stood out in his later memories more clearly than the other pleasanter masters at the grammar school. He summed up his experiences: "Of schools . . . I retain no cheerful memories. I loathed lessons and the paths of learning led through a vale of tears and fears."

As might be expected in schools presided over by pious sadists, there was much bullying of the younger boys by the older ones. And once free from these tyrannical masters, the boys of Mitchell's generation became idle and dissipated in the University. He records four who ended up as complete drunkards.

Of his brothers and sisters it was Elizabeth who was nearest to him in age and temperament. Like her brother, she too was an omnivorous reader. Together they would pounce on any new poetry or fiction. Elizabeth had a keen wit in repartee, a quality she never lost in the pain and illness of her later life. Oversensitive, she was inclined to imagine slights or neglect. When aroused she had a dangerous temper. Weir, too, seems to have shared this quality, but in later life learned to discipline it.

On the whole it seems to have been a healthful, cheerful environment for a child. Philadelphia itself still occupied but half the area laid out by Penn between the Delaware and the Schuylkill. Children skated on a pond at Broad and Walnut streets, an area which during Mitchell's lifetime became the center of the downtown district. Before he could remember, the family moved from Fifth Street to South Eighth, and then to a large house at 1100 Walnut Street. It is this home which the boy chiefly remembered. From here he could walk the three or four blocks to school or to his father's laboratory. The library was only six blocks (or, as the Philadelphian says, "squares") distant. Nearly everybody of importance lived within an area not more than ten squares long and three wide.

The big brick homes with white marble steps, religiously

scoured, were built in the famous frying-pan design with the "back buildings" forming the handle. Usually the formal parlor and drawing room occupied the downstairs front. In Dr. Mitchell's home, the room back of the parlor was used for an office. However, office practice was not in vogue; physicians usually called at the home. The dining room and kitchen were in the handle, that is in the back buildings. Here too was the Mitchell bathroom with its huge green tub, so high that it required steps. As the traditional Saturday night bath was still in vogue, the location of the room was not felt as an inconvenience. It was on the third floor back of such a house that young Weir had a room of his own. Here he kept the collection of coins, minerals, and autographs inherited, along with the room, from his brother Alexander, who died in childhood.

In Weir's boyhood the city still retained something of Penn's green country town. There were shade trees on the sidewalk, and on summer nights the fireflies glimmered in city gardens. There was so little traffic that the boys played in the streets. On Sunday afternoons the Mitchell boys rowed out to Smith's Island in the Delaware or went hiking along the Wissahickon Creek. With his friends Henry and Charles Lea and Henry Carey Bird, young Weir went botanizing along the Schuylkill and the Wissahickon.

On hot July evenings Dr. Mitchell would take two or three of the boys for a drive into the country, where they were turned loose to play by the roadside. Sometimes the family spent two weeks at Cape May, a few hours' boat trip down the Delaware. Here they could enjoy gargantuan breakfasts of fish, clam fritters, oysters, cranberry sauce, "split chickens, that looked exactly like Austrian double eagles," honey, and "an archipelago of little dishes." During part of several summers Weir visited his relatives in Jefferson County, Virginia (now West Virginia). Here he fished or lay meditating for hours under the trees. With his friends the four Tucker boys, who lived on a neighboring plantation, he played circus and learned to ride and shoot. At the Tuckers there were daily prayers at which a pious great-grandmother kept order. A drowsy or inattentive boy or servant got a sharp jab from her green umbrella. Evenings were spent in reading or conversation.

A long composition written at the age of twelve tells of a trip to Newport with relatives. Even at that age the boy showed a literary bent: the account is filled with detail unusual in a youngster's writing. The spelling, however, is obviously that of a twelve-year-old. The trip involved a boat trip to Bordentown, "the cars" to Amboy, another boat trip to New York, from where they took a third steamer for Newport. Weir's uncle took him on an omnibus tour of New York. On the boat to Newport everybody got seasick and was tormented by bugs, but the boy noted a beautiful sunset over the East River. He was much impressed by the beauty of Newport, the mysterious stone tower, the bathing and fishing. He tells of people he met, of antiques he saw, of scenery in the neighborhood. Obviously the trip was an eye-opening experience.

By the age of fourteen he was trying his hand at poetry. "The Evening Walk" is a nature poem in the eighteenth-century style. Other unpublished verses during the next few years show experiments with stanza forms. He also tried his hand at prose tales. His first published work was a brief verse, "To a Polar Star," which appeared in the *Nassau Monthly* in 1846.

At fifteen he entered the University of Pennsylvania, then a small school at Ninth and Chestnut streets, only a few blocks from his home. His way of life did not change greatly: he remained more of a schoolboy than a college man.

Thus when at sixteen he spat blood, he was allowed to buy a boat so that he might spend as much time as possible outdoors. He and two of his companions, Wharton and Richards, had saved up twenty-five dollars. With it they bought a bateau which they kept at the South Street Wharf on the Schuylkill. For four years he rarely passed a weekday without a row or a sail, or a game of cricket. He used to lie for hours, daydreaming on the reedy river. Here he learned that aesthetic appreciation of nature which was to last throughout his life.

He was not, however, a solitary recluse. With his companions he went fishing and sailing, sometimes as far as Newcastle. Although he was by nature quiet, he was sometimes led into mischief by the other boys. A favorite sport was stealing peaches and melons from Jersey farmers. In his old age, Mitchell remembered with some pride that he had once stopped a pursuing farmer in his tracks by hurling a melon which broke on the man's head.

Sometimes his companions took too much to drink. On one occasion at Newcastle, a lad they had taken along drank too much whiskey and nearly wrecked the boat. The boys kept the offender standing neck deep in water for a half-hour. Weir himself once drank too much with results which taught him an enduring lesson.

His college life seems to have meant little to him. For one thing he was very young; for another he was late in maturing —a point he mentions more than once. His set devoted their time to billiards and complete idleness. In speculating upon his own escape from such a life, Mitchell thought it was due to the fact that his friends had more money to spend than he had. Also he had "a certain modesty . . . as distinct as that of a girl," which kept him from seeking the local prostitutes. His love of reading gave him resources which many of his companions lacked.

At first his own record was not distinguished. During his freshman year he was twice reprimanded for disorder and once for poor scholarship. During his first term he stood thirteenth in a class of twenty-seven; next twenty-first in a class of thirty. From this low point his work improved, and during the next two years he was on four occasions first in his class. Even so he was reprimanded during his sophomore year for trifling and disorderly conduct in class.

Perhaps the faculty member who most greatly influenced young Mitchell was Henry R. Reed, Professor of Rhetoric. Reed was an admirer of the Lake poets and edited an American edition of Wordsworth. He it was who gave a critical insight into modern literature and encouraged the young man's literary aptitudes. However, because Reed was a gentle person, the gay young men of the college created an uproar in his classes. Mitchell looked back regretfully on opportunities he had missed. Altogether, the University of his day was not a center of intellectual activity.

In his junior year Mitchell entered an oratorical contest with a speech called "Labor." Before he delivered it, the Provost made pedantic corrections, labeled by Mitchell, "Notes by Provost Ludlow, d..n him." In it Mitchell attributed the greatness of England and America to the willingness of people to work with their hands. He took as his text:

> When Adam delved and Eva span,
> Where were a' the gentles than?

On the whole it represented more democratic opinions than were characteristic of his later life.

Life in the Mitchell family seems to have been more challenging than that in the university. There would be evenings when over a bowl of Scotch punch Dr. John would read aloud: Pope, Akenside, Dryden. Then they would sing, led by Dr. John's delightful tenor.

At the end of three years he was withdrawn from college, September 1847, because the illness of his father made it necessary that Weir as the eldest living son should find an occupation. He welcomed the break as an escape from mathematics, which he hated. The young man suggested entering a chemical factory, but Dr. John vetoed this on the grounds that capital would be needed. He favored a mercantile career for his son. Although Weir had no inclination for this, he narrowly missed it. A bachelor cousin of his mother's was a member of a large firm in Manchester, England. He offered a partnership in the business with the promise that Weir should be his heir. Such a chance seemed too good to miss. Without much consultation with Weir, the family accepted the offer. Two weeks later the cousin was lost on the *Lexington*. In later life Mitchell shuddered at the thought that he might have been a British millionaire and an M.P. He was at that time sure he would have gone to the top in any line.

But in 1847 young Weir was much less sure of his own capabilities. When he suggested the study of medicine, his father objected: "You have no appreciation of the life. You are wanting in nearly all the qualities that go to make a success in medicine. You have brains, but no industry." When Weir persisted, Dr. Mitchell gave in, with the condition that there should be no changing. "You have always been an undecided person," he told his son.

Much troubled over his father's words, Weir determined to learn habits of application. Heretofore he had often failed for want of energy. It is probably that Dr. John's own physical energy made it difficult for him to understand his frail, imaginative son. On the other hand, Weir always felt inferior and inept beside his father. With a guilty conscience Weir set about memorizing the names of bones.

In 1848 he entered Jefferson Medical College. Like many another young man in professional school, he found that in college he had not learned how to study. Many a night he fell asleep over the bones he was trying to learn. It seemed to him he could remember nothing. He tried drinking strong

coffee and taking cold showers at night. As his father wanted
him to become a surgeon, Weir fought his own horror of
surgery and attended operations. Time after time he fainted.
His hands were awkward. The young man was in despair.
However, he began to find things to interest him, such as
Dunglison's lectures on physiology. These, like the other lectures, were presented without experiments or illustrations.

This was typical. Within the next thirty years both medicine and medical education were to go through a revolution.
In America in 1848 medical education was still conducted in
the eighteenth-century manner. The lectures were delivered
by practicing physicians who took chairs of medicine as a
means of adding to their prestige as physicians. As late as
1877, Dr. William Welch, in comparing European and American medical schools, said that because of low professorial
salaries a man had to practice to earn a living. "A professor-
ship in a medical college is generally sought as an advertisement in acquiring practice rather than as an opportunity for
study and investigation." In fact, laboratory investigation was
rare. In 1878, when Welch went to the New York College of
Physicians and Surgeons, the leading school in New York, he
found that in the one hundred years of its history it had never
had a laboratory. During the late 1850's John Shaw Billings
found his own medical education to consist of the same lectures repeated year after year. At the University of Pennsylvania Hospital as late as 1887 there was only one microscope
in use, that belonging to Dr. Osler, who had recently come
there. Microscopical studies were so rare that the necessary
equipment was not for sale. In the 70's Dr. Welch found it
necessary to improvise his own, using darning needles for
teasers and a razor brought from home for cutting sections.

It was not until 1869 that President Eliot of Harvard began
the regeneration of medical education in America by raising
entrance requirements, prolonging and increasing the courses

of instruction, and introducing practical methods of clinical teaching and some laboratory training.

Nor was Weir Mitchell the only young man who found himself ill prepared for medical study. He knew a little Greek, some Latin, and could read French poorly. He was more fortunate than most in that he had attended his father's lectures on chemistry and had done a little experimental work. Most young men, said Thomas Huxley at Johns Hopkins in 1876, "come to medical schools without a conception of even the elements of science. They learn for the first time that there are such sciences as physics and chemistry, and are introduced to anatomy as a new thing. . . ."

The saving feature of the medical education during Weir Mitchell's student days was what amounted to the preceptorial system—really an apprenticeship. Young men followed their teachers into the clinics and postmortem rooms. John Billings said that as a student he practically lived in the dissecting room and in the clinics.

During his first year of medical school, Weir studied ten to fourteen hours a day, including lectures. His determination and efforts finally convinced his father that he was in earnest. This and their common interest in the profession drew them together. As Weir learned habits of application, the ennui which had plagued him through the years began to disappear. His health suffered, however, and in the spring of 1849 he developed severe jaundice, due, he believed, to overwork and lack of exercise.

During the next winter he found time to attend several balls and to go to the Assembly in January and again in February. This hallowed Philadelphia institution was then as now open only to those of duly accredited ancestry. In addition, he fell in love with a Miss Chapman of Doylestown—"not a half or a quarter," he wrote his sister, "but wholesale, neck and heels in, beyond the reach of Doctor or Humane Society." The young lady at the moment was visiting in Philadelphia. We do not, however, hear of her again.

At his father's insistence he spent part of the spring and summer of two years in an analytical laboratory. Weir believed this taught him a very necessary lesson in accuracy. One summer, again at the insistence of his father, he worked in Fred Brown's drugstore, an experience he disliked. At the time he felt it a sort of degradation.

In March 1850, Mitchell, aged barely twenty-one, finished his two-year medical course. As his graduating thesis he presented a paper on the Intestinal Gases. During these two years Dr. John's health had improved so that he was able to carry on his practice. In fact, as we have seen, he was hale enough to risk his life skating above the Fairmount Dam. He had, however, abandoned original research. This was not unusual for a practicing physician, but Weir believed that his father's real genius was for research rather than for practice. Certainly his influence and example gave his son a direction which was to hold throughout life. Weir Mitchell was to be a pioneer in developing the scientific spirit in American medicine.

II

Wanderyear

"On the French coast the light gleams and is gone."
—ARNOLD, *Dover Beach*

UNTIL LATE in the century, European medicine was far in advance of that in America, especially in research. Most of the great figures in American medicine during this period studied abroad: Holmes, Pepper, Welch, Billings, and Osler. Fortunately Weir Mitchell also had this opportunity.

The autumn following his graduation from Jefferson he embarked for England accompanied by his sister Elizabeth, she to visit a married sister in England, he to go on to Paris. They sailed on the clipper ship *Tuscarora*, which in mid-ocean caught fire from an accident in the galley. For five hours they were in serious peril, but calm weather made it possible for the sailors to put out the blaze. They made the Channel in fifteen days, but were another six in reaching Liverpool. Weir, not completely recovered from jaundice, was seasick the whole way. He was also homesick. And at home Dr. John was writing, "What a chasm in our means of enjoyment!" The Mitchells were a close-knit family.

In England Weir visited the country seat of a wealthy kinsman, Mr. Alexander Henry. It was the Henry firm for which Weir had once been destined. That the young man was beginning to get a sense of his own importance is shown by an incident during the visit. He and Mr. Henry's son were playing billiards when at ten-thirty the dictatorial parent came in, said it was time for bed, and turned off the lights. Weir relighted them and went on playing. For some reason Mr. Henry took a fancy to his bumptious kinsman, and on parting presented him with one hundred pounds for books and scientific instruments. Weir, much troubled by the gift, wrote to his father for advice. Dr. John counseled him to use it to buy a microscope.

In London Mitchell stayed with a cousin, Dr. Mitchell Henry. Through Dr. Henry the young man met and dined with men who were becoming notable in British medicine: William Carpenter, Richard Quain, James Paget, and William Jenner. Thirty years later Weir Mitchell, famous in his own right, was to dine with Paget and Jenner again. He found that neither remembered the earlier dinner.

In his long letters home he told of visits to Westminster, St. Paul's, and other points of historic interest. With his love of history and literature he found them fascinating. He went also to visit British hospitals, which did not impress him, and listened to an acrimonious debate among a group of physicians. He commented on the low social position and consequent lack of polish of British doctors.

Late in November he left for France. The night before embarking he did not go to bed, for he wanted to see the famous chalk cliffs and the sunrise. As the crossing was rough, everyone but Mitchell got sick. He held a baby for a charming French matron, who was too ill to care for the child.

In Paris he looked up some American students, one of whom, Barnet, found him a fine large room in the Latin Quarter next door to a student named Pearce from Providence, Rhode Island. It had comfortable armchairs and a sleeping alcove which could be closed off. As he found the landlady's *table d'hôte* good, he took his meals there, the expense for board and room being only twenty-six dollars a month. To his mother he described his routine. He arose about seven, had *café au lait,* went to the hospital, and returned about eleven for "breakfast": beefsteak, chops, or omelette; potatoes, fruit, coffee, and of course *vin ordinaire.* If he wished, he could have a bite of lunch. Dinner was at six, with soup, fish; beef, chops, or poultry; salad, vegetables, wine, and cheese. He was comfortable and happy.

Paris fascinated him: the places of historic fame, the bridges at night with thousands of lights, the petite, stylish women— so different from the big-footed, graceless English women he had seen. "You begin to love Paris with all the love which enthusiastic admiration can inspire," he told his mother. But he added that she was not to be alarmed at his admiration for the French girls.

He visited museums, attended the opera, and was entranced by the acting of Mlle. Rachel in the plays of Racine, although he was somewhat shocked on hearing of her illegitimate children. Once on the street he saw Byron's famous mistress, the Countess Guiccioli, now remarried and respectable, but still handsome and looking no more than forty. It was a glimpse into the fabulous past.

Nevertheless the distractions of Paris did not keep him from medical study, for he was an ambitious young man. As he told his mother, he hoped he and his brothers could build up a family name and reputation.

At first he had difficulty in understanding the lectures, but he could get along in the clinics and still better in the operating theaters. However, as the classes of popular lecturers were 250 or more, it was often difficult to get more than a glimpse of a patient. He used every opportunity to speak French and took a month of lessons for twelve dollars. In the evenings he studied or went to cafés and theaters. One café in particular was his favorite because of its associations with Rousseau and Voltaire. Here students, professors, and mustached officers gathered to drink and play dominoes. "In we walk and cry gar-r-r-con, rolling the r." The waiter would hurry over, take their orders, and sprinkle bread crumbs on the table to make the dominoes slide easily. It was all very different from Philadelphia, different and fascinating.

His innate puritanism and his mother's teachings kept him from plunging into the dissipations of the city. He told her that she need not fear that he would disregard her wishes about Sunday night; he never went to places of amusement on that evening. And when he went with some fellow students to a *bal masqué* at the Grand Opera he wrote a description of it to his mother. The *can-can* he compared to a witches' sabbath. It was characteristic of him that when he went with Professor Robin to a friend's rooms where they found half a dozen men "and two females," Mitchell did not join in the card game. (Once when he had won a hundred dollars from a man who could ill afford to pay, he had dropped it into the collection plate at church.) Robin, who started with twenty francs, ended up with eight thousand, much to Mitchell's delight, for it had been won from two bankers who proposed the game. Robin took Pearce and Mitchell to dinner, where the latter taught the waiter to make tomato salad.

Robin, the professor of microscopy, seems to have liked the young Americans, who were generous about buying him dinners. He was a bachelor, who made a small income by teaching. On Sundays he dined with Pearce and Mitchell at the Café Maguy, where he ate and drank for three. On one occasion when a student asked why he used only one eye in microscopy, Robin gouged out his glass eye, to the amusement of the class. With one hundred and forty dollars of Alexander Henry's gift Mitchell bought the best microscope that could be obtained, and for his father he hunted up books on microscopy. In America this was a relatively unknown field, as is shown by Osler's experience at the University of Pennsylvania and Welch's in New York.

Another man who had an important influence on Mitchell was Claude Bernard. Throughout his life Mitchell was to have stupendous luck in meeting men who were to become famous. Paget and Jenner, whom he had dined with in England, are cases in point. Claude Bernard was another. Here was a man who became one of the leaders in European medicine of his generation. During the 1850's he made famous investigations of digestion and the functions of the pancreas. Along with his German contemporary, Rudolph Virchow, he formulated the standards of methodology which were to become standard in modern medicine. Young Mitchell had a memorable example of this when on one occasion he stated that he thought this or that to be the case. Bernard's answer was, "Why think when you can experiment? Exhaust experiment and then think." The remark deeply impressed the young man. In fact, it sums up the European point of view, a point of view which men like Mitchell and Welch were to introduce into America.

However, Mitchell's studies were interrupted by an almost tragic illness. At the hospital one day, Chomel called him and another student in to observe a smallpox case. Mitchell felt the patient's pulse. Fifteen days later, after a Christmas dinner with his friends the Walshes, he came down with the disease. He spent two weeks in bed, cared for by his friends Barnet, Pearce, and Bache. Bache, hearing him curse over the hard French pillows, had a softer one made for him. A Miss Phillips brought him jelly, and the elderly consul, Mr. Walsh, traveled two miles daily to inquire about him. Even the landlady was sympathetic. "Never again talk to me of men being selfish," he wrote his mother. After he recovered, he developed an eye infection which made it impossible to study. Altogether he lost about six weeks of precious time.

There were other complications. His mother wanted him to deliver letters of introduction to American friends. Protestingly he did so. To her he listed the disadvantages:

Item a cab to and fro 62 cts.
Item Kid gloves 30 to 62 cts. à discretion
Item a card: value unknown
Item a dinner
Item its consequence: a headache
Item Bored to death.

By March he was spending four, five, or more hours a day experimenting with the microscope, studying tumors, or whatever he could lay his hands on. Shortly after this he arranged to take one or two private courses, one of them on auscultation. He pitied the poor consumptives who had to allow five or six students to thump their chests. Such courses, although forbidden, were commonly offered by professors trying to add a little to their incomes. He also practiced with the catheter and, at his father's suggestion, made some clinical study of gynecology. As Holmes had discovered eighteen years before, medical students in Paris had a wealth of post-mortem material for study. In addition he did some work in ophthalmology. Considering the variety of subjects he tried to cover in a few months, it is small wonder that he felt "lamentably deficient" in many branches of medicine. His brilliant Boston friend, Bigelow, seemed by comparison to have scientific knowledge in almost every field.

It is remarkable that he got any work done at all. Almost daily he wrote long letters to his mother, father, brothers, or sister. And scarcely had he recovered from smallpox than he had to face the problem of Lizzie. Every few days she wrote him long accounts of her unhappiness at the Neilsons. The letters, frequently written crisscross, must have taken hours to decipher and still other agonized hours to answer. They are not pretty reading. Elizabeth constantly charged her sister Saidie (Mrs. Neilson) with being unsympathetic. Thus:

It has given me much pleasure to be with Saidie this winter and contribute to her happiness as far as lay in my power, but it is very hard after making sacrifice for those you have loved to find your honest efforts unappreciated and yourself misjudged.

The irony of this is that the Neilsons were in desperate financial straits; Saidie bore a seven-months baby, and then became so ill that she could not travel to America. They had enough to worry about without a complaining guest.

Elizabeth would have visited Cousin Agnes, who, however, did not renew an earlier invitation. This again

. . . wounded me deeply . . . I never prided myself on my powers of attraction but now begin to believe I am positively disagreeable. What would I not give for women's sole valuable dower beauty. I have a loving heart but it only seems to make me miserable.

The next plan was to visit Weir and travel with him on the continent. Letter after letter protests her willingness to return home if she will be a burden, but every letter tells of the great disappointment it will be not to see Europe. She wrote her father and got permission for the trip. To him she was most obsequious:

Yours being the wisest head I would prefer having your advice to "going my own gait" which is but a lame one when I lose your guiding hand.

Then there was the problem of lodgings. If she went to France before mid-June, it meant that Weir had to give up his rooms in the Latin Quarter and find others more suitable for a woman. He also had some hope of studying in Vienna. In fact, he suggested to Dr. John that he would like more time to study abroad. When Elizabeth heard this, she was horrified:

The very idea of your remaining abroad for another six months after my return makes me miserable. What should I do without you for a long dreary winter?

She said she hoped their father would consent, but she was sure he would not, that he had his heart set on having Weir's professional help. Therefore if Dr. John refused, Weir should bear his disappointment cheerfully. After all, it would break their mother's heart to have him away for another winter.

So it was that by the end of April she sailed for Havre. This meant that Weir had to make a day's journey to meet her, and had to take rooms distant from the hospital where he was studying. There is no doubt that Elizabeth was partly motivated by genuine affection for her brother, selfish as she might be. In fact her protestations of love are much more those of a sweetheart than a sister.

You may love Saidie as much as you please so that I stand number one. She does not need your love and I do most desperately.

From an adolescent such letters would have been less indicative of neurosis. But Elizabeth was twenty-five, four years older than her brother.

To his mother Weir wrote that it would be necessary to give up many of his studies in order to play the "gentleman cicerone" to his sister, a task he would undertake with "a sort of willing reluctance." He rejected his father's proposal that Elizabeth's travels be postponed so that he might study a little longer. She deserved to be rewarded for "a gloomy, yet dutiful winter." With the rather ostentatious chivalry which he sometimes used he stated that, "One kiss from her would pay for a greater sacrifice."

Soon after Lizzie's arrival Weir was able to write home that she was happy as a queen. In June they started on a three months' tour of the continent. Dr. John added a credit of one thousand dollars to the twelve or fifteen hundred dollars (Weir wasn't sure which) that he had deposited in the fall for his son's use. Weir had spent only about seven hundred dollars of the original amount.

Before they left, he searched for a telescope which his father wanted, and he bought some medical books to send home, among them two or three on "animal magnetism." Dr. John, who had long been an experimenter with this, had unusual ability to hypnotize subjects. Apparently he used it more for parlor tricks than as a form of medical treatment, but he seems to have been interested in its possibilities.

Weir and his sister went to Italy, where they visited Naples, Rome, Florence, Bologna, Terrara, Padua, Venice, Verona, and Milan. It seems to have been a rather eventful journey. At least part of the time a pugnacious young American named Johnston was with them. Thus, when at Naples they were cheated by the police and the American consul, the two young men went back and forced both parties to restore their ill-gotten gains. Here too they got into a row with a cab driver. This time they wound up in the guardroom of the palace, whence they were extricated after an appeal to the minister, Mr. Morris. They were warned to leave the country lest a stiletto be stuck into their backs. Instead they went on to Capri, where Mitchell, angered by a boatman who tried to drag Lizzie into the boat, knocked the man backwards into the bay. Again they were warned to leave before they were murdered. Instead they stayed out of crowds and remained indoors at night. In Rome Weir saw French officers run their swords through a young peddler accused of selling explosive cigars. In Tuscany he stood in his carriage while a young peasant was shot by Austrian soldiers—a scene which long haunted him. Europe in 1850 seemed a pretty savage place to a Philadelphian. In the Papal States conditions seemed worst of all. His experiences stirred up his patriotism. After complaining of the lying and extortion he met with so often in Italy, he wrote home:

All this teaches one to love and honour our own free home where passports are not and honesty is. I am more a democrat than ever.

I have always been for free trade. I am now yet more so and as
for monarchies I begin to think regicide a noble virtue.

Despite all this he found much to enjoy: St. Mark's Cathe-
dral, the works of art in the Vatican and the museums of
Florence, the beauty of the countryside. In Florence he stood
before the Venus de Medici and reconstructed in his mind the
Grecian temple with beautiful girls bowing before the statue
of the goddess. He especially enjoyed the paintings of
Raphael, and studied the development of the painter's work.
But the thing that most appealed to him was the Apollo Belvi-
dere. When the party visited the studio of the American
sculptor, Hiram Powers, Weir found that Powers agreed with
him, that this was "the king statue."

At Verona, where they had a two-hour stop-over, they
took a carriage to the tomb of Juliet. Weir laid a copy of
Shakespeare upon her tomb. At Lake Geneva he looked out
of one window toward Ouche, where Byron wrote *The
Prisoner of Chillon;* from another he could see Clarens, where
Rousseau had lived. They took a boat out to the castle and
visited the dungeon where Bonivard had been imprisoned and
where Byron's name was carved on one of the pillars. Weir
traveled with Byron often in his mind.

It was a sentimental journey, and the Americans were very
young and a little naïve. Weir admired all the right things,
and wrote home guide-book descriptions of what he saw. But
he traveled with alert eyes and surprisingly few prejudices.
Despite occasional dirt and smells, and dishonest officials, he
found much to admire in both scenery and people. Throughout his life Italy remained a land of enchantment to which he
always returned with pleasure.

From Italy they went to Switzerland. Here too the young
men got into a row. At one point while the horses were being
changed they walked over to admire a bridge. The surly
German driver of the coach started off without them. Weir

seized the bridle of the lead horse while the driver applied the whip. The young man was dragged about twenty paces before Johnston came to the rescue. Thinking that the driver had hit Weir with the whip, Johnston was about to beat him up when Mitchell shouted that he had not been touched. The party drove off amid laughter by some Swiss officers at the driver's defeat.

In Switzerland they climbed mountains and glaciers. One day they traveled on muleback for ten hours and a half. After a day spent climbing the glacier to the Jardin Vert of Mount Blanc, Weir wrote that it was the most terrific feat he had ever undertaken. "How Sis stood it I know not." And she had also partaken liberally of the cognac with which they had refreshed themselves during a pause for rest. They returned to London by way of Brussels and Paris. In London Weir complained of the change from light wine to malt liquors and from "good cuisine which half digests one's food to the cannibal habits of England." His European travel had also made him critical of British taste. The arrangement of furniture, the statues in museums, even the jewelry, were "inconceivably poor."

He had written home pleading for a second year of study abroad. Because of the loss of time due to smallpox and subsequent abscesses, he felt that he had not accomplished much. Before leaving Paris he had written: "The little I have done here is child's play. I have learned next to nothing. I feel unsettled, and instead of a year of fair work which would show results, what have I to exhibit?"

However, Dr. John wrote that he needed Weir at home, and Mrs. Mitchell reinforced this by telling of the pressure of work: three or four consultations a day in addition to his usual practice. Dr. John's health was again failing. So it was that on September 17, 1851, Weir set sail for home to become his father's assistant. He had managed to keep almost enough money to pay for his own and his sister's passage, so that he was able to decline his father's offer of more funds. It may be that he was right in thinking what he had done was mere child's play, that he had learned next to nothing, but his horizons had widened. He had breathed a freer intellectual air than that of Philadelphia. Above all, he had learned how much there was to learn and how to go about getting knowledge.

III

The Young Doctor

1851 - 1861

"What fairer seal
Shall I require to my authentic mission
Than this fierce energy?"
—BROWNING, *Paracelsus*

BY MODERN STANDARDS, Weir Mitchell was ill trained for the practice of medicine. It was not only that medical knowledge was limited and medical education lacking in genuine scientific methods; there was also his lack of hospital experience. He had never served an internship. He wanted to do so at the Pennsylvania Hospital, but because of a controversy between Dr. John and some of the trustees, he never received an appointment. Instead, he had to accept the position as physician to the poor at the Southwark Dispensary. Thus he acquired experience but, as he says, "at the cost of very great labor."

As Dr. John wished, Weir still struggled to become a surgeon. In France he had against his own inclinations studied surgery rather than medicine. At home he performed a number of operations, one or two of importance. But he found that he had neither the nerve nor the hand for operating. That this disability was physical rather than psychological is suggested by Mitchell's handwriting. Relatively early in life it developed the characteristic tremor which became very marked in his last forty years. Thus even in years of physical

34

and intellectual vigor Mitchell's handwriting looks like that of an aged man. Apparently his nervous temperament led to a lack of precise muscular control. During the 1860's Dr. W. W. Keen observed that Mitchell's hands trembled during operations although he never saw him injure a nerve, blood vessel, or tissue he desired not to cut. Much to his father's disappointment, therefore, he abandoned surgery for general medicine.

Inspired by his father's example and by his experiences in France, Weir plunged into a program of research. Within a year after his return to America he published a paper "On the Various Forms of Uric Acid Crystals." It is probable that this was the result of work begun under Robin, his professor of microscopy in France. It will be remembered that Mitchell and Robin usually dined together on Sundays. Certainly it was not his older American colleagues who inspired a program of research. Among those who discouraged him was Professor Samuel Jackson, who warned that every experiment in the laboratory would lose Mitchell a patient.

It was a strenuous program the young man of twenty-three worked out for himself. He would get through his medical work at three or four in the afternoon. Leaving his servant at home with orders to come to the laboratory if he were needed, Weir would work through the evening, sometimes until one in the morning. He would have a light supper brought in from a neighboring inn. For in Mitchell's day even a young professional man could afford services a man today would have to perform for himself. Telephones which must be constantly answered and motor cars which must be parked, garaged, and taken here and there for servicing are not entirely labor-saving devices.

Obviously such a program left little time for social life. By 1855 Dr. John had to give up practice entirely, although he continued to hold the chair of Medical Practice at Jefferson.

Thus at twenty-six Weir Mitchell was carrying the whole burden of the family. He gave up his summer vacations in order to have time for research, and began a series of studies of the nature of snake venoms. In this work he became associated with William A. Hammond, who was to become Surgeon General of the United States during the Civil War. Hammond, who was only a few months older than Mitchell, had something of the same type of mind. He was energetic, original, and facile with a pen. Like Mitchell, he published both medical papers and fiction. In addition, he wrote plays. Both became leaders in the new field of neurology. Their early work in the study of snake venom was the beginning of an association which was to be of great importance to both men.

The results of their work did not begin to appear in print until 1859, when their first paper "On Carroval and Vao" came out in the *American Journal of Medicine*. Shortly afterward a second paper on the same South American snake venoms was published by the Academy of Natural Sciences. During their work, Hammond mentioned that in Texas he had successfully used a certain antidote for rattlesnake poison. At the same time, a man knowing of Mitchell's interest in snake venoms offered to sell him half a dozen rattlesnakes. In order to test the truth of Hammond's statement Mitchell bought the snakes. He soon proved to his own satisfaction that the antidote had no value.

Mitchell thus began a study of rattlesnake venom which was to occupy him for many years and in the end to open up new paths in toxicology and immunology. Some of the results were published in 1860 by the Smithsonian Institution in a 150-page treatise. A list of Mitchell's publications, independently and with Hammond, shows that this was part of a larger area of study: the field of alkaloids.

Mitchell gives an interesting account of the thought processes which go into the working out of a scientific problem:

Ideas about snake poison, how to do this or that, the phenomena it causes in animals, occupied my mind incessantly. I took it to sleep with me and woke to think about it, and found it hard to escape when in church or conversing with people. It is something like being haunted, this grip a fruitful research gets upon you. You come upon a difficulty, try to think a way out of it. This happens continually. You are like a cat watching a mouse. . . .

The process is not very unlike that which is present when in fiction or verse you wait, watching the succession of ideas that come when you keep an open mind. And acquiring the habit of an open mind is not always an easy matter especially if you have occupations outside of your work. In fiction and poetry, the form of expressing a thing has to be considered. In science, this is primarily of little moment, but always I think that I think best when, having come to a critical point, I state a theory which I am going to accept or reject as experiment decides. I must always write it out, sometimes again and again. This is a favorite method with me for fruitful thought. Above all, when engaged in any form of production, my mind is turned on to it as one winds a piece of machinery and waits to see it grind out results. I seem to be dealing with ideas which come from what I call my mind, but as to the mechanism of this process, beyond a certain point it is absolutely mystery. I say, "I will think this over. How does it look? To what does it lead?" Then there comes to me from some inward somewhere criticisms, suggestions, in a word, ideas, about the ultimate origin of which I know nothing.

It is interesting to note that for Mitchell, at least, the same mental processes are involved in scientific research and in the writing of fiction and verse. In *The Road to Xanadu*, Professor Lowes has described this process in the mind of Coleridge as he produced *The Ancient Mariner*. And in *Green Laurels*, Donald Culross Peattie argues that most great scientific discoveries originate in the same manner. The inductive method, supposedly the source of such discoveries, is rather the tool by which they are tested. The discoveries themselves originate in thought processes which are little understood.

Mitchell himself had a dramatic experience of the strange workings of a mind engaged in a scientific problem. Over twenty years after the publication of the Smithsonian treatise, he was going up the steps of a house where he had once lived. Absorbed in thought, he took out his keys; then remembering he no longer lived there, he rang the bell. At his feet was a door mat whose partly unraveled ends reminded him of a serpent. Suddenly there came the idea that the poison of snakes must be a double and not, as then thought, a single poison. Whether this idea was the result of past thought or due to the activity of the subconscious mind he could not tell.

He went home, had dinner postponed for fifteen minutes, and sat down to write out his reasons for believing snake poison must be double. The next day, with the aid of Professor Reichert, he began experiments to prove his theory. It was five months before they succeeded.

This work was not without its hazards. On one occasion a six-foot rattler shipped from Arizona arrived at the office in a wooden box. Mitchell let it stay there overnight before sending it to the laboratory in the morning. During the evening, as he was reading in the office, the snake got loose, climbed up the back of Mitchell's chair and put its head over his shoulder. Mitchell sat still and watched the reptile, fascinated by the lamp, sway its head back and forth. Then the snake touched the hot globe and drew back in anger. The man and the snake watched each other while Mitchell cautiously reached over to his desk for a large metal paper cutter. Getting hold of it he struck the snake a quick blow on the neck knocking it to the floor. He escaped from the room until the snake could be captured in a net.

Characteristically Mitchell, on the publication of the study of 1860, had a copy sent to Dr. Holmes. Holmes reciprocated by sending a copy of *Elsie Venner*. "It is a little bit rattle-snakish as you will find out."

This is typical of Mitchell's habit of making the most of every important contact. Holmes had been a guest of Dr. John's and had written a long letter on his publication of the pamphlet "The Cryptogamous Origin of Fevers." Therefore when in 1858 Weir wanted to get some verse into the *Atlantic*, he sent it to Holmes, apparently asking for criticism and recommendation.

The following year he wrote Holmes about a very different sort of project: a study of the physical statistics of the native-born white population. He had already submitted the plan to the Philadelphia Academy of Natural Sciences. A committee of the members agreed to help, as did the Smithsonian Institution. Mitchell himself had already examined five hundred mechanics. He had worked out two forms for the collection of data: one for the trained examiner, the other and simplified one to be filled out by manufacturers or foremen. What Mitchell wanted of Holmes was aid in getting similar data on college students. He proposed that colleges keep a permanent record of height, weight, etc., of their students. Or if a permanent record was out of the question, perhaps colleges could aid in the collection of such information.

Mitchell seems to have had in mind a comparison of the physical characteristics of the working class with those of the upper classes. As he told Holmes fifteen years later, he believed that, as with the aristocratic class in England, the descendants of the upper class in America (for example, descendants of the Signers) would show finer physiques than would be found in the lower middle class. It was in the latter that one saw "the worst examples of bad types," whereas most of the Philadelphia families "of historical or social note are healthy and even vigorous." He went on to list the families represented in the ancestry of his own boys and to speak of their physical vigor. Mitchell had either forgotten or was trying to refute Holmes' idea that better diet and care may have had something to do with the superior physique of the more favored classes.

Mitchell's study has a modern quality, the gathering of a large body of statistics, and the use of the questionnaire method. It was the sort of thing which was to change medicine from an art based on subjective criteria to a science resting upon a mass of experimental data. But his point of view was pure Philadelphian. He chose wisely in his correspondent: it was a point of view a Bostonian could understand.

Mitchell's custom of following up important contacts is also shown in a letter of 1851 to Dr. John Warren of Massachusetts, recalling a conversation about etherization and reporting Dr. John's remarks in a lecture which gave credit to Warren for using and sanctioning the use of the new anesthetic. Weir Mitchell was to use this technique throughout his life. Sometimes it would be to send a recent book of his to a celebrity; sometimes to recall an introduction or to praise a man's work. In a number of instances this technique brought about further correspondence or a genuine friendship. It was in this manner he came into contact with Francis Parkman, James Russell Lowell, and George Meredith.

Weir Mitchell was no mere toady. It is significant that many of these exchanges of letters led to lifelong friendships. Frequently, as with Warren, Mitchell was eventually able to do the man a service. Thus, forty-three years after his letter to Warren, he used his influence to have Warren's son made an associate fellow of the College of Physicians, and a year later tried to help him get a position he desired. Parkman asked medical advice and Lowell became a patient of Mitchell's, writing descriptions of his symptoms and asking for advice. Meredith reported the results of a buttermilk regimen Mitchell had recommended.

These years when Mitchell was getting established in his practice and at the same time carrying a heavy program of research were also full years in his personal and family life. Much of the time they were troubled years. In 1855, only four years after Weir had begun practice, Dr. John suffered a stroke from which he never completely recovered. A school friend, Elisha Kent Kane, was lost in the Arctic. Weir's brother Walsh began to be a problem. And during 1856 Weir met and wooed Mary Middleton Elwyn.

As Miss Elwyn lived in a lovely colonial country house, "Reculver" near West Chester, Weir had to go to considerable trouble to do his courting. This involved getting up at six with "half a sleep, half a wash, and half a breakfast, up to the cars, tumble in, and so two and a half mortal hours to West Chester. . . ." Here he put up at a hotel, spent an hour smoking and observing the town characters. They proved to be very curious about the visitor's affairs. Then he hired a guide and went driving along the Brandywine. Here he met a friend who was fishing. They dined together and Weir tried to persuade him to go along to Reculver. The young man said that he had no desire to spend the afternoon talking to Mrs. Elwyn. This was exactly what Weir had wanted him to do. At five Weir drove out to the Elwyns' for tea. About eight, another couple started to drive back to town under a gorgeous August moon. Weir and Miss Elwyn rode halfway with them and then walked back by moonlight. At nine-thirty his carriage was brought round and he had to leave. He had no doubt he was in love.

At home he wrote verses and resolved on other visits. The next time he sent a basket of flowers as thanks for a pleasant evening. The couple soon became engaged.

Elizabeth Mitchell did not give up her brother without a struggle. In connection with an earlier flirtation of Weir's she had written, "I would rather you married an arrant fool than

so coarse a woman." And when Weir wrote of his journey
to Reculver, Elizabeth, who was in New England, wrote:

I think you were hasty. I wish I could be at home with you, for
you dear old boy, are my future. I cannot tell you what you are
to me and just now I feel so eager to be with you, I feel as if I
could almost fly to you.

Weir answered with heavy-handed jocularity and went on
with his plans. Before the date set for the wedding, Dr. John
died on Easter Sunday, April 4, 1858. Throughout his life
Weir, who ordinarily forgot anniversaries, remembered that
one. Fifty-four years later he was still noting it in his diary.
Weir had always stood somewhat in awe of his father and had
depended upon him for intellectual leadership. A few years
before, because of Dr. John's opposition, Weir had given up
plans to lecture during the summer despite the fact that "the
temptation to me is immense."

As his father had wished, the wedding took place on schedule. Weir married Mary Elwyn in September. They went to
Reculver for their honeymoon.

At once Weir had to assume the burden of two families.
Dr. John had lived in the lavish style of Virginia, so that there
was not enough of an estate to maintain his family in comfort.
Weir's practice had been bringing in about two thousand a
year; with his father's death, it dropped to one thousand dollars. Many patients, aware of Dr. John's failing health, had
continued to come in the belief that the older physician was
advising his son. Now at twenty-nine Weir had to establish
his own reputation. He was appointed that year to St. Joseph's
Hospital.

Immediately his vigorous personality involved him in a controversy. There were no trained nurses except sisters, who
at that time were very ill prepared for their duties. Mitchell
found that they were first given kitchen duties and then
brought into the wards, where under an older sister they

picked up their training in a hit-or-miss fashion. He charged that patients were sometimes "sacrificed to the presumed necessity of attending religious services." As the rules of their sisterhood forbade a man to live in the same house, there could be no resident physician. After several unfortunate accidents Mitchell tried to remedy some of these defects. When he failed in his efforts, he resigned. Partly because of this experience he became a pioneer in the movement for schools of nursing.

Somewhat later he tried teaching. He was invited to teach physiology at a summer school of medicine. Athough he had some leanings in that direction, he says he never became a good teacher. He disliked to lecture because of his poor memory; he found he had to relearn his material each year.

None of this brought in much money. However, in providing for his mother, sister, and three younger brothers he had some assistance from his English kinsman, Alexander Henry, who made the family an allowance of twelve hundred dollars a year for some time. This, however, was much diminished during the Civil War by American income taxes. Weir's own family was increased by a son, John, born in July 1859. A second son, Langdon, was born February 1862.

The burden of two families was psychological as well as financial. There were worries and problems. Thus in 1859 we find him advising Elizabeth, then in her early thirties. A letter of hers had caused him some tears. He speaks of "a baseless jealousy which has been the shadow of your life, not only now but always," and refers to Dr. John's warning about certain shoals on to which she might drift. The letter is a cryptic one, but it suggests that Elizabeth was high-strung and neurotic. This is borne out by the portrait of her as Anne in *When All the Woods Are Green*. When we remember that since childhood Elizabeth had been Weir's favorite, it seems possible that she may have been jealous of his new bride.

Another worry was his brother Robert Walsh, whom the family called Walsh or Wally. At his own wish, he was sent to Panama in 1859. From there he wrote to Weir about getting involved in a duel with a Spanish officer. The officer died, whether from a wound or from yellow fever, Walsh was not sure. There were other brawls, injuries, personal and financial difficulties. His long, misspelled, and often sprightly letters are filled with accounts of adventures with revolutionists in which Walsh was always a hero. Weir angered him by suggesting that his brother had a "slight tendency to vivify and expand" his statements. In other letters Walsh is contrite; Weir is an old stick-in-the-mud, but a fine fellow. It is too bad Weir had to sell some stock to support their mother, but there are all sorts of bright prospects with the Panama Railroad Company, or he will go to Aspinwall, or maybe to Rio. If there should be a war, he might distinguish himself in the army. He has altered his way of life and is reading the Bible nightly.

Each letter contains new promises, but the bright hopes never materialized. He sent trinkets, Indian relics, but no money. Nor could he ever seem to get hold of the poisons Weir wanted for experiment. Always someone failed to supply the "wooraro" (curare) which had been promised. Maybe he would come home and study medicine or divinity. He loved Fanny Butler, but would Weir find out who had reported them engaged? Someone must have read his mail; he was sure he had not talked too much.

So it went. In 1861 Weir had to pay debts of three hundred dollars for his brother, and he helped get him a lieutenant's commission in the army. At the same time he was paying Ned's college expenses and giving financial help to his mother.

There were, however, compensations. Several lifelong friendships began during these years. In September 1860 Mitchell hunted up young Dr. W. W. Keen, who had been a physician but three days. Mitchell asked Keen to help in the research with snake venoms. Thus began an association which continued during the Civil War and lasted until Mitchell's death. Keen stated: "Never have I known so original, suggestive, and fertile a mind. I often called him a yeasty man. His mind was ever fermenting, speculating, alert, and overflowing with ideas. . . . An hour in his office set my own mind in a turmoil so that I could hardly sleep."

About this same time Mitchell met Phillips Brooks, the new rector of the Church of the Advent. Hearing him preach, Mitchell was struck by the man's ardor, intensity, and imagination. After Brooks became rector of Holy Trinity, he lived near the Mitchells. Once or twice a week he dined with them, and about five evenings a week he would drop in about ten o'clock to chat and smoke before the fire in Weir's library. This too became a lifelong friendship.

Thus, by the time he was thirty-two, Weir Mitchell's pattern of life seemed pretty well determined: medical practice, research, family cares, and congenial friends. He wrote verse occasionally, but he gave no indication of becoming anything more than a kind of dabbler in literature like his father. Family cares and a growing practice, in the normal course of events, could be expected to leave him less and less time for research or writing. With his courtly manners, his love for entertaining, chatting, and dining out, he seemed destined to become simply another family physician on the nineteenth-century Philadelphia pattern.

IV

The War Years

"Such ghastly visions had I of despair."
—WORDSWORTH, *Prelude X*

WITH THE COMING of the Civil War, Mitchell entered a dark period, but one which was to transform his life. Like many Philadelphians, he was at first not enthusiastic about the war. In August of 1861 he wrote to his sister saying he thought all sides were insane. "If I were a nig I should go in for it all, but being white, I decline." After all, Mitchell's father had been a Virginian. Throughout his life Weir never took much interest in politics.

During the war, however, Mitchell became more partisan. In an unpublished, abortive novel he gives a picture of the confusion of mind in Philadelphia at the news of Fort Sumter. At the telegraph office as the news comes over the wire there is violent quarreling among the waiting men. The men to whom the South owes money hesitate to approve the assistance of the North, but the crowd is pro-Union. "The penny is prompt—the dollar doubts," comments Mitchell.

On the unfinished manuscript he later added the note, "incomplete—too painful for both sides." With relatives in the South, he knew something of the heartaches of divided loyalties and sundered families. It is an important theme in his last novel, *Westways*, in which the wife of a Union officer has many family ties in the South. At the time he was writing it he wrote to Osler, "[it] concerns the time of the Buchanan administration and the war. No one has sufficiently put on paper the home influences, the changes in families which that period brought on; or the extreme bitterness of party."

Not only was there bitterness at home. From his cousin Mitchell Henry in England came a long letter stating that neither side was believed to be sincere, and that most people looked on the war as they did one in countries where it was chronic as among the Turks, Montenegrins, or Mexicans. A few sympathized with the North on the slavery question, but had been disgusted by a long history of appeasement. Mitchell was so deeply wounded that for years he took no pleasure in visiting England.

Weir and his three brothers were all drawn into the struggle. As we have seen, Weir helped to get Walsh a commission. In 1863 Chapman was offered a commission in a Negro regiment. By that time Weir had lost prejudices against black troops and advised his brother to accept the post if it would not injure his status among other officers. Edward, or Ned as the family called him, was a constant worry because of his delicate health. Of all of them, Weir regarded his youngest brother as "the most earnest and perfect character." The second year of the war Ned, who was in the medical service, contracted diphtheria, and although he recovered, he never regained full health. Within two years more he was dead. Throughout the war Weir, with his strong family ties, knew the "never-ending anxiety" of scanning the casualty lists in the morning paper and the thrill of terror at a newsboy's cry in the dead of night.

In 1862 Weir took a position as "contract surgeon" in an army hospital. Because he felt that someone should remain at home with his widowed mother and because the income from his practice was essential, he declined a position as brigade surgeon. As a contract surgeon he could keep his private practice. He would go to the army hospital in the morning and again at three. Then he often would work until twelve or one making notes on the cases he had treated.

Some idea of the primitive state of medicine at the time can be gained from the reminiscences of Mitchell's friend, Dr. John Billings. Just out of the Medical College of Ohio, Billings became an army surgeon in 1861. With him he had a set of clinical thermometers, one straight, the other curved; a hypodermic syringe; and a Symes staff for urethral stricturotomy—instruments that none of the other surgeons possessed. They constantly borrowed his hypodermic syringe, but the thermometer was little used because it was troublesome. It was not until a year later that he had a microscope.

However, the Surgeon General, Dr. William A. Hammond, was a man of vision. It was he who had been associated with Mitchell in the early research on snake venom. Therefore, when he learned that his friend had become interested in cases of nervous disease and wounds of the nerves, Hammond created a small hospital for nervous diseases on Christian Street, Philadelphia. At first Dr. George R. Morehouse was put in charge. Soon this hospital outgrew its quarters, and Hammond set up one of four hundred beds on Turner's Lane near Nineteenth Street. Morehouse and Mitchell were transferred to this, and Mitchell asked to have another former associate, Dr. W. W. Keen, as assistant surgeon. In the same hospital Dr. Da Costa had a ward for the treatment and study of heart cases.

By special order they were relieved of much of the red tape so that they might engage in research. There were twenty-five thousand beds in army hospitals in the Philadelphia area. From these the nervous cases were sent to Turner's Lane. At one time there were as many as eighty epileptics, and every kind of nerve wound, palsies, choreas, stump disorders. After each battle the cases would flow in, forcing the physicians to work long hours. Late at night Mitchell would walk home with

Keen and Morehouse discussing the cases they were studying.

They took thousands of pages of notes, and planned essays to record their work. Here for the first time massage was used to restore action to limbs in which nerve wounds had impaired muscular action or which had become rigid from splints. They were the first to use atropine hypodermically for muscular spasms, and they discovered the counteraction of morphia and atropine. The young men shared the excitement of opening up new fields of knowledge.

Notes in Mitchell's handwriting are extant for at least eighty of the cases. These are written in a superbly clear expository style, a style so lacking in technical diction that a layman can easily understand it. A single case may take up five to nine pages of foolscap. For each there was certain standardized data: name, place of birth, general health before the wound, place (geographic) wounded, description of wound, length of time before treatment, nature of treatment, extent of recovery, sensation, motion (of limb), comparative sizes of limbs if wound was in limb. A single case might be followed for as long as two years. Sometimes there is a crude drawing, showing the nature of the wound.

A typical record is as follows:

Jacob Demuth age 21. Swiss. Enlisted July 1861. Co. D. 108th N.Y. Vol. A man somewhat below the average standard of height. Of lymphatic temperament—and very moderate intelligence. Reports himself as healthy up to the date of his wound which took place at Fredericksburg Dec. 13th 1862. He was marching at double quick when a fragment of shell as large as a musket ball struck his right thigh—at the junction of the upper and middle third directly over the femoral artery. The fragment did not enter deeply but merely lodged in the leg and was removed a day later without injury to the vessel. Effect of the wound. He fell half conscious and although aware that he was wounded he could not fix upon the site of the injury until he had examined the limb. He felt instantly a burning pain in both feet, in front of the right chest and in the right arm and in the right thigh about the wound. At first he was entirely powerless but after a few minutes the power of the left arm returned leaving him paralysed as to motion in the right arm and in both legs. He lay on the field twenty-four hours the weather being very cold. . . .

The muscles of the legs are about equally irritable to induced electric currents. Unfortunately no very perfect electric examination of their condition was made at the period.

Treatment: Regarding the case as one of reflex paralysis chiefly he was ordered to have rough frictions with cold to the spine and to take the twentieth of a grain of strychnia three times a day. Under this treatment the cramps and twitching increased so that after three weeks the strychnia was abandoned.

Later hot and cold douches to the spine were used plus electrical treatments. The patient was given iron and quinine. The electric treatment caused a rapid amelioration of his case so that he soon left his bed and began to walk on crutches. Still later the patient was able to walk unaided and was discharged after two years of treatment.

Notes such as these indicate the painstaking study and care of patients and the constant experimentation that went on at the Turner's Lane Hospital. Mitchell, Morehouse, and Keen were far from the old-fashioned sawbones of military hospitals. In no small degree they were pioneers in military medicine.

A number of important publications grew out of the researches of Mitchell, Morehouse, and Keen. They agreed among themselves to rotate their names at the head of these publications. The first important one, *Reflex Paralysis*, was a pioneer work describing cases of sudden palsy resulting from wounds in remote regions of the body. Seventy-seven years later the Yale Medical School republished it as an example of brilliant pioneering in medicine. At a time when the motor areas of the cerebral cortex had not been defined, these men recognized the presence of motor centers in the forebrain which controlled muscles on the opposite side of the body. This was five years before the work of Fritsch and Hirtzig was announced.

Another important contribution of this pamphlet was the clear-cut description of what is now termed "primary" and "secondary" shock. In addition, these men recognized the syndrome which in World War II has been called "primary blast," that is, collapse from proximity to an explosion when there is no sign of external injury.

In the same year they published *Gunshot Wounds and Other Injuries of the Nerves*, a book which in this and its later amplified form became famous. It contained the first distinct accounts of ascending neuritis, the treatment of neuritis by cold and splint-rests, and the psychic phenomena in those who have undergone operation. Three-quarters of a century later, in his introduction to the reprint of *Reflex Paralysis*, John F. Fulton called it and *Gunshot Wounds* "great milestones in the history of American neurology and American clinical medicine." Both of these, according to Keen, one of the co-signers, were principally by Mitchell.

Next came a study of malingering among Union soldiers. The writing of this was assigned to Keen. The three men laid great stress on the connection between malingering and the bounty system. They described the various types of malingering, and made recommendations for handling the problem. In doubtful cases, they believed that soldiers should be given the benefit of doubt, and warned against cruelties to really sick men. For clear-cut cases, they proposed a malingerers' brigade assigned to hard, unpleasant work. But here again the authors advised caution. In their own work they used careful observation and anesthesia to detect malingerers.

They also had very full notes on epilepsy, but Morehouse, who tended to become paralyzed when he held a pen, delayed writing them up, with tragic consequences. His library burned. Fifty years later Mitchell told an audience of physicians: "To this day I cannot think of it without regret." For in the lost notes were records of types of cases Mitchell never saw again.

Years later he spoke also of an "interesting psychic malady of soldiers," making men hysteric and incurable except by discharge. Obviously this is what in World War I was called shell shock. He recognized that the victim was not, as commonly supposed, necessarily a coward, for in *John Sherwood* he introduced a fine young man who had been such a case. Young Bob Cairns was always sick before a battle. Although he was branded as a coward, he later saved a man's life by jumping into a rough sea after him. Mitchell recognized that the "psychic malady" was not cowardice or malingering.

Most later commentators on the work of Mitchell, Morehouse, and Keen tend to credit Mitchell with the more penetrating ideas. This is born out by the statements of Keen himself, who said that at the time he was a "mere medical kid," and, except for the generosity of Mitchell, would have been listed as a research assistant.

He [Mitchell] was the guiding spirit of our "firm". . . . Soon after I joined them Mitchell plotted our work. He assigned to himself a paper on "Reflex Paralysis" . . . a book on "Gun Shot Wounds and Other Injuries to the Nerves," with several other papers.

The work of these men was, of course, part of that remarkable body of medical information which came out of the Civil War. The official record of this work, *Medical and Surgical History of the War of the Rebellion*, amazed European medical scholars like Virchow because of its wealth of statistics and scholarly statement. What made the work of Mitchell, Morehouse, and Keen stand out was their emphasis on research and experiment. And for originality of thought and clarity of exposition the two studies written by Mitchell are perhaps the most brilliant record of all.

The Civil War hospitals in which they worked were of course primitive according to modern standards, but they were far different from the medieval pest houses Florence Nightingale had found eight years before in the Crimean War. At Sutari she had met dirt and stench beyond any of the worst slums she had seen in Europe. The most ordinary drugs, even soap, were lacking. The mortality was forty-two per cent. By contrast at Turner's Lane there were long white pavilions with many windows. This was the design which Hammond had worked out for military hospitals. Inside there were long rows of iron beds, each with its little card identifying the patient and carrying information about the ailment and treatment. Beside each bed stood a small wooden table with medicines and sometimes books. Walls were whitewashed and floors scrupulously clean. As the wounded were brought in, each one was questioned by a surgeon, given iced lemonade or other refreshing drink, and assigned to a bed. The Sanitary Commission insisted on rigid inspections, and Mitchell was occasionally employed as an inspector of other hospitals. Not all medical care was as good as that in Philadelphia, but despite the absence of fly screens and any knowledge of asepsis, there was intelligent and humane management of military hospitals. Under Hammond physicians like Billings and Mitchell were given an opportunity to use the latest techniques.

One of the worst problems was "hospital gangrene." Fifty years later Mitchell described it to physicians who had never seen it. A slight flesh wound would develop a gray edge of slough which progressed rapidly until in some cases arteries and nerves would be laid bare. The patient was immediately removed to a tent, etherized, and the wound savagely cauterized with pure nitric acid or bromine, followed by dressings of powdered charcoal. Nevertheless, they lost at least 45 per cent of the cases. Erysipelas was another scourge in the hospitals. Here again, removal of the men to tents would check an epidemic. Even patients with pneumonia or bronchitis did better in tents. Out of this experience grew Mitchell's essay, "Camp Cure," a method of treatment he continued to recommend throughout his life.

Mitchell had another reason for hard work besides duty and the excitement of pioneering research: at almost the same time he became a contract surgeon, his young wife died of diphtheria. She had caught it from her older child, John, who recovered. Thus with his brothers in the army and his wife dead, Weir Mitchell was a lonely man. The long hours of note-taking and discussion with Morehouse and Keen must have been a welcome means of escape from personal grief. Not that research was ever for Mitchell a mere escape. To his sister he wrote: "I so much dread to find increasing practice or other cause removing from me the time or power to search for the new truths that lie about me so thick."

What time he could spare from his work he read endlessly: travel, biography, history, and some novels. His beloved sister Elizabeth, though in poor health, took over the care of the two small boys, one three, the other under a year at the time of their mother's death.

A year later, Mitchell wrote to Elizabeth that he thought he should keep the anniversary of his wife's death without bitterness and "think only with pure thanksgiving of all she was and is." However, he wanted to get away for a brief trip if he could get Dr. Da Costa to go along. He would be an understanding companion for a grief-stricken man. He could not face the prospect of a wedding anniversary at home.

There were also financial worries. In 1864 Mitchell paid four hundred dollars for a substitute for the army. With the responsibilities at home and his service in the hospitals he probably had no qualms of conscience about thus avoiding military service. Certainly as a surgeon doing important research for the army he was of vastly greater use than he would have been carrying a rifle. Then he had to buy a carriage, which cost three hundred and seventy-five dollars. His mother offered hers. Weir hesitated to break the news that she would soon have to do without one; he had large bills coming in for painting two houses. His salary of eighty dollars a month from the army did not cover many such items. Even so he was able to boast that he had invested fifteen hundred dollars.

Wally, having got into some sort of scrape, turned up for a visit in Philadelphia. His mother wrote to Lizzie that "it is needless to say what Weir has done for this boy, you know there is no end to his kindness." Wally was by turns most amusing and terribly depressed. Mrs. Mitchell decided that it was up to her to support him, although she had dark suspicions about what he did with his money. But of course it was Weir on whom the burden chiefly rested.

One of his few happy experiences during these years was the beginning of a friendship which was to last fifty years. Even this began under unhappy circumstances. At the Douglas Hospital in Washington, Ned Mitchell, who was a medical cadet, contracted the illness which was to lead to his death. On a visit to his brother, Weir met a tall athletic surgeon, nine years his junior. This was John Shaw Billings. Billings had a very different background from Mitchell's. He had been a poor boy who had worked his way through the Medical College of Ohio. Mitchell found him a man of "almost womanly tenderness," never impatient or irritable, a man who "left every bedside in the long sad wards the impression of being in earnest and honestly interested." Weir Mitchell had a knack for spotting unusual people. This young surgeon was to have a distinguished career. His biographer states that next to Mitchell, Billings became the best-known American physician of his time, especially in the eyes of Europe. Welch called his *Index Catalogue* of medical literature the most important of American contributions to medical science in the nineteenth century. He also became famous as a designer of hospitals, and was the first head of the New York Public Library. But when Mitchell first knew him he had neither fortune, family, nor fame. Mitchell, for all his Philadelphia sense of class, was no snob. This man became perhaps his dearest friend.

Of all Mitchell's experiences during these war years, one was to stand out in his mind. This was his assignment to Gettysburg just after the battle. In a letter to Professor Lounsbury in 1911 he states that he was on the battlefield at the end of the third day, but it seems likely that an old man's memory was inaccurate. His pass for the battlefield is dated July 5, 1863. Whenever he got there, the scene made an impression which was to be lifelong. There were twenty-seven thousand wounded to be cared for. Twenty-four hours after the battle all of these had received treatment and been placed under shelter. Thirty years later a forest blasted by fire and wind was to remind him of "the dead Confederates lying below Round Top the day after the fight, with arms and legs in rigid extension,—a most horrible memory." Even at eighty-four he remembered "that strange complex odour which rises from a battlefield . . . as horrible and as unlike any other unpleasant smell."

In his imagination he was able to reconstruct the battle itself. Thus in *Westways* he pictures the screams of the horses, mules, and the wounded. He shows the ambulance trains and a vivid moment in which a bursting shell wipes out a wagon driver and his load. There is no false glamour. In this last novel, as in a much earlier one, "war is a disgustingly dirty business. You don't realize that in history, in fiction, or in pictures. It's filthy."

He returned from Gettysburg almost immediately, in charge of a carload of wounded. Later he learned that his brother had been with John Reynolds at the time that General was killed. Billings was one of the surgeons during the battle. It may be that when Weir later used this material in novels, he drew upon his brother's and Billings' memories as well as upon his own.

Within a few weeks he was sent by the War Department to inspect the military prison at Fort Delaware on an island about ten miles below Newcastle. Before he went he was incensed over the reports of conditions there: overcrowding, lack of drinking water, twenty deaths a day from dysentery. "Thus a Christian nation treats the captives of its sword," he told his sister. However, he found conditions vastly better than the Copperheads had charged. True, he "smelt nine hundred smells" and saw dying men and scurvy; but fresh water was brought in tugs; the prisoners were well fed and well housed, though badly shod and ill clad. And he thought the location a bad one for a prison.

In his official report he pointed out that the prisoners needed clothing. The Quartermaster's Department ransacked the Schuylkill Arsenal and came up with a lot of ancient uniforms, some of them musicians' outfits from the War of 1812. The Confederates took off the buttons marked U.S. and docked swallowtail coats, but, as Mitchell said, for a time the fort resembled a fancy dress ball.

At the fort he found a number of Confederate surgeons. Earlier in the war both sides returned medical men, but after a Union surgeon had been held on some charge in Virginia the Union Army imprisoned some Confederate surgeons. In turn the Confederates held Union surgeons captured at Winchester, with the result that the Union held those taken at

Gettysburg. Mitchell thought the lot of those held at Fort Delaware was a sad one. Some of them were acquaintances. He gave them presents of tobacco and books, both at the time and later. It annoyed him that none of the loans of money he made were ever returned.

In 1864 he broke down under the strain of the work he was carrying. In addition to his hospital duties, his research, and his inspection tours, he was maintaining a heavy private practice. On a single Sunday he saw twenty city patients and four in the country. When his health gave way he obtained a two months' leave for a visit to France and England. The experience was not a happy one. During his few days in Paris he found an aggressive hostility toward the North. He sailed to London, where he found things much the same as across the Channel:

> Neither in travel, nor dining at the club which I frequented, a fashionable resort, did I hear a single person who was not our enemy. If I spoke to a man in a train, he was always for the South. All the literary folk of England, the banking-class, the professions, and generally the titled class, were against us, so that it became at last too depressing for a man in search of renewed vigor.

While he was in London, news came in of the impending battle between the *Alabama* and the *Kearsarge*. Mitchell, as was his custom, refused to bet on the result, but he warned an acquaintance against betting on the *Alabama*. The gentleman, following the advice, won three thousand pounds. However, most of "our English enemies" were unhappy at the victory of the *Kearsarge*. Mitchell was glad to sail for home.

A possible contributing cause to his breakdown of 1864 was a great disappointment the year before—in fact, two disappointments. When the Chair of Physiology at Jefferson was to be filled, Mitchell hoped to obtain it. He asked the help of Dr. Holmes, who not only wrote in his behalf but promised to speak to Agassiz and Wyman. A few weeks later Holmes wrote Mitchell again, expressing satisfaction that the Cambridge men had been willing to help. Wyman told Mitchell that Agassiz sat down immediately and wrote a "very handsome letter." Other friends, including Surgeon General Hammond, worked in his behalf. Mitchell failed, however, to get the post.

The same year he tried for a similar post at the University of Pennsylvania. Again his friends helped. They discussed the best way of influencing each of the twenty-four trustees. "Who were their clergymen, doctors, creditors, relatives? What church influence reached them? Which of them were believed to listen to advice from their wives, and who were their wives' clergymen? and so on." No wonder Mitchell later spoke of this "vile path to preferment." Again he failed. "I am disgusted with everything," wrote Hammond, "and can only say that it is an honor to be rejected by such a set of apes!"

Seventy-five years later the physiologist, Professor A. J. Carlson, wrote of the trustees of Jefferson and Penn: ". . . they rejected one of the ablest, if not the ablest man of their generation, a man who would have done honor to any faculty, in any school, in any country, at any age."

Even three years after the war Mitchell's Republican sympathies helped to cause yet another rejection for a medical chair. This time it was for the Chair of Physiology vacated by his former teacher, Dr. Dunlgison. Again Wyman, Agassiz, Holmes, and Hammond wrote in his behalf. Again he failed. When he learned of his defeat he went home with a sense that the world was at an end for him. That night he read himself to sleep with Clough's *The Bothie of Tober-na-Vuolich*, a book for which he long after cherished an affection.

Agassiz believed that Mitchell had been defeated because he belonged "to the small band which by original, independent research contribute to the advancement of science . . ." In

America, he said, the good jobs usually went to the fluent talkers who capitalized on the work of others. Mitchell himself believed that his political opinions cost him the post. As late as 1863 he had regarded himself as more of a Democrat than a Republican. During the war, however, he had become a Republican; whereas the majority of the trustees at Jefferson were violently Democratic.

Never a strong party man, Mitchell could describe himself in later life as "an unreconstructed Northerner." He had seen Lincoln on the way to his first inauguration and had been impressed by the unusual character of the face and the deep melancholy in the expression.

Whatever the reason for his failure to get a teaching position, the result may have been to his ultimate advantage. Holmes wrote him:

Perhaps it is hardly desirable that an active man of science should obtain a chair too early, for I have noticed . . . that the wood of which academic fauteuils are made has a narcotic quality which occasionally renders the occupants somnolent, lethargic or even comatose!

It is unlikely that Mitchell would ever have become lethargic, nor like Dr. Holmes a kind of playboy of science. As Holmes said of himself, ". . . my nature is to snatch at all the fruits of knowledge and take a good bite out of the sunny side—after that let in the pigs." He felt that he should have been compelled to learn the kind of patient, thorough investigation such as Mitchell had done on snake venom. Certainly Mitchell with his own love of research and his organizing ability might well have brought to Jefferson something of the same sort of vision which Eliot brought to medical education at Harvard, Welch to Johns Hopkins, and Pepper to the University of Pennsylvania.

One plan for improving medical faculties grew out of Mitchell's experiences. He saw no hope in reforming trustees.

Even though they might hear a candidate lecture, examine a list of his publications, and gather opinions from men of note, "such a course would [not] prevail against the grandmothers, church influence, insurance board associations, this or that railroad." The only solution he could see was to give faculties the power to elect or at least nominate. In the latter case, election should be by a joint committee of faculty, trustees, and alumni. He believed that representatives of both faculty and alumni should sit on boards of trustees. Seventy-five years later, faculties are still asking for the same thing.

Mitchell's ability as an executive and organizer was demonstrated by his work in helping to organize the first of the great Sanitary Fairs of the Civil War. These were designed to raise money for the work of the Sanitary Commission, an organization analogous to the modern Red Cross. Not only did he help to organize the Philadelphia Fair, he made a contribution to it in the form of a children's book. This was *Fuz-Buz the Fly*, published anonymously by Lippincott.

Fuz-Buz, the first of a number of children's books he was to write, is a pleasant but not inspired little tale. In it a fly caught in the net of Mother Grabem, the spider, saves his life by telling her children a series of fairy stores. The framework is thus reminiscent of *The Thousand and One Nights;* the stories themselves have similarities to traditional fairy tales like "Jack and the Beanstalk." One thing that makes them remarkable among Victorian children's stories is their lack of moralizing. And in one tale is a bit of satire—rare in Mitchell—when a giant refuses to eat a congressman for fear of being poisoned.

Mitchell's Civil War experiences also led to the publication of his first short story, *The Case of George Dedlow*. It grew out of a discussion with his friend, Henry Wharton. Mitchell spoke of a man who had lost both legs and arms in the battle of Mobile Bay. Wharton suggested that a man might lose some part of his consciousness of individuality with the loss of parts of his body. To amuse himself Mitchell worked up a story on this theme. The name Dedlow he picked up from a sign over a jeweler's shop. He showed the story to Mrs. Caspar Wister, whose literary judgment he highly valued. She in turn gave the manuscript to her father, Dr. William Henry Furness, who, unknown to Mitchell, sent it to the editor of the *Atlantic*. To his surprise he received a check for eighty dollars. The story was printed anonymously in July 1866. So realistic was the account that many people accepted it as fact and sent contributions to the mythical Dedlow at the Stump Hospital in Philadelphia, where he was supposed to be.

A few poems also appeared during the war years, among them *Kearsarge* and *How Cumberland Went Down*. Thus during these years Mitchell began to show that versatility which developed with age. Poems, a short story, a fairy tale, the book on gunshot wounds, and numerous scientific papers —all these he produced during five years of driving labor and anxiety. *Gunshot Wounds* and the paper on *Reflex Paralysis*, both done jointly with Keen and Morehouse, were works of major importance.

Certainly these years had changed his whole life. He had lost two brothers in the war, and a wife through illness; he had had a desperate financial struggle, a physical breakdown, and some bitter disappointments. His friend Hammond had been brought before a court-martial and dismissed from the service because of a controversy with Stanton. Possibly this is the reason that in the same year, 1864, Mitchell had resigned as a contract surgeon. The suffering he had seen in military hospitals and on the battlefield had made a lasting impression upon him. He could never assume toward the war the light-minded attitude of Holmes who, after writing him about his son's wounds, added, "O for a triumphant issue to this war— and the second Volume of Allibone!" For Mitchell the war always remained tragic and horrible. Yet these war years were the ones which transformed him from a struggling family doctor into a physiologist and neurologist whose reputation soon became worldwide. And they gave him materials for some of his best writing. His own summing up was that the war had brought "an increase of life, a freshening of national vitality, which was felt most in the centers of population. . . . Certainly, no period in the history of our race was ever more interesting."

V

Recognition

1866 - 1880

"And every winter turn to spring."
—TENNYSON, *In Memoriam*

THERE WAS nothing of the hermit about Weir Mitchell. Even when engaged in research he liked to have the association of congenial minds: Hammond, Keen, Morehouse. He had the knack of keeping friends. Fifty-five years after his first work with Keen on snake venom the two men were still discussing new ideas for study. Hammond, Billings, Osler, Phillips Brooks were lifelong friends. As Mitchell put it in a letter to Mrs. Mason, "He who would have friends must put up with what they lack." A corollary to this is Anne's remark in *When All the Woods Are Green:*

"I never found any one human being who, at all times and under all stress of needs, was able to give me everything I want of a man or woman." [To which Lindsay adds], "I think with you, Anne . . . I could never quite comprehend those all-satisfying alliances one reads about, those friend-love affairs such as Shakespeare had with Herbert, or whoever it was."

Because Mitchell expresses similar ideas elsewhere there is little doubt that he is here talking through his characters.

Throughout his life he put these principles into practice. He had a knack for spotting a man's special talent and putting it to use as he did many years later with Noguchi. Thus he could enjoy discussions of religion with Phillips Brooks, of

64

sculpture with Augustus Saint-Gaudens, of Shakespeare with Horace Howard Furness, of history with Parkman and Bancroft. He could even enjoy people whose points of view or personalities clashed with his. Thus he could discuss women's education with Agnes Irwin of Radcliffe or listen to Walt Whitman. He even read Whitman, though much of *Leaves of Grass* offended his Philadelphia sensibilities.

During the 60's Mitchell's most intimate friend was Phillips Brooks. At least once a week and usually twice, Brooks dined with Weir and his sister. Five evenings out of seven Brooks dropped in about ten o'clock for a talk and smoke before the fire in the library. He referred to himself as the Mitchells' house dog. Brooks, who was intellectually sympathetic, liked to talk with men about their own work. Thus the lonely widower had someone to whom he could talk of his own problems and achievements. At this period Brooks had an ardor and intensity combined with imaginative qualities, qualities he later subjected to the rule of his rational faculties. Mitchell during his life knew many well-known or even famous men, but Brooks was the only one who seemed to him "entirely great."

In the summertime the two men took many trips together, one a long canoe voyage from Moosehead Lake to the sea. It was three weeks before the guides discovered that Brooks was a clergyman. Physically strong, he delighted in swimming and paddling, but refused to kill game or fish. Mitchell's bleak mood of this period appears in some verse, "Rain in Camp," written during a trip with Brooks:

> The camp-fire smoulders and will not burn,
> And a sulky smoke from the blackened logs
> Lazily swirls through the dank wood caves;
> And the laden leaves with a quick relief
> Let fall their loads, as the pool beyond
> Leaps 'neath the thin gray lash of the rain,

And is builded thick with silver bells.
But I lie on my back in vague despair,
Trying it over thrice and again,
To see if my words will say the thing.
But the sodden moss, and the wet black wood,
And the shining curves of the dancing leaves,
The drip and drop, and tumble and patter,
The humming roar in the sturdy pines,
Alas, shall there no man paint or tell.

And in some lines on a storm he describes Lake Nipigon as:

> . . . sweet as the dream of hope
> What time despair is nearest . . .

As Brooks grew older he gave up such excursions. Mitchell warned him repeatedly that his failure to take any exercise would bring disaster, warnings which only annoyed the younger man. It is characteristic of Mitchell that he did not confine himself to medical advice; he also suggested themes for sermons, and on one occasion helped to compose one. Apparently Brooks did not preserve it. He did, however, ask Weir to write a Christmas hymn. For once Mitchell felt that here was something he could not do. As a result of his refusal, Brooks wrote one himself: "O Little Town of Bethlehem."

Frequently the two men were joined in their discussions by Weir's sister Elizabeth. His portrait of her in the Autobiography and elsewhere is of a witty person, heroically bearing suffering. Daily for an hour or two she shut herself in her room to wrestle with torturing pain, presumably from cancer. That Elizabeth was witty and well-read seems clear. Books for her were a world of release from pain, for she refused opiates. She became learned in biblical literature and church history. Phillips Brooks found her a brilliant and stimulating companion. He once told Weir that no one else had influenced his opinions so much as she had. Weir remembered her death-bed remark: "All life laughs for me; I must laugh, dear. I would not feel that the other world was the good place I think it is if I did not believe I could laugh there too." She even called pain a strange sort of joke.

Even when in 1869 Brooks was called to Boston, he long remained homesick for Philadelphia and the Mitchells. In Philadelphia he had found "The temperate zone of religious life. Free from antagonism, among a genial and social people, with just enough of internal debate and difference to insure her life . . . the Church in Philadelphia was to the Church in Boston much like what a broad Pennsylvania valley is to a rough New England hillside." Boston, he told Weir, took a pretty large-sized man to stand. Ninety-nine hundredths of the people seemed "awful failures—priggish, prudish, pedantical, pragmatical." For him Philadelphia remained the city of joy and beauty, the home of immortal youth.

Three times within the first three months of his Boston pastorate he returned to visit the Mitchells. To Weir, and especially to Elizabeth, he wrote his intimate thoughts, his problems and doubts. To her he could speak with a freedom and sarcastic wit he could not exercise with others. At her death in 1874 he wrote to Weir that his friendship with her had been the kind few people ever have and no one has more than once.

Elizabeth meant a great deal in Weir's life also. She ran his household; she looked after his two boys when they were not away at school; she gave him intellectual companionship. He introduced her in two of his books. She is Anne in *When All the Woods Are Green*, and in *Doctor and Patient* she is a case history of a woman who by humor, fortitude, and intellectual vigor triumphs over a painful mortal illness.

Her letters to John, who was at St. Paul's School under Dr. Coit, show that she was a devoted foster mother to the boys. Perhaps she was inclined to be over serious and to dwell too frequently on the need for better academic work. For John's reports were often far from satisfactory. Still it was Aunt

Lizzie whom he thought of as his mother, and for whom he had a lifelong memory of affection. It is hard to recognize in the self-sacrificing, motherly woman the complaining person of Weir's student days in Paris. Pain and responsibility had matured and ennobled her.

Now it was she who looked after Weir and worried over him when he came home too tired to eat. Lany, who did not go away to school until later, was also a worry, for he was inclined to get into scrapes. Nor did Aunt Lizzie approve when Horace Furness took his own boys and Lany to see *The Black Crook*. Because it was Mr. Furness who asked, she consented, hoping that the boy was "too young to see how bad it is."

It was a devoted but somewhat somber home. Mitchell, with many burdens upon him, often had a fit of the blues on Sunday, the day he wrote to John. And he could not read an account of a child's death without a moment of terror for his own children.

As with many people brought up with numerous brothers and sisters, Mitchell had a strong sense of family. Thus in 1871 his budget carried an item of seven hundred and twenty dollars for his ne'er-do-well brother Walsh. In addition there was six hundred dollars interest on a mortgage, and a life insurance premium of six hundred and sixty dollars. The policy was for ten thousand dollars with his mother as beneficiary. In turn he asked that she make a will in favor of his sons. His concern, however, was not merely financial. His heart ached for Walsh's "moral degradation."

The burden of Walsh was finally lifted in 1872. The wanderer had drifted to Alaska, whence he wrote an appeal for money to pay medical expenses. "I don't think it will be long," the ill man wrote. "You will have your greatest disgrace taken from you. . . . I could fall down and bless you for what you have been to me." It is characteristic of Weir's affection and family pride that he kept Walsh's sword over his mantelpiece and built up a legend of a gallant soldier.

In July of the same year Weir's mother died. It is small wonder that the harassed and unhappy man had an attack of neurasthenia. He became very weak and was troubled with insomnia. As was his custom, he went to Newport. On the way he stopped off in Boston, probably to visit Brooks. He also called on Holmes, who proved to be poor company for a gloomy man. An old servant had died; his son's wife had rheumatic fever, and Holmes himself had dyspepsia. Twice Mitchell rose to go, but Holmes held on to him, pouring out his woes and ideas. He argued that Christianity was a failure because of its inability to relate itself to natural and social science. As usual with the Autocrat, the conversation was one-sided. Whatever its effect on his audience, it raised Holmes's spirits. When Mitchell finally got out the door, Holmes sat on the top step for ten minutes making "chirpy remarks" which followed his caller far up Beacon Street until he was out of earshot.

With his mother's death and the increasing illness of his sister, Mitchell turned more and more to his sons. The necessity of sending John away to school was a bitter sacrifice for the lonely father. "It seems to me I shall never, never get used to that empty chair on the far side of my table," he wrote the boy. On Sundays it was his custom to write long letters of advice, exhortations to work hard, and family news. He passed on some advice his own father had once given:

Next time take off your glasses when you mean to hit a fellow, and above all in a row never slap anyone's face. If a blow be needed, strike hard with the fist. The insult is no more and it prevents or interferes with a return.

More unusual was the frankness with which he discussed his own life and ideas. He told of his youth, his expenditures for Walsh, his difficulties in choosing a profession, his reaction to the rejection at Jefferson, his attitude toward death—things he realized were queer fare for a schoolboy, but which he hoped would be food for more mature reflection.

Thus when he went to Europe in the summer of 1873, he wrote to the boys of loitering among the theaters and singing cafés at night and of prowling the streets of older Paris around Notre Dame. At a hotel in Swizterland he found only two Americans and one hundred and fifty English, whom, as he told the boys, "your grandpapa might like but who I do not. All the women have huge feet and dress horribly. . . . Two only are handsome and not any who have come in my way are very intelligent." One of them annoyed him exceedingly by stating that she supposed he was used to seeing people killed on the streets in America.

To his brother Chapman he complained of the priggish education of British children. In a conversation with four of them he discovered to his consternation that they were not permitted to read fairy tales. He recommended *Alice in Wonderland* as suitable because it was written by a clergyman. One eight-year-old little lady answered that the clergyman would have been much better employed in writing sermons. Englishmen at home were sometimes pleasanter. Near Tintern Abbey he met two clever young men with whom he drank whiskey punch until midnight. The next day he rode on top of a great coach for two hours with a handsome girl on each side of him. But in an open steam ferry crossing the Severn he found the British less charming. A sudden storm sent waves over the deck, terrifying a group of children. Mitchell wrapped two of them in his waterproof, but the other men on the boat seemed indifferent to the women and children.

As had long been a custom in the Mitchell family, Weir asked that letters to his brother or sisters be passed around. Thus in effect each letter was written to all members of the family.

He had the habit of picking out the things of especial interest to each correspondent. Thus to his sister Lizzie he wrote of the church dignitaries he met in England, of the points of historic and literary interest he visited, and of hearing Disraeli and Gladstone cross swords in Parliament. In Paris he met the neurologist Charcot, and hunted up his old teacher Robin. He envied their laboratories. He also looked up the publisher who was bringing out a French edition of his book *Injuries to the Nerves*. It was pleasant to listen to the flattering things said about it. But when he saw his old rooms, now a bookstore, in the Latin Quarter, he had a sense of youth gone by.

Taking the letters as a whole, one gets a picture of an alert gregarious, self-assured man of forty-four, who found places and people interesting. Always too there is the keen eye for the beautiful: Tintern Abbey, a bit of English countryside, a stained glass window, a graceful French girl, or "that loveliest of pictures, Correggio's Marriage of St. Catherine." He returned refreshed and ready for work.

As his father had done, he spent whatever time he could with his boys. In the summer, when they were at their grandmother's in the country, he took the tiresome trip out to see them. On occasions when there were interesting guests at dinner, the boys were allowed to sit while their elders chatted over the doctor's Madeira. There was considerable formality, of course. If a question was put to the boys, they were required to answer it; but their opinions were treated with respect. It was good conversation the boys listened to, the sort which Mitchell later reproduced in *Characteristics* and *Dr. North*. The guests were interesting and able people: physicians, scientists, poets, historians—such men as Brooks, Holmes, Hammond, and a little later Lowell, Bancroft, Billings, Saint-Gaudens. It was a rare person of importance who, coming to Philadelphia, missed sitting at Dr. Mitchell's dinner table.

There were less formal contacts. He spent a happy afternoon with Lany at the zoo. They went hiking in Fairmount Park and came home facing a ruddy moon. The great number of expensive horses and turnouts seemed to them lacking in taste. Mitchell was not one to be a part of the gilded age. He liked comfort, even luxury, but not ostentation; and his own youth had given him a genuine love of the outdoors. He taught his sons to see "the changes of light and tints of sun and cloud and leaf and flower."

Still he was lonely. And with the death of his sister in 1874 he was very much alone. Within a dozen years he had lost a wife, three brothers, a mother, and his beloved sister. Phillips Brooks was in Boston, and the boys had to be away at school.

After his wife's death his friendships with women tended to be with those he found intellectually stimulating. These were chiefly married women of his generation or older. There is no hint of scandal in any of these friendships. Perhaps nothing could better illustrate the gulf between the 1860's and the period after 1920 than the complete sublimation of Mitchell's sexual drives. That he was attractive, even fascinating to women, is attested by the reactions of his feminine patients. The Philadelphia propriety of his life during these years influences characters in his novels and has bearing on the psychiatric theories of the time. In a society which so carefully overlaid sexual forces with rationalizations, it was difficult for even a specialist in nervous ills to understand some of their origins.

Mitchell's feminine friends during this period were chiefly the actress Fanny Kemble, her daughter Sarah Butler (Mrs. Owen Wister), and Mrs. Caspar Wister, the sister of his friend Horace Howard Furness. After the separation from her husband, Pierce Butler, Mrs. Kemble lived for a time at

York Farm outside of Philadelphia. Mitchell, who became a constant horseman, used to ride over to dine with her. On one occasion, after first stopping at Sarah Butler Wister's and finding her out, he rode over to call on the mother. Mrs. Kemble, having quarreled with her butcher, was unprepared for guests. But when Mitchell started to leave she detained him:

No, do not go yet. I am old and lonely, and never again will you have these chances to talk with a woman who has sat at dinner alongside of Byron, who has heard Tom Moore sing, and who calls Tennyson, Alfred.

It was an appeal few men, and certainly not Mitchell, could refuse.

Mrs. Kemble's daughter Sarah Wister, the mother of the novelist Owen Wister, was, Mitchell said, the most interesting woman he had ever known. "We had many contentions, but never a quarrel." Her friendship meant much to the lonely man. There is reason to believe that she furnished the model for several of the heroines of his novels.

The two Mrs. Wisters became his chief literary advisers. Sometimes he jokingly said Mrs. Caspar Wister wrote half his stories. She was a woman with a "magically beautiful voice" and with a knowledge of literature and the arts. In fact, she made many translations of German novels.

During these years Mitchell seems not to have thought seriously of remarriage. As he told his sister in 1868, ". . . it is a gray old scalp of mine and won't dry in any woman's wigwam."

Thus, although he found Miss Lena Peters "perfectly exquisite," he let it go at that. On the train to Boston a few years later he lost a corner of his heart to a married woman with two fine boys. He took a cinder out of the eye of one of them and received gracious thanks. She seemed to him a "family-made thoroughbred." There is, however, no record of any serious involvement during these years.

Then, less than a year after his sister's death, Mitchell wrote his son that he intended to marry Miss Mary Cadwalader. He had met her seven years before at the same time that he was introduced to the perfectly exquisite Miss Peters. He had not quite got her name, and had to ask his sister whether it was Emily, Mary, or Maria. With this marriage Mitchell stepped from the gentry into the Philadelphia aristocracy.

The available evidence suggests that the forty-five-year-old physician had made a sensible rather than a romantic alliance. It proved to be not only a wise but a happy marriage. With it came a "fresh hold on life." Her social position opened new doors for him, and her practical good sense enabled her to provide the sort of smooth-running home needed by a busy and socially active celebrity.

On their honeymoon they took along the fifteen-year-old John and Mrs. Mitchell's sister.

Mrs. Mitchell immediately set about winning the affection of her two stepsons, aged fifteen and twelve. She told Weir that he scolded John too much in his letters—a charge that was well founded, for there had been a constant stream of exhortation to do better work and write home more often. The lonely father had been rather demanding of affection. When John entered Harvard, Mrs. Mitchell sent money for horseback riding, John's chief enthusiasm. Then Lany got into a scrape at St. Paul's and was expelled. He had fastened the door to a room so as to imprison Dr. Coit and some of the faculty. Dr. Mitchell's appeal to the humorless Dr. Coit for reinstatement failed, and Lany came home in disgrace. Mrs. Mitchell worried over the boy so that she did not sleep, and Dr. Mitchell lost weight during the period of anxiety. On receiving the fateful wire from Dr. Coit, Mitchell found

himself slightly deaf, apparently the first intimation of a
malady which was to become increasingly troublesome.

At Harvard John continued to be the same sort of erratic
student he had been at St. Paul's. There were letters of warning from the dean, and hortatory letters from his father. On
one occasion Phillips Brooks went over to Cambridge to see
how matters stood. He reported that the boy simply hadn't
studied. Dr. Mitchell warned John that if he flunked out he
would have to go to Penn.

Mitchell also worried about his son's habit of running over
to Newport and of writing to young ladies. With his extreme
Victorian ideas of propriety he believed that a proper mother
would forbid her daughter to correspond with young men. It
hurt him that John wrote home seldom, but every day or two
to a Miss D. It was this sort of thing which led Mrs. Mitchell
to tell her husband that he scolded his son too much.

He was, however, not without provocation. Not only did
he receive warnings from the dean that John's grades were
dangerously low and that he was cutting chapel and classes,
but he got large bills. In figuring up a year's expenses he found
that his son had spent nearly fifteen hundred dollars, which
was then regarded as a large amount for a college year.
Mitchell promised not to spoil the boy's homecoming with a
parental diatribe, but he asked for greater moderation in the
future.

Despite the complaints there was nevertheless a note of
warm affection running through Mitchell's letters to his son,
and John seems to have treated his father with considerable
frankness. Thus he told of a college friend's venereal disease.
Mitchell answered with medical realism and Victorian naïveté
which so often characterized him:

I . . . wonder on what principle of justice it can be that so horrid
a punishment cames of so brief an offence and of one the natural

temptation to which exists as the most deeply rooted of man's physiological peculiarities.

He hoped John would avoid "all such uncleanliness," but if he ever did get into a scrape, he was to come to his father without fear. Whether it was "a row or a disease, always let me share your trouble."

He confided that he was riding horseback daily, and added, "I consider it a painful and dangerous form of gymnastics— but I do it." He was discovering one of the penalties of marrying into the Philadelphia aristocracy.

Furthermore, during the 70's Weir Mitchell was becoming a celebrity. His neurological work in the Civil War began to bring patients with nervous disorders, and it was not long before he largely dropped regular medical practice in favor of this specialty. As a regular physician he had made as many as fifty-two calls in a day. At the beginning of the decade he was appointed physician to the Orthopaedic Hospital, which occupied two small rooms over a shop of an instrument maker on Ninth Street. A few years later the institution moved to Seventeenth and Summer streets, changing its name to the Orthopaedic Hospital and Infirmary for Nervous Diseases. The change of name indicates the change of function which Mitchell brought about. He believed that the addition of the neurological department was particularly desirable because of the close relationship between bodily deformities and diseases of the nervous system.

Here he instituted some important innovations in hospital management and the treatment of patients. The clinic for nervous diseases was, he believed, the first in the country. But he found the board of managers apathetic; it was difficult to obtain a quorum for meetings. Mitchell got them together with some difficulty, told them the hospital was a mismanaged public trust, and threatened to carry the story to the newspapers. He pointed out that the board had not, as required, asked the Governor of Pennsylvania to appoint members. Therefore the board was illegally constituted. Upon this two of the older members of the board resigned, and Mitchell asked the Governor to appoint others. Gradually Mitchell built up a board of active younger men.

Another change was that instead of turning over the out-patient service to juniors, he insisted that, except in summer, it be handled by senior physicians and surgeons. He required his assistants to make careful notes on cards for each case, to have present an ophthalmologist and an electrician (one who applied the electrical treatments then in use). If necessary a physician from the orthopaedic division would be brought in. Then the notes were read aloud and Mitchell made his suggestions. Because of the amount of care and attention given to each case, he could say proudly that this "could not have been exceeded, were the patients millionaires."

In addition, this was one of the first hospitals to supply private rooms where physicians not members of the staff could bring cases. More important was the fact that Mitchell brought in a series of able men as his assistants: Warren Sinkler, Morris Lewis, William Osler, and his own son, John K. Mitchell. With these men he carried on a program of research which led to important discoveries.

Thus in 1869 he published what Mettler calls "a classic paper on the physiology of the cerebellum." It was based upon a series of experiments on pigeons, in which he studied the effects of various types of injuries to the brain. He reached the conclusion that the cerebellum functions as an augmenting organ to the cerebrospinal motor system.

The study is a continuation of his pioneering work in localization of brain function, a problem he had dealt with in *Reflex Paralysis*. It is significant that two of his protégés, W. W. Keen and Charles Kasner Mills, later did important work in this field.

In the ten years from 1870 to 1879 Mitchell published at least thirty-five papers and three books on neurology and related subjects. There were other papers on physiology, venoms, alkaloids, and diet. Of course he also found time to write some short stories and verse.

One of the books was *Injuries to the Nerves and their Treatment*, an amplification of the earlier *Gunshot Wounds* done in conjunction with Morehouse and Keen. The new work, by Mitchell alone, was translated into French two years after its American publication, and it was this work which helped to establish his European reputation. In fact, the book was still in use by the French in World War I.

Another was *Wear and Tear*, a little book on mental and physical hygiene intended for the general public. In it he attacked the working habits of Americans and their inability to play. To a certain extent Mitchell was opening up a new field, the discussion of medicine written in the language of the layman. He had a gift for clear non-technical exposition. This had appeared as early as *George Dedlow* when, in explaining the reason for the illusion of pain in amputated limbs, he wrote:

. . . the nerve is like a bellwire. You may pull it at any part of its course, and thus ring the bell as if you pulled it at the end of the wire; but in any case, the intelligent servant will refer the pull to the front door, and obey it accordingly.

To get material for *Wear and Tear* Mitchell had questioned patients and friends who had studious habits to discover the extent to which they suffered from mental fatigue. From Holmes he had received an account of his working habits. Holmes said that his physical discomforts warned him when he had been concentrating too long. He described his state as mental nausea rather than mental fatigue. He found that a fifteen- or twenty-minute walk cleared up his restlessness and disgust. (Two days later he sent a request that his name not be attached to the confessions in his "free and easy letter." He felt that he might, in the judgment of some people, be condemning his own intellect.) On the basis of this and other reports, Mitchell concluded that for people in health there is no such thing as mental fatigue. What was commonly taken for mental fatigue was merely physical discomfort arising from prolonged writing or constrained positions. "Eat regularly and exercise freely and there is scarce a limit to the work you may get out of the thinking organs." The real enemy was worry or anxiety. Then "the whole machinery begins at once to work, as it were, with a dangerous amount of friction."

From Holmes he borrowed the theory that the American climate makes greater demands upon the physical and mental machine than does the European. To support this view he cited the experience of immigrants and of American students in Europe. He particularly attacked long school hours and heavy assignments in homework, especially for girls. On this point he presented statistics on the health of students in various schools. In one boys' school fifty-nine out of eighty-one suffered from headaches or constant weariness. On the subject of women's health he was particularly vehement: "Today, the American woman is, to speak plainly, physically unfit for her duties as a woman . . ."

To some extent he foreshadowed the teachings of modern psychosomatic medicine. He warned that palpitations and a disordered stomach were the first danger signals of nervous overstrain. In overwork, business anxiety, and the like he recognized "the fertile parents of dyspepsia, consumption, and maladies of the heart."

Much of his teaching is as good today as it was three-quarters of a century ago. This is all the more remarkable when it is seen against its background of obsolete medical theory. Mitchell's ideas of the physical capacities of women grew out of a period of overcorseting and underexercise. Yet he was an advocate of much more physical activity for girls than was then customary. A more startling example of the limited medical knowledge of the time is his listing of certain diseases then believed to be of nervous origin, among them apoplexy and tetanus.

So vital did the book seem in its own day that the first edition was sold within ten days, and four more editions were published. A third book, *Fat and Blood* (1877) was even more popular.

Among the neurological papers published during these years, several were of great importance. In one of them he first showed the relation of headaches and other neurotic symptoms to eyestrain. In another he recorded the first study of what the medical historian calls "the effect of meteorological changes upon the traumatic neuralgia, particularly in old amputation stumps." Mitchell himself simply called his paper "Relation of Pain to Weather."

He had noted that his old war patients would write in waves. He would get a batch of letters from California, another from Denver a day or two later, and then in a day or two another from Chicago. The former patients complained of their old wounds. He then got in touch with the weather bureau and found that a wave of rain and a wave of pain were crossing the continent at the same rate. The rain area and the pain area were concentric, but the pain area was the larger. The radius of the first was between five hundred and fifty and six hundred miles; that of the second, one hundred and fifty miles greater.

The following year he published his discovery of *erythromelalgia* or red neuralgia, which came to be known as Weir Mitchell's disease. This is a neurosis of the feet or hands characterized by redness of the skin, with burning pain. Most famous of all in their day were those publications describing what came to be known as the Rest Cure or the Weir Mitchell Treatment.

There are at least three different accounts of the origin of this treatment. In an article on the subject in 1904 Mitchell said it was first developed in his Civil War hospital work. On the other hand he gave Osler a more dramatic account of its discovery. As the two men walked home from the Biological Club one December night in 1887, Mitchell told of an intelligent woman patient who had taken a four-year course in a Boston school in three years; she had then married and had four children as fast as possible. The result was a breakdown of mind and body. Boston and New York physicians had all advised exercise. Standing at the foot of her bed Mitchell felt that every suggestion he might make had been forestalled. On the inspiration of the moment he advised her to remain in bed. She recovered and bore several other children.

His friend Dr. Keen told still another story. He believed that Mitchell began to evolve the theory after having two patients whose nervous ailments were greatly alleviated during an enforced rest in bed because of broken legs. These various accounts are not necessarily in conflict. All these experiences may have played their part in the evolution of the treatment. Mitchell himself used that term rather than "discovery." Furthermore, the treatment itself underwent various modifications. It was not a single-barreled method. In addition to rest it included massage and a fattening diet. Electrical treatments were later added.

However it evolved, the Rest Cure was announced in the 70's. In a paper in the *American Journal of Medical Science*, July 1873, Mitchell discussed the "Favorable Influence of Long Rest in Bed on Neuralgia of Locomotor Ataxia." Two years later he published a more general discussion, "Rest in Treatment of Disease." These papers, plus the work at the

Orthopaedic Hospital, attracted to Mitchell a group of enthusiastic young men and caused considerable discussion in medical circles, not all of it favorable. The treatment of nervous and mental ills has ever been a field of violent controversy.

The interest in Mitchell's theories led to an invitation to be chief speaker at the memorial meeting in 1877 of the Medico-Chirurgical Faculty of Maryland. Here under the title "On Extreme Measures in Therapeutics," he gave an outline of the history of therapeutic measures in the treatment of nervous ills, and then a clear, non-technical exposition of his own methods. His little book, *Fat and Blood*, in the same year gave a more complete discussion of the topic. Its style is one reason for its great success. In addition to going through eight editions in America it was translated into French, German, Spanish, Italian, and Russian.

A large part of the discussion in *Fat and Blood* is devoted to that characteristic phenomenon of the Victorian era, the semi-invalid woman who, although having no organic disease, suffered from "nervous exhaustion."

. . . the woman grows pale and thin, eats little, or if she eats does not profit by it. Everything wearies her,—to sew, to write, to read, to walk,—and by and by the sofa or the bed is her only comfort. Every effort is paid for dearly, and she describes herself as aching and sore, as sleeping ill, as needing constant stimulus and endless tonics. Then comes the mischievous role of bromides, opium, chloral, and brandy. If the case did not begin with uterine troubles they soon appear, and are usually treated in vain if the general means employed to build up the bodily health fail, as in many of these cases they do fail. The same remark applies to the dyspepsias and constipation which further annoy the patient and embarrass the treatment. If such a person is emotional she does not fail to become more so, and even the firmest women lose self-control at last under incessant feebleness.

One thinks immediately of Elizabeth Barrett, of Mrs. Dante

Gabriel Rossetti, of the invalids in countless novels. This was the heyday of Lydia Pinkham and Peruna.

Mitchell's approach to the problem had none of the elaborate theoretical structure of Freud's system. *Fat and Blood* has no mumbo-jumbo of terms like *id* or *super ego*. Instead, Mitchell has used a typical American pragmatism. If he lacks Freud's philosophical search for fundamental concepts, he has the same recognition of the relationship between physical symptoms and psychological states. His first concern was to alter "the moral atmosphere which has been to the patient like the very breathing of evil." This moral atmosphere was usually "the self-sacrificing love and over-careful sympathy of a mother, a sister, or some other devoted relative."

It is easy to see where this all leads to,—the nurse falls ill, and a new victim is found. I have seen a hysterical, anaemic girl kill in this way three generations of nurses. If you tell the patient she is basely selfish she is probably amazed, and wonders at your cruelty. To cure such a case you must morally alter as well as physically amend, and nothing less will answer.

Therefore Mitchell's first step was to substitute "the firm kindness of a well-trained hired nurse." The next step was a rest in bed of a month to six weeks. At the end of this period the patient was usually eager to accept the order to get up and take some exercise. There is, however, the famous anecdote of a woman who refused to follow Dr. Mitchell's edict. After considerable persuasion he threatened, "If you are not out of bed in five minutes—I'll get into it with you!" He removed his coat, then his vest, but the patient did not move. When he started to take off his trousers, a very angry woman leaped out of bed. The comment of a young woman in 1947, "She should have called his bluff," suggests some of the reasons why the whole social fabric reflected in *Fat and Blood* now seems archaic.

The anecdote also reflects some of the empiricism characteristic of Mitchell. This he shows throughout the book. Most patients needed to be denied alcohol; some were given a daily ounce of whiskey or several glasses of dry champagne. For most, rest was prescribed until they were fattened up, but certain others were advised to exercise. One patient refused to take her daily walk. So Dr. Mitchell courteously offered to drive her home from his office. A good way from her home he sternly told her to get out and walk. Such incidents are useful footnotes to *Fat and Blood*. They show an older and more assured man than the conciliatory author of the first edition, but they also show the personality behind the treatment.

Its success in Mitchell's hands was perhaps as much due to his personality as to the rest, massage, diet, and electrical treatments. There is considerable testimony to his dominating and stimulating personality. He had an influence over women not entirely accounted for by his medical skill. A granddaughter describes him as "electric with fascination." His fan mail from women testifies to this quality. Therefore certain remarks in *Fat and Blood* must be read with an understanding of the man who wrote them:

If the physician has the force of character required to secure the confidence and respect of his patients he has also much more in his power, and should have the tact to seize the proper occasions to direct the thoughts of his patients to the lapse from duties to others, and to the selfishness which a life of invalidism is apt to bring about. Such moral medication belongs to the higher sphere of a doctor's duties. . . .

It is obvious that the genuine and often remarkable success of the methods described in *Fat and Blood* are not entirely due to the system of treatment. Mitchell himself recognized this; he was not one to put the machinery of a system above the human element. In a later edition he wrote:

Mere hygienic advice will win a victory in the hands of one man and obtain no good results in those of another, for we are, after all, artists who all use the same means to an end but fail or succeed according to our method of using them.

Undoubtedly the Rest Cure was useful in overcoming the underweight and anemia related to neurotic states. The system of massage and electric stimulation was an ingenious way of meeting a practical problem: "How to deprive rest of its evils . . ." These were indigestion and constipation. Characteristically Mitchell was open-minded enough to get a clue from a local charlatan who had achieved remarkable results by the use of massage in a case of paralysis. It is probable that today Mitchell would have recognized the contribution of osteopathy without subscribing to its dubious theories. Always his approach is pragmatic. *Fat and Blood* is a remarkable account of applied therapeutics for ailments of neurotic origin.

The controversy over Mitchell's ideas foreshadowed that of several decades later between the neurologists and the psychiatrists. Mitchell was not a psychiatrist in the modern sense of the term. He was a neurologist, and in America neurology was far ahead of psychiatry both in point of time and in the development of research techniques. The neurologist's approach to the problems of nervous disease was primarily physiological. He looked for nerve lesions; like Mills, he plotted the areas of the brain which controlled various functions. The superintendents of asylums performed hundreds of autopsies in search of lesions in the brain and nervous system. The Civil War had given great impetus to this approach, as in the studies of Keen, Morehouse, and Mitchell. The neurologist deals with measurable, demonstrable data. A nerve wound causing paralysis of function is obviously physiological; claustrophobia or a psychosis is apparently not. But in the nineteenth century the neurologists were looking for physiological or somatic clues to all neurotic phenomena. Thus a purely empirical treatment such as the Rest Cure smacked of pseudo-science and quackery.

Today, when at least fifty per cent of the more serious cases, the psychoses, have no demonstrable somatic pathology, the psychic orientation of treatment is generally accepted. In the 1870's the important American investigators such as Hammond, Edward Sequin, Edward Spitzka, George Beard, J. S. Jewell, along with Keen, Morehouse, and Mitchell himself, were all neurologists. The very productiveness of their work suggested that the somatic approach was the only valid one. Thus it was the neurologists who at the turn of the century became the chief opponents of Freud and his followers. It is to Mitchell's credit that, neurologist though he was, he realized the need for a psychic approach as well. He learned to recognize, in environmental factors like education, the sources of good or bad mental health.

Another point worth noting is that Mitchell and his fellow neurologists concerned themselves with the ambulatory sufferer from mental or emotional disorder. They were the first to recognize and treat the mentally ill who were not committed or committable to mental institutions. *Wear and Tear*, like the later *Doctor and Patient*, is essentially a discussion of physical and mental hygiene. The Rest Cure was a method of treatment for the type of cases the medical profession had long treated with contempt and bread pills. Mitchell was one of the first to stress the relation between physical and mental health, and to recognize the neurotic as an ill person rather than as a nuisance or a malingerer.

Mitchell's growing prominence and the resulting flood of patients did not prevent him from aiding the work of others. His own office might be, as a friend commented, "the ghoul-haunted woodland of Weir," but he found time and energy to help Dr. Charles Kasner Mills in his attempt to start a department for nervous diseases at Blockley, the vast, ancient charity hospital of Philadelphia. Mitchell had earlier seen the great value of the neurological material which was available there, but had been unable to get anyone to do anything about it. When in 1877 Mills took up the project, all sorts of obstacles were thrown in his way. Mitchell came to his aid and helped to get the department started. When necessary, Mitchell could pull useful wires. Nor did his efforts stop with aiding Mills in getting started; throughout his life Mitchell continued his interest in the clinic and the studies in cerebral localization and all forms of neurological work at the hospital. The fact that Mills had been a surgeon at the Battle of Gettysburg gave the two men another link. They spent many hours discussing the war. Mills also enjoyed listening to Mitchell's conversational clinics and conferences at the Orthopaedic Hospital. Like almost all Mitchell's other friendships, this one was lifelong.

In this same year Mitchell moved to 1524 Walnut Street. This handsome, four-story row house had been his wife's home. Here, as he had done from childhood, he lived south of Market Street. In the nineteenth century this boundary had much the same significance as the railroad tracks in other towns. One lived on the right side or the other side. In a satiric novel of the period a mother refuses to invite to her home the child of a Southern family which had moved to Spring Garden Street:

No, we have our rules, and we cannot break them even for nice people who have been so foolish or so ignorant as to settle above Market Street.

This cleavage, "as distinct as the brass line of the equator on a globe," is alleged to have governed social distinctions as far away as Bryn Mawr College.

At 1524 Walnut Street, two squares below this important

equator, the Mitchells entertained lavishly. Their claw-footed extension table with its ten leaves held the choicest delicacies and the rarest wines. The service was elaborate and the butlers always in uniform. After dinner the tablecloth was removed and the Madeira circulated from left to right in good British fashion. Later Dr. Mitchell took the gentlemen to his office for cigars and conversation. Here in season blazed a wood fire. On both sides of the fireplace were shelves of rare books. In the center of the room stood a handsome Chippendale flat-top desk covered with manuscripts, papers, books, magazines, and one or two medical instruments. The other furniture was a mixture of eighteenth-century pieces and Victorian atroc-ities. A life-sized portrait of Sir William Harvey hung on the wall. There were engravings and a water color of a huge rattlesnake. Everywhere there were photographs of friends and patients. In the center of the room was a huge glass chandelier. It was a rich, heavy, and somewhat messy room. Patients were ushered in by a doorman in knickerbockers and a red vest with brass buttons and a swallowtail coat. With the move to 1524 Walnut Street, Dr. Mitchell had definitely arrived.

In the summer the Mitchells went to Newport, where the Doctor found the nearest approach to what he regarded as true social life. This was the period when Henry James found there a way of life with "a faintly European expression." No-where else in America did "business seem so remote, so vague, so unreal." Much as Mitchell enjoyed it, he never, like James, confused it with ancient Athens. "How delicate, how wise, how discriminating they should become," James wrote of the summer residents. "What excellent manners—what enlight-ened opinions—their situation should produce! How it should purge them of vulgarity! Happy *villeggianti* of Newport!"

Mitchell later became bored with Newport, but at this period he found interesting companions. He rode constantly

Office at 1524 Walnut Street

with George Bancroft. Their mutual interest in history did
not carry over to roses. Mitchell was forced to admit that his
were "poor devils anyway—not worth listing." There were
also Colonel Higginson, Alexander Agassiz, and some relatives
of Mrs. Mitchell's: the Willings and her uncle George Cadwalader and his wife. Without James' exclamation points,
Mitchell spoke of "our large, highly-cultivated, intellectual
life." There were trips to Boston and New York. "Weir
Mitchell has been here curing all the dilapidated Bostonians,"
Phillips Brooks wrote in 1878. "His coming makes a great
sensation, for he is a very famous man." In New York there
was William A. Hammond, who was also becoming well
known as a neurologist.

He kept in touch with John Shaw Billings, who was in
Washington developing the Surgeon General's Library and
filling it with rare books from all over Europe. During these
years Billings too was becoming famous. In 1876, out of five
designs for the Johns Hopkins Hospital, his was the one
accepted. He began publication of the *Index Medicus* and in
1880 issued the first volume of the *Index Catalogue* of the
library, both of immense importance. In the same year he
proposed that medical data be recorded by means of holes
punched on a card, and that the cards then be assorted and
counted mechanically. Like Mitchell he was a great reader,
devouring a novel or two every evening. He was interested
in philosophy and theosophy, delving into Plato, Spinoza,
Cornelius Agrippa, Paracelsus, and the Cabala. It is quite likely
that his interest in William Blake was the source of Mitchell's
discovery of that poet. He was the master of a vigorous, clear
style. As early as 1871 he was investigating the germ theory
of disease. In his discussions of hospital design, the care of
patients, or the various types of physicians, he went right
to the fundamentals, the philosophy of any problem. Of all
that remarkable group of medical philosophers which in-

cluded Mitchell, Osler, and Welch, it is Billings who often seems the most profound.

Of course he and Mitchell discussed other things besides literature and philosophy. Sometimes it was so crass a subject as patients who failed to pay bills. Thus in answer to an inquiry about one who had apparently moved from Philadelphia to Washington, Mitchell wrote:

. . . I used to attend him here but was idiot enough to attend his old mother until she owed me a few hundreds . . .

Billings, however, did not share Mitchell's fondness for discussing the Civil War. He had seen too much of it: the Wilderness campaign and the blowing up of Petersburg. Anyone who talked about the war in Billings' home was silenced under threat of being shown the door.

Mitchell kept in touch with these men by letter and saw them at medical meetings. In 1879 he managed to get away long enough for a trip to Yellowstone Park.

With a widening circle of friends came even more letter writing. Francis Parkman asked medical advice and, when Mitchell asked for a book or two, sent a whole set. "I felt as if I had gotten tremendously the better of a live Yankee," Mitchell said in his letter of thanks. He went on to tell of beguiling himself with Parkman's works during sad and bitter hours earlier in his life. There was correspondence with Brooks and Holmes and Billings.

At home, medical practice continued to increase, and other physicians asked for consultations. People with causes to promote came for contributions and aid. To the College of Physicians Mitchell presented copies of portraits of Harvey and Jenner. In 1875 he was elected a trustee of the University of Pennsylvania and president of the American Neurological Association.

In addition to entertaining at home he loved to dine out at

various clubs. The Biological Club was one of his favorites. Here he could see Joseph Leidy, whom he "greatly loved and honored." Osler became a member soon after coming to Philadelphia. A wit remarked that the function of the club was the worship of the sacred tortoise. Leidy, however, instead of eating a dozen terrapin presented to him, dissected them and discovered three intestinal parasites previously unknown. "Never give Leidy anything that is edible and worth dissecting," Mitchell warned the donor. He summed up their meetings: "We had science of the highest; good talk; never were gayer dinners!"

Thus at the end of the 1870's Weir Mitchell seemed destined to the life of a fashionable Philadelphia physician: he had a full and satisfying social life, a charming wife, two promising sons and a lovely small daughter; he had a large practice and a reputation in science. He was in a position to coast upon his social standing and medical reputation.

VI

A New Career

1880 - 1889

"Each life converges to some center
Expressed or still."
—EMILY DICKINSON

IN 1880 Weir Mitchell was fifty-one. His professional and
social prestige might well have satisfied him. Instead he began
a new career and added distinction to his earlier one. He became a novelist, and he participated in the medical researches
which made the decade "the most wonderful, perhaps, in the
history of medicine." Thus Flexner spoke of it, and Cushing,
writing of this and the next two decades, called it "the most
remarkable period in the annals of medicine." In addition to
writing, medical practice, and research, Mitchell brought
Osler to Philadelphia. This was the beginning of another
warm friendship, one that lasted over thirty years.

Before 1880 Mitchell had published four stories in the
Atlantic, one of them, *The Autobiography of a Quack*, long
enough to require two issues. Only one of the stories carried
his name. Another, *Thee and You*, published by Lippincott,
was signed Edward Kearsley. His reason for anonymity was
probably the advice of his conservative elders in the profession who warned that patients might distrust a physician
who wrote. Philadelphia has always regarded writers and
artists as rather queer fellows. Mitchell's chief encouragement
came from Holmes, who in 1862 wrote, ". . . remember

Haller and Goethe and make the most of both your talents by either of which I have no doubt you can achieve reputation." Years later, however, when he had achieved literary success, Mitchell was still a little defensive in telling of his decision to continue writing. "Feeling that I could not be injured by literary success, and trusting the good sense of the American people to know whether I was any the less a good doctor because I could write a novel, I continued to thus amuse myself."

In 1880 he published a volume of fiction called *Hephzibah Guinnes*. In addition to the novelette of that name it reprinted *Thee and You* and added *A Draft on the Bank of Spain*. With *Hephzibah Guinnes* Mitchell entered two areas of fiction he was to develop throughout his life: historical romance and the study of neurotic personality. The story is laid in Philadelphia at the end of the eighteenth century. There is careful representation of costume, furniture, local scenery. Miss Howard's parlor is described as having a half-dozen portraits by Copley and Stuart. There are nests of Chinese teapoys, carved chairs and India cabinets. "The walls were covered with small crimson squares of wall-paper, then just introduced, and the Quaker's foot fell noiselessly on the rich brown and yellow and red of a Turkey carpet." When Arthur Guinnes takes a walk, he goes along the willowy margin of the river, then across the floating bridge at Gray's Ferry, and so up to the high ground back of Woodlands. Though the floating bridge had been replaced, a Philadelphian would instantly recognize the scene.

Not only is the background carefully represented, but also the speech and customs of the time. Two overseers from the Society of Friends visit a home to make sure that discipline was being observed in the matter of dress and furniture. It was a period of "great searchings of the searchings of the heart." Mirrors were taken down and brass clock faces painted over.

The story is filled with such details obviously based on research.

In the character of Hephzibah, Mitchell has drawn the portrait of a religious fanatic, so convinced of her own righteousness that she lies and hides important letters to hold her young ward to the Quaker discipline. Hephzibah has all the Freudian implications of a character in one of O'Neill's plays. They are, however, implications only; Mitchell gives no analysis of the springs of her neurotic personality. That sort of thing came later in his work.

The plot is pure nineteenth-century romance: mysterious noble origins, dramatic rescues, a family cursed with inherited insanity, noble rejections and romantic love. Mitchell was seldom good at plots.

There are several recognizable elements from Mitchell's own experience. Elizabeth Howard has resemblances to his sister Elizabeth Mitchell. Both are essentially tragic figures and both are witty, laughing persons. "I should laugh at a jest if I were dying," Miss Howard tells Hephzibah, "—ay, and fear not that God would frown." The remark is very like that of the dying Elizabeth Mitchell (pp. 66-67). Another reworking of Mitchell's own experience is found in the skating scene, this time on the Delaware, in which a mass of ice filled with skaters breaks off and floats away. One is reminded of the adventure of Dr. John and Walsh on the Schuylkill. In any case the scene is extremely vivid:

> Here and there on the ice were bonfires, from which in every direction fell broad flaring shafts of rosy light broken by the long shadows of the skaters as they flew around the blaze. Many of the coasters carried pine knot torches, as they dashed by the little party with cry and laugh the lights flared, and then sped away over the ice until they became but as red stars in the distance.

With *Hephzibah Guinnes* Mitchell had learned to blend his

own experiences, his knowledge of Philadelphia history, and
his study of neurotic personality.

Mitchell once jokingly told some students that having read
all the novels there were, he decided to write some. Certainly
he had read a lot. There had been the long childhood hours
in the Library Company; the lonely evenings of the sixties
when reading was an anodyne; the summer holidays when
he came under the spell of Thoreau. Throughout his life he
read one or two novels a week, and twenty or thirty volumes
a year of other kinds. Although he could read in other languages, especially French, he found little enjoyment in them.

The real reason he began novel writing was boredom during
summer vacations at Newport. He disliked games, especially
golf because it involved walking continually over the same
ground. He much preferred his spring salmon fishing at Riste-
gouche in Canada, where the "air . . . is like that ideal wine
which cheers but not inebriates but alas keeps me awake," to
Newport's "capuan atmosphere which inebriates and does not
cheer." In fact, enforced idleness gave him "intestinal neuralgia." There was no opportunity for scientific work, and as
with success his holidays grew longer, he felt that he must
have some occupation in the mornings. "One can read but not
all the time." He wondered what other men did with their
idle hours. So it was that he began to devote his mornings to
writing. In the afternoons he rode or went striding over the
hills.

For material he now turned to the Civil War. There exists
an unfinished manuscript of 107 pages dealing with the conflict of loyalties within Philadelphia at the outbreak of hostili-
ties. Because of the similarity of certain names to those in
Roland Blake it would seem to antedate that story. It is unlikely that having an Octopia Darnell in *Roland Blake* he
would have a Lucia Darnell in a later work. It is safe to assume,

then, that the unfinished manuscript belongs to the late seventies or early eighties. The handwriting would support this view. On the back in Mitchell's later tremulous hand there is the notation: "An aborted novel but a fair account of Philadelphia at the news of Sumpter."

It is probably this to which he refers in his letter to Thomas Bailey Aldrich when he submitted *In War Time:*

. . . I ought to have explained to you that had this been my first novel you would not have been bothered with it—but besides the volume called Hephzibah Guinnes I have burned one novel and have another which will not see the day—so that this is my third. I have had it on hand two years and have nothing to add or subtract—but I am not yet satisfied with the manner I mean the form of the closing of it.

The *Atlantic* published it in twelve numbers beginning in 1884. It was then republished in book form.

In writing it Mitchell drew heavily upon his own war experiences. The scene opens with the arrival at the Filbert Street Hospital in Philadelphia of the ambulances from Gettysburg. Certainly this was an unusual beginning for a novel in that period of saccharine love stories and cloak-and-sword romances.

Much else in the book is unusual. Perhaps the most interesting character is that of the young physician, Dr. Ezra Wendell. Here is a man of unusual sensitivity and imagination, but with a fatal strain of weakness. Thus after Wendell has lost a patient he might possibly have saved, Mitchell comments: "A less imaginative man would have suffered less; a man with more conscience would have suffered longer, and been the better for it." As Wendell is walking home brooding over his carelessness, he stumbles over a piece of bad sidewalk characteristic of Germantown. His meerschaum pipe falls and breaks ". . . a shock which, as he reflected with amazement a moment later, seemed to him—nay, which was—quite as great as that caused by the death of his patient, an hour before."

Obviously Dr. Wendell is no stereotype. In fact there are hints that in this character Mitchell exorcised some of his personal devils. The process may be like that in *The Excursion*, where Wordsworth in the person of the Wanderer solemnly lectured the younger free-thinking Wordsworth in the person of the Solitary. Mitchell is less pompous. Wendell has his love of books and fine antiques, his keen eye for color in leaf and flower—even an early inclination toward the profession of teaching. Certainly, as Wendell walks home on that unhappy evening, Mitchell shares his feelings: "There is probably no physician who cannot recall some moment in his life when he looked with doubt and trouble of mind on the face of death."

The book is filled with other well-drawn people besides Wendell. There is his righteous, unimaginative sister, who runs his household efficiently, yet torments him with her ritualistic tidyings-up. She carries the same qualities into her personal relationships with disastrous results. There is Mrs. Grace, the busybody, who is a fearful nuisance to the other ladies working for the Sanitary Commission; and Mr. Grace, "who believed in the Pennsylvania Railroad." In Mrs. Grace, Mitchell has drawn that bugbear of every physician: the woman who has determined opinions on medicine and runs from doctor to doctor in search of one who shares her prejudices.

The Morton family is another interesting group. Mrs. Morton is the able, determined woman, frustrated by her marriage to a less able person. Colonel Morton, who had "the amiability so common among selfish people," has found in mistresses a refuge from his strong-minded wife. Thus when the war came he entered the army with enthusiasm and became an able soldier. Mrs. Morton in turn lavished her affection on her semi-invalid son, Edward. Edward, too, is an interesting study of the effects of invalidism. Originally a boy interested only in physical activity, he was injured by a fall from a horse. Gradually he changes into a person who loves books and who lives vicariously in the person of his dashing brother Arthur.

Arthur is a much more typical character, the romantic young soldier. His elder counterpart is Colonel Fox, a Quaker who has abandoned his pacifistic heritage to become the very gentle, perfect knight. Twelve years later Mitchell drew him again as Hugh Wynne. Much more vivid is Alice Westerley, the charming and witty widow, very feminine in her perceptiveness, her loyalties, and her provocativeness. She too is a prototype. Anne Vincent in *Characteristics* and *Dr. North* is much like her. Mitchell obviously admired her greatly, except for her feminine inability to care properly for her fine Madeiras. She is very much the chief woman character in the novel, quite overshadowing the charming young girl, Hester Gray, who provides the necessary romantic counterpart for Arthur Morton. In all his major characters Mitchell is conscious of the complex nature of human motives. It is one of his favorite themes.

In addition to penetrating character studies, *In War Time* is filled with interesting and often provocative ideas. There is the discussion of the effect of the Civil War on medicine and on American life in general. (Cf. p. 63.) Most important is that war is not glamorized. Eleven years before Crane's *Red Badge of Courage*, Mitchell caused Colonel Fox, a thoroughly brave man, to tell Mrs. Westerley that he has been terribly afraid in battle. And the daredevil young Arthur Morton tells his brother:

But don't think I like it at all. Anyone who says they like it is stupid or lies. I don't. I never realized until now how dreadful is war; but I think I know that I ought to be here, and why.

Then there are such incidental comments as ". . . manners have a good deal to do with business success in medicine," and

again, "a doctor's life has in it . . . a good deal to harm his
moral growth and needs watching. It is difficult not to become
despotic from mere habit of control, and still harder to be
tender and yet decided . . ." A school for girls was condemned
because it "applied alike a common system, which admitted of
no recognition of individualities," a point of view the "pro-
gressive" educators have since claimed as their own invention.

Thus in his first full-length novel Mitchell combined certain elements that became characteristic of him: realistic
background, complex and often neurotic personalities, skilfully drawn minor characters, historical material, intellectual
discussion, and stereotyped romance. The style is rarely colloquial, never fast moving, but with occasional clever turns
of phrase and epigram. Certainly *In War Time* is a novel of
more intellectual vigor than most of its contemporaries. It is
interesting and alive.

Mitchell sent a copy of the book to William Dean Howells,
who some years before had accepted "Miss Helen" for the
Atlantic. At that time he had suggested that Mitchell resume
psycho-physiological writing. In 1885 Howells, no longer editor, was working on novels of his own. *In War Time* had the
kind of antiseptic realism he liked. As he said a few years later
in a celebrated essay, the novelist who had the smallest hint
of naughtiness held his readers in the hollow of his hand. Life
had, he believed, become comparatively decent, and the novelists had learned to keep "the realities of life" in proportion
"to the space and place they occupy in life itself, as we know
it in England and America." Therefore he wrote Mitchell
about his novel: "I like nearness to life, and this is Life, portrayed with conscience, with knowledge, both deep and
quick . . ."

Mitchell also sent a copy of the novel to George Meredith,
who responded enthusiastically:

... I find it a piece of psychology wrought into a production of art. The story is excellent; and you have done what I constantly protest should be done to give a fruitful report to cultivated readers. You have evolved the story from characters. I look about me in my country vainly for an author who is up to that high-water mark of fiction. The characters are so clearly drawn as they are forcibly conceived, and for that reason the crux of the position between the young medicus and Mrs. Westerley, (to whom my heart is vowed) has the stamp of highest nobility. . . . My wife, my girl, my friends, the fair and masculine alike, are of my mind that the book is both noble and interesting.

Speaking of it to a lady beside me at a dinner-table, I was met by the exclamation, "Why that must be the Dr. Weir Mitchell of Massage!" I praise it on all hands. I shall consider it a privilege to read more of your work and to meet you again.

With such praise from such a source, Mitchell had no further need to hesitate about a literary career. Two years later he published *Roland Blake*. Again Meredith was enthusiastic; he read it twice (Mitchell later said three times) and came to regard it as Mitchell's best novel. The title was a combination of the names of the chivalric hero Roland and the mystic poet and artist William Blake. As might be expected, the book shows therefore some confusion of purpose. And its most interesting character is not Roland Blake at all; it is Octopia Darnell, a superb study of a neurotic woman.

What Mitchell has done is to dramatize the situation described in *Fat and Blood* (p. 83) in which a neurotic woman becomes a chronic invalid and, through her selfish demands, turns her nurse into a neurotic. Thus the twenty-year-old Olivia finds that because of her care for her distant cousin Octopia,

Her life was absorbed by Octopia, who directed her studies after a fashion, and who was supremely affectionate so long as there was no resistance; when that came Octopia was hurt or nervous, or both, or else, when defeat was near, gave way to such distressing symptoms as commonly routed Olivia and made Mrs. Wynne too uncomfortable for continuous opposition.

This has its inevitable effect upon Olivia:

Her head ached, and with the consciousness of constant fatigue, the outcome of a life of strain and repression, began to come its certain result, irritability.

The elder woman has "an importunate craving for expressions of love and pity," and her "fondness for physical petting" repels Olivia. The homosexual implication in Octopia's feeling for her cousin is of course carefully veiled, but it is there: Mitchell speaks of the unhealthiness of the relationship, and vividly portrays Olivia's physical repulsion. Not many writers in 1886 could or would have handled such material.

Like its predecessor, *Roland Blake* gives an unglamorous picture of war. There are vivid scenes from the Wilderness Campaign. Mitchell's intimate friend Billings had gone through this campaign as his letters to his wife testify. One wonders if Mitchell overcame his friend's reluctance to discuss the war, for certain scenes have a first-hand realism. There is the dull thud of bullets hitting trees and "the duller sound on limb or trunk of man." Waiting for an attack, one man incessantly wipes his gun-barrel; another buttons and unbuttons his coat. We see men shot, stabbed, beaten down with clubbed muskets, and there are ghastly pictures of the battlefield after a charge. The whole attitude toward war is much more like that of novels after 1920 than of the Charge-of-the-Light-Brigade era. Blake says of war, "It was for me merely a sad duty. I hated it."

Throughout the novel there are provocative ideas such as, "Character is more subject in women than in men to changes physiologically produced. . . ." Or, "The engineer speaks of the breaking-strain in material: the breaking strain in morals was near for Octopia." Or, "The surgeon's idea of 'shock' as a result of sudden physical injury should be imported into the domain of criminal psychology." This last is essentially an anticipation of the trauma theory of psychosis.

There are excellent studies of minor characters: the aged Mrs. Wynne, using her age as a screen against the demands of Octopia and allowing Olivia to assume the burdens, yet at times becoming the great lady who had danced with Lafayette; the ex-slave Judith, malevolent, cautious, unable to shake off her servility to Octopia, yet using a furtive cunning against her.

Despite all these merits, however, the novel is in many ways less good than *In War Time*. The hero is too much the very gentle, perfect knight; the plot thoroughly Victorian. Roland Blake as an intelligence officer in the Union army has received information from the Southern traitor, Richard Darnell, who then attempts to murder him. Yet because of a pledge of secrecy, Blake will not expose Darnell to Olivia, whom they are both wooing. Old Mrs. Wynne allows Octopia to blackmail both her and Olivia in order to prevent the revelation that Olivia's father committed suicide. At almost any point the plot would evaporate if some character did a little sensible plain speaking. Too often coincidence brings important characters together. The elements in the novel which led Meredith to call it noble are the same which a modern reader would call Victorian. Thus *Roland Blake* is a somewhat ill-assorted mixture of realism, psychological brilliance, and Victorian sentimentality.

In 1889 Mitchell published a very different sort of novel, *Far in the Forest*. The scene is laid in northern Pennsylvania early in the century. Here Elizabeth Preston has brought her husband in the hope that in the woods he will conquer his addiction to opium. He takes to whiskey and soon dies. Because of her near poverty she remains in the backwoods where she gives shelter to a mysterious German gentleman, later

revealed as a baron interested in lumber and coal lands. From
there on the love story follows an expected pattern.

What gives the story life is the fast action, rather unusual
for Mitchell. There are good minor characters: Philetus Richmond, blind and insanely jealous; Ance Vickers, drunken,
hardboiled, but with a sense of fair play; and the group of
backwoodsmen associated with him. Ance, in trying to seduce
the lush Mrs. Richmond, accidentally shoots her. Riverius, the
German, who had been to see her, is blamed. After a series of
melodramatic adventures, including a forest fire set by Mrs.
Preston to aid the escape of Riverius, everything ends happily.

Obviously the material is less original and significant than
that of the two earlier novels. There are occasional characteristic Mitchell touches such as the theory that children are
very complex personalities or that "The friendship of a man
and a woman . . . for those past their first youth . . . has or may
have qualities which give it values beyond a like tie between
two of one sex." More unusual for the eighties is the analysis
of the charming Mrs. Preston: "She mistrusted the stormy
passion of which she knew herself to be capable, and acknowledged with a wild joy that she was competent to love
with such energy and intensity as once would have seemed
to her impossible." On the whole, although it is a readable
novel, it is not an important one.

The year before the publication of *Far in the Forest*
Mitchell brought out a half-dozen medical essays under the
title of *Doctor and Patient*. It was, as he described it, really a
series of lay sermons, most of them addressed chiefly to
women. Its clarity, good sense, and wealth of illustrative anecdote drawn from his practice made it sufficiently popular to
go through four editions. Sixty years after its first appearance
it is still readable, and to a great extent valid.

In the introduction there is a long and most remarkable
paragraph on the treatment of neurotics:

The position of the physician who deals with this class of ailments, with the nervous and feeble, the painworn, the hysterical, is one of the utmost gravity. It demands the kindliest charity. It exacts the most temperate judgments. It requires active, good temper. Patience, firmness, and discretion are among its necessities. Above all, the man who is to deal with such cases must carry with him that earnestness which wins confidence. None other can learn all that should be learned by a physician of the lives, habits, and symptoms of the different people whose cases he has to treat. From the rack of sickness sad confessions come to him, more, indeed, than he may care to hear. To confess is, for mysterious reasons, most profoundly human, and in weak and nervous women this tendency is sometimes exaggerated to the actual distortion of facts. The priest hears the crime or folly of the hour, but to the physician are oftener told the long, sad tales of a whole life, its far-away mistakes, its failures, and its faults. None may be quite foreign to his purpose or needs. The causes of breakdowns and nervous disaster, and consequent emotional disturbances and their bitter fruit, are often to be sought in the remote past. He may dislike the quest, but he cannot avoid it. If he be a student of character, it will have for him a personal interest as well as the relative value of its applicative side. The moral world of the sick-bed explains in a measure some of the things that are strange in daily life, and the man who does not know sick women does not know women.

Here in germ is an outline of the psychoanalytic method. Here is the recognition that remote causes may have bearing upon mental and emotional ills. And here is the suggestion that a study of abnormal psychology can shed light upon normal behavior. All this at a time when for most physicians the neurotic patient was at best a nuisance and was often suspected of being a malingerer. Such patients were likely to be treated with bread pills and amused contempt.

He recognized that in his day a writer of a popular book on the nervous woman was bound by the same limitations as the Anglo-Saxon novelist. He hoped that clever readers would interpolate the unsaid. And as the book is designed for a lay audience, he left out the technical reasoning behind his advice.

The opening essay, "The Physician," is a little classic. In it he pays tribute to the great physicians of the past like Harvey, Cardan, Sydenham, and Rush. He cites Cardan's advice in 1551 to an asthmatic to avoid feather pillows, and Rush's letter telling how to treat cancer of the breast in the aged mother of George Washington. Throughout all the discussion Mitchell emphasizes the need for accurate observation. Family physicians are apt to take too many things for granted. It was careful observation which often enabled the great physicians of the past to transcend limited knowledge. Although the modern physician has many precision instruments to improve his opportunities for observation, Mitchell warns of a too narrow specialization. The specialist must not confine his observation to a single organ: all are parts of a complicated, interrelated mechanism. The properly trained specialist must have a thorough understanding of the whole body. The essay is filled with practical advice on the practice of medicine and on the relationships between patients, their families, and their physicians. There is scarcely a line which could not be written today.

The second essay, "Convalesence," contains, as might be expected, the same sort of practical advice. In addition, there is a discussion of the way in which novelists and playwrights have handled doctors and medical matters. On the whole, Mitchell is dissatisfied: too often illness is used by the novelist as a mere device to gain time. And why should heroes in battle always lose an arm in preference to a leg? "Is it more romantic to get rid of one than the other?—considering also that a one-armed embrace of the weeping, waiting lady-love must be so utterly unsatisfactory." And he snorts over the novelist who poisoned a character with a drink of rattlesnake venom. "She might as well have drunk a glass of milk."

The chapter, "Pain and the Opium Habit," should be required reading for those who think our grandmothers lived in a less neurotic age than the present. Mitchell in his fashionable practice had seen many cases of opium, morphia, or chloral habit, and says he believes these are becoming increasingly prevalent. And it is the fortunate woman who does not add alcoholism to her disorder. The source of the trouble, he believes, lies in a faulty system of women's education. A man may go through life with little pain; a woman is much more likely to experience it. Yet boys are trained to endure pain; a girl is trained to expect sympathy, and learns that to weep is her prerogative. Physicians are too ready to give sedatives to women for minor ailments. Wives of physicians are especially liable to become victims of morphia or chloral. The husband cannot bear to see his wife suffer when he can so easily give relief. Mitchell advocates a better physical and emotional training of girls, and more sense of moral responsibility on the part of physicians. He cites the case of a woman who learned to live with pain: the description makes it clear she was his beloved sister Elizabeth.

As in the preceding essay, there are literary references. Mitchell argues that Coleridge and De Quincey have spread a false notion that opium gives pleasant dreams and that it carries one into the land of poetry. Most people get merely relief from pain followed by ". . . next day's remorses. . . . There was more of Coleridge than opium in 'Kubla Khan,' and more of De Quincey than of the juice of poppies in 'The Vision of Sudden Death.' " In a recent paper based on both a study of *Kubla Khan* and of present-day medical research, Elisabeth Schneider has reached exactly the same conclusion as did Mitchell sixty years earlier.

Essay four, "The Management of Sick Children," is a polite but severe warning to indulgent mothers. The reasonable mother is rare. Too often, "Disease has crippled [the child's] body and the mother has crippled its character."

The chapter "Nervousness and Its Influence" reworks some of the material of *Fat and Blood*, particularly the discussion of the Octopia Darnell type of neurotic who makes an entire household wretched. Then there is a discussion of shock as the source of neuroses. Most of the essay, however, is devoted to the subject of mental hygiene. After warning against charlatans and faith healers, Mitchell launches into a favorite theme:

The strong animal is, as a rule, the least liable to damaging emotion and its consequences. Train your girls physically, and, up to the age of adolescence, as you train your boys.

During the years of adolescence he recommends a more cautious use of exercise, but once past the critical years women should live their own lives as men live theirs. Most women, he says, exercise too little.

Along with much sound advice, especially to the women of the eighties, there is some which is outmoded. To an age accustomed to higher education for women, Mitchell's fears on the subject seem quaint. For although he believed a woman was "better in mind and morals for the larger training," he felt that many girls ran grave risks of being injured by it. Therefore, although a majority of healthy women ought to be able to stand the strain, there was much greater need for watchful care. A girl with any tendency to nervousness should not go to college. Mitchell on the whole concurs with "the belief held by physicians, that there are in the woman's physiological life disqualifications for such continuous labor of mind as is easy and natural to man."

The last essay, "Out-Door and Camp-Life for Women," continues the discussion of physical training. Mitchell even goes into the subject of expense. He points out that for very little money one can vacation in a tent, or better still hire a boat and go camping up and down the inland waterways of the Jersey coast. Out of doors, men and women lose the sense of pressure and hurry; they have time to work out their intellectual problems. Also they develop their esthetic sensibilities. It is here that Mitchell speaks of Thoreau and Whitman, Wordsworth and Clough, and the "out-door plays of Shakespeare." He talks of the delicate tracery of the tamarack, the sunlight on a sloping bank, and the shining changeful orange light on the water, through which gleam the mottled shadows of stones below; the shining bark of birch and beech after a storm—all the varied changes of sun and shower. For Mitchell out-of-door life was a rich and joyous experience.

Doctor and Patient is a charming blend of Mitchell the physician and Mitchell the man of letters.

During this decade there is a brief blank-verse masque, *The Miser*, written in 1884 and a much longer verse drama, *The Cup of Youth*, published in 1889. The latter especially is reminiscent of Browning's *In a Balcony* and *Pippa Passes*. The scene opens on a moonlit beach near Ravenna in 1632. As in Browning's dramas, there are songs, long speeches, little action, a diction and sentence structure never heard on land or sea. Galileo is introduced into the story, and there is some discussion of his use of the pendulum to measure the rapidity of the pulse. This sort of material was later handled more successfully in his monograph, *The History of Instrumental Precision in Medicine*.

During these same years Mitchell published a number of short verses, including a poignant lyric on his brother Ned. Certain lines suggest the character of Edward Morton in *In War Time:*

> Painfully
> He sickened, yearning for the strife of War
> That went its thunderous way unhelped of him;
> And then he died. A little duty done;

A little love for many, much for me,
And that was all beneath this earthly sun.

It is significant that Mitchell gave his fictional character the
same first name as his brother, that both yearn to go to war
but are prevented by illness, and that both center their affections on a brother.

The eighties were not, however, devoted exclusively to
literary activity. Early in the decade Mitchell returned to the
study of snake venoms. It was at this time that he had the odd
experience with the doormat which suggested the dual nature
of snake poisons. (Cf. p. 38.) He wrote of this experience
both in his manuscript autobiography and in *Dr. North*. The
day after it happened he asked Professor Edward Reichert to
aid in the study, which after five months was to demonstrate
the truth of his hunch. His claim that this became the foundation for all future research in this field is probably correct.
In 1901 Hideyo Noguchi was to demonstrate his work in antitoxins for snake venoms. Noguchi's biographer states, "It is
good work, but it is Mitchell's theme." As we shall see (p.
153) Mitchell's research had bearing on the whole field of
immunology, which was of such vast importance in the last
two decades of the century. As Noguchi's biographer says,
"Thus Weir Mitchell at the tired close of a day has made a
discovery possibly more important than any Noguchi will
ever make in this field."

During these investigations Mitchell again kept a cage of
rattlers on the premises despite the protests of his wife. Dr.
Holmes, who continued to find the subject of snakes a fascinating one, avidly read each new report and asked for a snake
skin. Mitchell sent one ten feet long. Holmes was delighted:
". . . What a parlous worm it was, to be sure! I didn't know
that pizen sarpents ever grew so big as that." Two weeks later
he wrote again, having just "swallowed your little poison-

pamphlet at a mouthful." He wished Mrs. Holmes were a little taller so that she might wear the snake skin along the back of her cloak, the head coming up as if to a hood. ". . . what a sensation it would make, to be sure, as she walked along Beacon Street."

The Autocrat was almost equally pleased with an ivory paper cutter which Mitchell sent along with a rhymed riddle. Holmes pronounced the latter one of the best in the English language. He doubted if there were "ten, or even five—I am not sure there are three, which can compare with it in finish and in the perfection of its double meanings." He thought it would be a fitting present for the Queen, the President, or Mr. Gladstone or Victor Hugo! Neither the praise of the puns nor the hierarchical list seems to have been ironic.

Including the publications on snake venom there are more than a score of medical papers during this decade. They cover such subjects as "Facial Tic," "Knee-jerk and Muscle-jerk," "Spastic Paralysis." Thus in addition to fiction, verse, and research in venoms, Mitchell was continuing his studies in neurology.

Another subject of investigation was wished upon him. Henry Seybert, a believer in spiritualism, gave the University of Pennsylvania a sum sufficient to establish a chair of philosophy with the stipulation that the University appoint a commission to investigate "all systems of Morals, Religion, or Philosophy which assume to represent Truth and particularly of Modern Spiritualism." The University must have needed the money, for it appointed a commission filled with outstanding people:

William Pepper, Provost of the University and Professor
    of the Theory and Practice of Medicine
Joseph Leidy, anatomist and biologist, Professor of Zöology
    and Comparative Anatomy
George A. Koenig, Professor of Chemistry

George S. Fullerton, first incumbent of the Seybert Chair
of Philosophy
Robert Ellis Thompson, Professor of History and English
Literature
Coleman Sellers, an engineer
J. William White, Director of Physical Culture at the
University
Calvin B. Knerr, a homeopathic physician
Horace Howard Furness, Shakespearean scholar, acting
chairman of the Commission
S. Weir Mitchell

Although each member expressed his readiness to accept
any conclusion warranted by the facts, Furness had a definite
leaning in favor of the truth of spiritualism. Mitchell, although
very fond of Dr. Furness, who after all was the brother of
Mrs. Caspar Wister, nevertheless snorted at the naïve scholar's
beliefs in homeopathic medicine and table-rapping. The minutes of the meetings show that Mitchell, contrary to his custom as a member of committees, attended rarely. The commission, employing some of the most prominent mediums of the
day, investigated such things as slate-writing and table-rapping. The result was the unearthing of a series of frauds and
legerdemain. Furness, after sitting daily for six weeks with a
New York medium, was undaunted:

I would go on to three months. Does not a hen sit for three weeks?
Where a hen gives a week, shall I not give a month? Is not a
medium worth more than a chicken?

But after six months the closed slates remained virgin. Unhappy over the frauds and the failures, Furness still refused to
pass a verdict. Not so the rest of the commission. The *Preliminary Report* published in 1887 is written with an irony which
Mitchell may have had a hand in producing:

For some cause or other the atmosphere of Philadelphia is not favorable to this mode [slate-writing] of Spiritual manifestation.

A much more congenial and important activity developed during a trip to Europe in 1884. The setting, however, is not important; the series of events was pure Philadelphian. Upon the retirement of Dr. William Pepper from the Chair of Clinical Medicine at the University of Pennsylvania, the Medical Committee of the Trustees recommended that a member of the existing teaching staff be elected to fill the vacancy. The question was raised why the committee had not looked further; for instance, there was Dr. William Osler at McGill. Dr. Tyson thought it too late to move in the matter. At that point Mitchell entered the picture. He got from the committee power to act as emissary. Osler, who was vacationing in Germany, received a cable from friends in Philadelphia telling him to get in touch with Mitchell. Osler tossed a coin; it fell heads and he went to wire Mitchell, only to find he had no money. After almost accepting this as an omen, he finally decided to accept the verdict of the coin.

Mitchell cabled Osler to meet him in London. Here he and Mrs. Mitchell tested the candidate's social graces. According to Osler, "Dr. Mitchell said there was only one way in which the breeding of a man suitable for such a position, in such a city as Philadelphia, could be tested: give him cherry-pie, and see how he disposed of the seeds." Osler, having read of the trick, disposed of them in his spoon.

Therefore Mitchell bombarded the committee with letters urging Osler's appointment. "Osler is socially a man for the Biological Club if we can get him," he wrote Leidy. And to James C. Wilson:

He has every social need; his age is 35. He has won distinction as an investigator and writer and will therefore add to our illustriousness, and as to competence as a teacher if anyone can be believed he must be a really unusual instructor.

He added advice on how to manage the campaign for Osler's appointment. Thus Osler came to Philadelphia and duly became a member of the Biological Club.

A jocular, sociable man, he enjoyed the Madeira and terrapin on the second and fourth Friday of each month. Much as Mitchell liked him, he often found the Canadian's jokes hard to take. But when Mitchell discovered that the younger man was struggling for consultation work, he saw to it that he was brought in on interesting cases. He also probably saw to it that Osler was almost at once elected to the College of Physicians and put on his own library committee. Both men shared an interest in rare books on the history of medicine.

Mitchell, on finding that Osler was becoming interested in diseases of the nervous system, had him appointed one of the physicians at the Orthopaedic Hospital, where he himself worked. In addition he made available his own clinical data. In 1888 Osler, on the basis of his own work and that of Mitchell and Sinkler, prepared five lectures on cerebral palsy. The publication of these the following year gained for Osler a high place among American neurologists. As Osler said of Mitchell many years later, "Had I been a son he could not have been kinder to me during the five years of my life in Philadelphia."

Other Philadelphians were rather pleased with having for once set aside what a member of the University of Pennsylvania medical faculty, Dr. Howard A. Kelley, described as "that tendency to nepotism—a form of paternal pride seen in all successful institutions." In a dither of mixed metaphors he described the university as having "broken her shackles, thrown tradition to the winds" and substituted "Fresh invigorating currents of life . . ." so that every "sturdy expectant youngster in short order lined himself as a satellite to the new star."

Certainly the new Canadian professor raised some startling

questions. A friend, Dr. Richard Maurice Bucke of London, Ontario, wired, "Please see Walt and let me know how he is." As early as 1883, Bucke had published a biography of the poet. Osler had no idea who Walt was, but he made inquiries. And when Bucke visited Philadelphia, Osler took him to dinner at the Rittenhouse Club where he got the elderly visitor to launch into a dithyrambic account of "The spiritual enlightenment" he had found in *Leaves of Grass*.

This was strange doctrine to the men of Mitchell's set. This was the period in American literature when the editors of *Harper's*, the *Atlantic*, and the *Century* were the arbiters of literary taste. Thus it was the verse of Thomas Bailey Aldrich, Bayard Taylor, Richard Henry Stoddard, Edmund Clarence Stedman, and Richard Watson Gilder which got published. At a time when Mitchell could get his verse into the *Atlantic*, Whitman could not. Aldrich, on meeting the latter, was pleasant but made no offer to publish. *Scribners* rejected him with an offensive note. *Harpers* accepted one poem and rejected four or five others. Walt decided he was not welcome there. Nor were other critics more favorable. "I think Stedman likes me as a critter," Walt told Horace Traubel, "but when it comes to my books he shies some." According to Walt, Gilder of the *Century* felt as Stedman did, but he bought Walt's work for the magazine. Horace Howard Furness refused to edit Whitman's work, saying that if they were unexpurgated the works would sell and the editor be blamed; if expurgated they would not sell well. He told Mrs. Wister that "No man with self-respect, or with children, could edit those so-called poems unexpurgated." He had spoken to Walt about his "shocking impropriety," but the poet had been "as deaf as an adder to my conjurations." He told Furness that Emerson had spent two hours under the elms on the Boston Common arguing in the same way.

Mitchell, however, was interested. Shortly after Osler be-

gan to inquire about Whitman, Mitchell got in touch with
Furness to find out if Walt needed money. Furness thought
not at the moment, but assured his friend that "you shall not
be debarred the privilege of coming to his aid, if required."
When a year later Talcott Williams and Thomas Donaldson
arranged for Walt to give a lecture on Lincoln, Mrs. Weir
Mitchell and a party, described by the press as brilliant, occupied a box. Furness, despite his opinion that Walt was a poseur,
was there. Mitchell's subscription was $100. In addition, he
gave Whitman $15 a month for over two years.

Both Mitchell and his son gave medical advice without
charge. Walt told Traubel his impressions of both as he knew
them in the eighties:

> Harned was in today. Also Dr. J. K. Mitchell. The young man
> Mitchell did not take me by storm—he did not impress me. I know
> J. K.'s father somewhat— Weir: he is of the intellectual type—a
> scholar, writer, and all that: very good—an adept: very important
> in his sphere—a little bitter I should say—a little bitter—touched
> just a touch by the frosts of culture, society, worldliness—as how
> few are not! . . . It is true Mitchell has written poems—a volume
> at least or two—I am moved to second you when you say they
> don't come to much (I guess they don't)—they are non-vital, are
> stiff at the knees, don't quite float along freely with the funda-
> mental currents of life, passion.

And two months later, when Traubel mentioned Weir
Mitchell, Walt stated:

He is my friend—has proved it in divers ways: is not quite as easy
going as our crowd—has a social position to maintain yet I don't
know but he's about as near right in most things as most people.
I can't say that he's a world-author—he don't hit me for that size—
but he's a world-doctor for me—leastwise everybody says so and
I join in.

For his part Mitchell, although thinking Whitman's poetry
too free-spoken, learned to admire it:

Certainly some books get fresh flavors out of doors . . . I should frankly name Walt Whitman and Thoreau . . .

In 1906, when Mitchell read Traubel's *Reminiscences,* he was highly incensed at Walt's remarks. "I thought Him self-pleased as a god and with no good opinion of any but those who flattered or admired a poetic tramp."

Mitchell, who described Whitman as having a head "like that of the Capitoline Jove," advised him to live outdoors and take no physic. Walt, pleased with the advice, asked the fee. Mitchell, with his gift for histrionics, answered, "The debt was paid long ago; it is you who are still the creditor." Walt thanked him and left the room, only to reappear without knocking a moment later. Placing two large hands on the table, he stated, "That sir, I call poetry."

A stout lady patient who had just come in, asked, "Is the gentleman insane?" The doctor answered yes, that he was a poet and therefore of course cracked at times; his name was Walt Whitman. The stout lady, who was head of a school, declared that his books were not fit for young ladies. However, she wished she had known his name in time to ask for an autograph. Mitchell consoled her with a note of Walt's.

On one occasion Mitchell exposed some of the literary snobbery of the editors by means of a trick almost every writer has dreamed of. He sent a poem anonymously to Gilder, who rejected it. Mitchell then resubmitted it under his own name. This time Gilder not only accepted it but praised it highly. Mitchell took great delight in telling the story.

As Whitman's remarks indicate, Mitchell's son John Kearsley Mitchell had begun to share his father's practice. The young man, after graduating from Harvard, had obtained his M.D. at the University of Pennsylvania in 1883. Then he had studied for a year in Vienna. The new ideas and techniques he had learned there greatly interested his father. Not only did John K. begin to share his father's medical work, he acted as co-host at the famous Saturday evenings at home. Mitchell's younger son, Langdon, also graduated from Harvard and began a career in literature. In 1888 Whitman discovered some of the young man's verse in *Lippincott's Magazine* and asked Horace Traubel about the author. Walt thought the verse better than the general run; it had "more snap and go." Mitchell was more enthusiastic. It was his belief that after several generations of talent, the family had finally hatched a genius. For despite the fact that Lany was often the problem child and that John increasingly became his father's chief support, it was the irresponsible Lany who was the favorite.

Despite all this varied activity Weir Mitchell had by no means abandoned the development of his specialty. In addition to his work at Orthopaedic Hospital he had, as we have seen (pp. 86-87), found time to help a colleague in the field of neurology. Charles Karsner Mills attempted to start a department for nervous diseases at Blockley, but Philadelphia conservatism and politics stood in the way. Mitchell, recognizing the value of the neurological material which was going to waste, gave Mills encouragement and aid. In 1884 Mitchell accepted a place as consultant in this department, hoping to make it a great hospital and school for mental hygiene; but the guardians of the poor thwarted this ambition, and Mitchell resigned. Thus, with a number of the ablest neurologists in the country, Philadelphia through politics and inertia failed to become a great center for neurology and psychiatry. The achievements in this field remained those of individuals. Mills, for instance, became an authority in cerebral localization. In this work he had the continued interest and support of Mitchell.

When in that same year Mills and others organized the Philadelphia Neurological Society, he nominated Mitchell for the presidency, to which he was unanimously elected. Mills was made vice-president. Both served for five years.

Mitchell's own work during this period included research in the knee-jerk. Westphal's recent discovery of this was being recognized as an important diagnostic sign in diseases of the nervous system. Mitchell and Morris J. Lewis demonstrated that the knee-jerk could be reinforced by sensory stimulation. Mitchell's important paper on this work was read at the inaugural meeting of the Association of American Physicians in Washington in 1886.

Thirty years later Osler described this meeting as "the coming-of-age party of internal medicine in America." He read a paper on the valves of the heart; William Welch and W. T. Councilman, both of the new and flourishing Johns Hopkins, also read important papers.

The following year Mitchell and Mills were active in trying to organize an International Congress of Medicine. Billings was chosen president, Mitchell chairman, and Mills secretary. However, some persons described by Mills as "disgruntled politicians" in the American Medical Association attacked the program. Nearly all those listed in the announcement, including Billings, resigned. The Congress was held, but proved to be a failure. As a result there was a movement to organize a new national medical society, the Congress of American Physicians and Surgeons, as a revolt from the American Medical Association. In 1889 Mitchell became president of the new body.

Another friendship which bore fruit during these years was that with his cousin Henry Charles Lea. As boys they had botanized together. Lea became both a wealthy publisher and a learned historian. Unlike Mitchell, he took much interest in civic reform. When he made the discovery that for some reason the Union League lacked enthusiasm for reform of Philadelphia's celebrated corruption, he organized the Municipal Reform Association and became active as a member of the Committee of One Hundred, founded in 1880.

Then for a period of six years Lea's work was interrupted by the threat of a nervous collapse and blindness. Fearing his work was at an end, he consulted Mitchell, who gave him a schedule of life which restored health and enabled him to go on with his writing. So grateful was Lea that he wished to dedicate to Mitchell the first volume of the definitive three-volume work, *A History of the Inquisition*. For a week Lea held up the title page; then he wrote Mitchell, saying he felt so much doubt about reception of the work by scholars that he had decided not to connect his friend's name with a work which might prove a failure. After all, Aldrich had rejected for the *Atlantic* Lea's article on torture as being too horrible. Mitchell praised the scholarship, but suggested that Lea wouldn't be set in bronze beside ex-mayor McMichael in the park.

Much of the association between the two cousins consisted in attempts by Mitchell to extract money for his pet causes. Lea, who feared that the excitement of a successful business career would turn him into a mere machine for making money, had channeled his energies into scholarship and public service. First he offered to contribute $5,000 toward a university library. Mitchell then got him to promise $2,500 toward a Leidy chair at the University. Leidy objected to the scheme, so Mitchell asked Lea to transfer the gift to a department of biology which Leidy wanted. A prominent Philadelphia merchant whom Mitchell approached asked if Leidy wasn't a great musician. Mitchell said yes without explaining further.

Next Mitchell picked up a passing remark of Lea's about a library and, "with the reasonable desire all men know to spend other men's money," proposed that his friend build the University a Lea Library. Mitchell was particularly likely to write such letters when he was caged up with a cold and had "leisure

to annoy my friends." Lea in turn picked up a remark of
Mitchell's about enlarging and liberalizing the Library Company, and urged this scheme. It was his opinion that "our good
community is somewhat intellectually stagnant." He next
proposed a consolidation of the Library Company and the
Mercantile Library, the whole to be thrown open to the public
under conditions similar to those of the Boston Public Library.
If the matter could be settled by January 1, 1887, he would
erect on Juniper Street a forty- or fifty-thousand-dollar
building.

When the Mercantile Library offered objections, the two
men thought perhaps the Library Company with public support might be able to carry out the project. Mitchell promised
to renew the fight in the fall, but by November he came to
the conclusion that it would be years before they could realize
their dream of a free library. He therefore proposed that Lea
give $20,000 to the College of Physicians Library, which at
that time had forty thousand books and twenty thousand
pamphlets. Lea refused, urging his friend not to abandon the
larger object. In the end he gave $25,000 for one of Mitchell's
favorite projects, a hygiene laboratory at the University of
Pennsylvania. Mitchell was a hard man to refuse. It is significant that it was his pet schemes rather than Lea's which were
realized. He himself had given to the College of Physicians
$5,000 for an entertainment fund and $5,000 to the library.
Mitchell was more interested in the University and the College of Physicians than in a free library.

Like Franklin, to whom he was increasingly compared,
Mitchell was coming to be looked upon as an indispensable
man when any project was proposed. He said that his epitaph
should read "Committeed to the grave." Honors began to
pour in upon him. Perhaps the one he valued most was a LL.D.
from Harvard, presented at the celebration of the University's
two hundred and fiftieth anniversary in 1886. As he had told

Holmes a decade before, "I like praise from Boston . . . Indeed I am un-American enough to think that a degree from Harvard would nowadays be worth more than one from Oxford. . . ." Next to the M.D., he most often used the Harvard degree after his name on title pages.

The same year he was elected president of the Philadelphia College of Physicians. Because the College was celebrating its centennial in January of 1887, the election carried with it the implication that Mitchell was the physician regarded by his colleagues as the outstanding member of the profession in Philadelphia. Certainly he was the central figure at the memorial celebration. For the occasion he gave an address on the growth and position of the medical profession in Philadelphia. No one else had such a wide knowledge of both local history and medical history; Mitchell was rapidly becoming a real authority in both fields.

The centennial was a proud one. Allowing for the customary exaggerations of such occasions, there were grounds for the statement by one speaker that the powerful triumvirate—William Pepper, Weir Mitchell, and William Osler—made Philadelphia without rival in the country or possibly in the world as a medical center. Many years later Harvey Cushing quoted the statement with apparent agreement.

Another honor came in the summer of 1888, an honorary M.D. at the celebration of the eight-hundredth anniversary of the University of Bologna. At that celebration he was also the representative of the Smithsonian Institution and the National Academy of Sciences.

The affair seems to have gone off in considerable confusion. As for the city itself, "Ten ant nests would not describe it," Mitchell wrote to his wife. The buses were full; there was great confusion and cracking of whips, and when he did find a cab, it broke a spring. At the University there were flags, crowds, pretty women, students, soldiers, and more confusion.

Mitchell discovered that the degree in letters and arts was to go to an obscure Reverend Mr. Allen, whereas James Russell Lowell was to receive none. Lowell was there, apparently in his capacity as ambassador to Great Britain. Then Mitchell found himself seated next to "a pale little man" who turned out to be the obscure Allen. Upon investigating the reason for all this, Mitchell discovered that Allen was a friend of the brother of the rector of the University, and the rector had chosen the recipients for degrees. When Mitchell turned to William Story, who was behind him, and related his discovery, ". . . it was as good as a bomb shell." Story went to the minister of instruction; the court interfered; the Reverend Mr. Allen disappeared from the program; and Lowell got the degree.

However the contretemps were not over. To his annoyance Lowell found himself listed as professor; Mitchell was listed as Mitchell Weir of Washington; Buenos Aires was described as being in Canada. At a dinner for three hundred and fifty people, a waiter spilled half a tumbler of meat jelly on Mitchell's head. He leaned over and let it drip while six waiters mopped him off. The next day when the degrees were conferred, Lowell misunderstood the Latin citations and nudged Mitchell at the wrong time, saying, "There, that's your name." Mitchell got up and walked through the crowd of gowned celebrities, only to discover his error. According to his own account he "pretty coolly walked on up to the Rector on the left of the Queen," where he took a seat and "waited close to the Queen and a little below." Weir Mitchell was becoming used to being a celebrity.

The Queen stared at him to such an extent that some Oxford professors teased him about it that evening. Later he was presented to her and she chatted with him for about twenty minutes. For him it was a very happy week with dinners, honors, and good conversation with Lowell, William Story, and Professor Crane of Ithaca.

Later, when he went to Baden in the hope that the baths would relieve his rheumatism, the Grand Duchess of Baden asked him to call. He noted proudly that she was a sister of the Emperor Frederick. The old lady chatted with him for about two hours, discussing among other things the rest treatment, which two of her cousins had taken. They also talked of the social position of physicians in Europe. When she suggested that it ought to be enough for a person born in a certain rank in life to rise to the highest position in "the place in which God has put them," Mitchell after some hesitation answered that if an ancestor of hers had not been discontented with his station in life ". . . you could not today have been Grand Duchess of Baden." She threw back her head and laughed.

It was during the week at Bologna that Mitchell and Lowell became warm friends. They had been acquainted for some time. Lowell was a distant cousin of Mrs. Mitchell's, and when he was minister to England, Mitchell had treated his wife. During the week at Bologna Lowell became ill and Mitchell treated him. Lowell continued to write accounts of his symptoms during the three remaining years of his life. He sent an edition "de looks" of his poems, and Mitchell in turn asked permission to dedicate a volume of his own verse to the more famous poet. Lowell visited the Mitchells in Philadelphia. "Why did we not know Mr. Lowell years ago?" Mrs. Mitchell asked her husband. Of course Mitchell had to introduce the celebrity to Sarah Butler Wister. The poet, although dying of Bright's disease, found her delightful.

As if all this professional and social life were not enough, Mitchell began his custom of going to Canada in May for salmon-fishing. He became quite proud of his exploits and never failed to mention them in his letters. It is typical that in a letter to Col. Higginson asking for an opinion on his verse, he should first describe his situation in a tent on a rocking scow while he pursued the "salmo ferox."

In 1889 when the letter was written, Mitchell was sixty. In that year alone he published five medical papers, a volume of verse, and a novel. And to Billings he wrote asking for a bibliography of John Call Dalton. At Billings' request he was doing a biography. That was only one of his projects as he entered his seventh decade.

VII

The Crest of the Wave

1890 - 1899

"I warmed both hands before the fire of life."
—Landor

In 1890 Philadelphia had become a city of a million people, over five times the size it was in Mitchell's childhood. And the boundaries of medicine had expanded at least as much. Pasteur, Koch, Ehrlich and others had proved the bacterial theory of disease in the seventies; in the eighties Koch and his pupils had discovered the germs of tuberculosis, Asiatic cholera, diphtheria, typhoid, and other infectious diseases. Pasteur had demonstrated the effectiveness of his immunization for rabies. As Flexner says, those living today can scarcely realize the enthusiasm and youthful spirits stirred by these advances. It was a new world in which Mitchell found himself.

He had no intention of taking a back seat, however. He continued to do important medical research and to encourage the work of others. He made new friends and extended his activities on committees and hospitals. He dined out more frequently, wrote more letters, and made more speeches than ever. He learned to ride a bicycle. He stirred up a resounding controversy among psychiatrists. Still it is for his literary work during this period that he most often is remembered: he wrote a celebrated poem and a best-selling novel.

Yet during these same years he was the Philadelphia aristocrat married to a wealthy and socially prominent wife. In this role he entertained lavishly and traveled abroad, making five trips during the decade, two of them for six months each. The Mitchells traveled in style with a courier, a maid for Mrs. Mitchell, and a governess for their daughter.

The record of his social life taken alone suggests a man resting on his laurels. As will appear, it was only one part of the picture, but for Mitchell it was an important one. Out of it grew two unusual novels and an odd little book called *A Madeira Party*.

It was a close-knit social world to which the Mitchells belonged. In the midst of the great sprawling city it inhabited a small area south of Market Street. Most of the group lived within walking distance of each other. There was of course Horace Howard Furness, whose winter home was on Washington Square. In the summer he came in once a week from his country home. Talcott Williams described him as "a sturdy erect figure, the full ruddy face shaped and blocked as of a man of many tasks, the resolute mustache, the solid chin, the stiff short, aggressive hair early whitened." Williams had come into the circle in 1881 when he had joined the editorial staff of the *Philadelphia Press*. He was a sincere, harried, melancholy man, described by the editor of the *Atlantic* as always having the ten commandments pasted in the top of his hat. His interests included literature and the improvement of the status of Negroes. Though Whitman denied that he was a prig, Williams was the author of such remarks as, "True freedom in marriage is submission to law, and the first law is the bearing of children," and again he quoted with approval the remark of a friend that "a woman after two or three engagements must be pretty well kissed up." It may have been with a bit of mischievous malice that Mitchell took Williams along on a professional call to a house of prostitution. The night hostess, seeing a newspaper man, genially called out, "Go right up, Mr. Williams; you'll find Jennie." Mitchell's

friendship with a man so different in temperament and points
of view is characteristic of him, a characteristic he did not
lose as he grew older. As he said, those who would have
friends must put up with what they lack.

Williams was one of those invited to Mitchell's "Saturday
evenings after nine." There might also be Harrison Morris,
Felix Schelling, Morris Jastrow, Charles E. Dana, Frank Gum-
mere, Owen Wister, and many others, especially visitors like
Osler or Augustus Saint-Gaudens. The first question would
be "Scotch or rye?" Mitchell presided like a benign Prospero,
aided by his sons John K. and Langdon.

In 1890 Dr. John had married Miss Anne Williams, a girl
Dr. Weir found charming:

. . . she is very intelligent—has a conscience, there will be three
such consciences in my home circle—how shall I stand it? She has
a certain mingling of sweetness and dignity which is very cap-
tivating. What a Father-in-law I shall make.

Talcott Williams hankered for a salon. He enlarged the
circle somewhat with other members from the arts and pro-
fessions. When the guests stayed to dinner, Mrs. Williams
wore ropes of ancient seals given by her husband. He was
almost embarrassing in his politeness, especially when he insisted on removing the guests' overshoes, muddy from Philadelphia brick sidewalks. After dinner he would pick up his
green bag and set off at a lope for the *Press*, over thirteen
blocks distant. Mrs. Williams, finding that her Philadelphia
guests did not take kindly to the exotic dishes she had learned
in the Orient, such as couscous and pilaff, went to cooking
school. She arranged an outdoor dining room in the back
buildings, where she gave select little dinners with the hot
things always hot and the cold things cold. For this Philadelphia circle took dining seriously.

Mrs. Mitchell's dinners were especially famous. There
would be terrapin and champagne; then the cloth would be

removed and the Madeira circulated to the left. Away from his own home Mitchell tended to be, according to Furness, the Autocrat of the Dinner Table, even moving his seat if the conversation bored him. But at home he was the gracious host, giving the guests a chance to talk. If a promising young man needed the right contacts, he would find himself seated beside the man or woman who might prove helpful. For much as Mitchell valued family and social position, he was always ready to help a talented young man or woman.

At the Mitchell table one could meet Cadwaladers, Biddles, Wisters. Mitchell was especially fond of his wife's brother John L. Cadwalader. Agnes Repplier lived a few blocks away on Pine Street. Mitchell's kinsman, young Owen Wister, married and took a house across the street from her. Williams once got the witty, sharp-tongued Miss Repplier, Felix Schelling, and Mitchell on the same platform at the Contemporary Club to discuss literary criticism. She was also a frequent guest at the Furness country home.

Two other clever women in the group were Agnes and Sophy Irwin. They had come to Philadelphia in 1869 to take charge of a girls' school on Penn Square after the two former principals were drowned at Bar Harbor. Mitchell may have had something to do with bringing them. In any case, it was the beginning of lifelong friendships. It was the able, sarcastic Agnes who interested him most. As Agnes Repplier says, "Her friendship with Dr. Weir Mitchell was the perfect flowering of sentiment and understanding." Miss Irwin and Mitchell disagreed on many subjects, especially on the proper type of education for women. But the friendship survived Miss Irwin's translation into dean of Radcliffe College—an institution Mitchell disapproved of as heartily as did any Harvard undergraduate.

The association was one which continued through the summers. In 1891, because of the influx of new rich who built big

houses and lived extravagantly, the Mitchells largely gave up
Newport in favor of Bar Harbor. The Irwins also spent their
vacations on Mount Desert Island. President Eliot of Harvard
was a neighbor. Like Mitchell, Agnes Irwin was a tireless
hiker. She was a good talker and an admirable raconteuse.
During the summers there was much visiting back and forth
between the Bar Harbor group and those at Northeast Harbor. There were supper parties at Somesville "where were
made the best popovers in America," and gay luncheons and
dinners at Jordan Pond midway between the two summer
colonies. Sometimes they would gather at the cottage of
Mitchell's literary mentor, Mrs. Wister, to hear her brother
Howard Horace Furness give his celebrated readings from
Shakespeare. Mrs. Wister invited as many guests as could
crowd into the place. The readings were excellent, but Miss
Irwin could not resist one of her satiric remarks. Noting Mrs.
Wister's rapt expression, she leaned over and whispered, "He
didn't write it, you know, Nannie. Shakespeare did." Bar
Harbor was a summer version of Philadelphia.

Out of all this social life grew Mitchell's books *Characteristics* (1891) and *Dr. North and His Friends* (1900). Really
two parts of the same story, they are difficult to classify. He
told the editors of the *Critic* that *Characteristics* was not a
novel—yet there is no other name for it. To Sarah Butler
Wister he wrote that it developed from her suggestion that
he write a book of characters. "Of course," he added, "it is
not at all the book of your hint." Somewhat ungraciously she
answered:

Before I read it I want to tell you that I shall not like it, because
I detest the form you have cast it in. There are a number of well
known books in this plan, of which I suppose the most justly
popular has been Friends in Council which I have never been able
to read.

Whether or not Mitchell had read *Friends in Council* or whether he had in mind Holmes's *Autocrat of the Breakfast Table*, the book is very much his own. The wit is not equal to the Autocrat's, but the characters are more fully rounded.

There is Vincent, the successful and slightly priggish lawyer. According to Talcott Williams' biographer (who was his secretary) he is the model for Vincent. Nevertheless, Mitchell hinted that John Cadwalader was the model, a suggestion that greatly pleased Cadwalader. Although Mitchell said that only Vincent was drawn from an actual person, Clayborne, the scholar, is almost certainly Horace Howard Furness. But the attempt to identify St. Clair, the poet-sculptor, mercurial and provocative, with Augustus Saint-Gaudens is a mistake. The two men were very different. Mitchell himself is in the books as Dr. Owen North. Possibly his lame secretary, Miss Combs, is the model for Clayborne's secretary Sybil, a neurotic, brilliant, psychic person.

Of the women, Anne Vincent stands out. Intelligent and restive in an over-formalized society, she is occasionally a disturbing influence. At times she is reminiscent of Alice Westerley in *In War Time;* at other times she suggests Sarah Butler Wister, whom Mitchell described as "the most interesting woman I have ever known." One thing must be made clear: whatever real persons acted as models, the characters are fictional combinations and projections of traits; they are not portraits. Mitchell's method was essentially that of all literary artists—a method which always baffles the literal minded, who look for familiar faces and exact transcriptions from life.

Into this ordered world Mitchell brings Xerxes Crofter (who first appears in *Characteristics* as Xerxes Z—), the millionaire builder and wrecker of railroads. Mitchell, while deploring his business morals, admires his crude power and fearless realism. The man will shamelessly trick an opponent, but keep his pledged word. He too is not a portrait, but a composite photograph of such men as Collis P. Huntington, Andrew Carnegie, Commodore Vanderbilt. In *Dr. North* he is thrown into contact with Vincent, a man with an extreme sense of honor and refinement. In the eyes of the modern reader Vincent does not always come off best in the comparison, whatever Mitchell may have intended. And to her husband's disgust, Anne Vincent finds Crofter interesting and attractive. It is partly her curiosity about a type of person new to her, partly the instinctive attraction a vital woman feels for a forceful male. There is of course no hint of scandal: Anne is deeply in love with her husband, but Mitchell's psychological insight often transcended his social prejudices.

In these two conversation novels the people spend endless hours over good food and wine, in drawing rooms or at summer resorts—just talking. There are the clever, interesting anecdotes of traveled, important people; the puns and charades of nineteenth century fashion. But what gives the books substance, in addition to the characterization, is their wealth of interesting discussion. All sorts of things are talked about: medical theory, extra-sensory perception, women's education, philosophy, literature, abnormal psychology—in short these people live in a world of ideas.

Characteristics, the first of the two, is much less well done than *Dr. North*; Mitchell was a better writer at seventy than at sixty. For one thing, the first has less interplay of character, less tension, less drama. For another, it is more provincial, more Philadelphian. In it are such local jokes as that about the conservatism of Philadelphia being due to the fact that its chief cemetery drains into its drinking water. Here too is Mitchell's theory that although a woman has a right to enter any profession, she loses her essential femininity by going into medicine.

In *Dr. North*, on the other hand, one finds such things as a thoughtful discussion of the evidence for extra-sensory perception. Mitchell has Vincent report an instance in which a man seemed to be able to read cards he could not see. This was based upon an experience of his own. At a party a Mr. Van Gaertner had been able to guess the denominations and suits of cards he could not see. To his astonishment Mitchell found that he too could often guess the denomination and color, although he sometimes confused hearts with diamonds. And in his own person as Owen North he says:

All our abilities, all sensual perceptivity, must have gone through endless ranges of acuteness, and always, in their evolution, certain persons sense in a larger degree than the less developed mass of their fellows.

Mitchell discusses such things as the compulsion to confess or to continually wash the hands. And characteristically, after a penetrating psychological insight, he has Alice North say, "You are a dangerous man, Owen." One of his beliefs is that there should be a psychological consultant for schools.

There is also a good bit of autobiographical material: childhood memories; the account of his experience with the doormat which led to the discovery of the nature of snake venom; incidents from his medical practice. He quotes appreciatively from his own verse and illustrates remarks with quotations from El Din Attar, a reputed contemporary of Omar's. This is of course Mitchell himself, but it caused people to try to buy the works of the mysterious poet. The book department of Wanamaker's, unable to find him listed, asked Mitchell where to obtain the work of El Din Attar.

The two conversation novels, especially *Dr. North*, are by no means an unsuccessful experiment. Like Holmes' *Autocrat*, they are the product of a man with wide-ranging curiosity and breadth of knowledge, a man who is rather vain of his ability as a talker.

Somewhat allied to these novels is an odd little book called *A Madeira Party*, published in 1895, but written at least three years earlier. Despite the eighteenth century setting, the conversation is essentially that which Mitchell heard as a child at his father's table and reproduced at his own. The scene opens with a mahogany table set with silver candlesticks, buff and gold Nankin china, glass, and polished plate. A servant is putting decanters near the hearth. A small group of gentlemen arrive for supper of terrapin (without wine in the dressing) and breast of canvasback. Then they engage in "an honest and refined study of Madeiras which are new to the palate." At each place is a crust of bread to clear the palate after each vintage. Beginning with a rather ordinary wine, "a grape juice," they progress to finer and rarer types. Cigars are forbidden until the wines have been tasted. Each decanter is passed to the left accompanied by the phrase "With the sun." For hours these men sit and discuss the lore of wines: proper methods of "fining," the reason Madeira is never good in England (the British kept it in demijohns), the difficulty of making a "correct palate" at the age of forty, the ill effects upon wine if a woman entered the room where they were kept—the whole mixture of epicurianism and legend that centered around wines. There is the anecdote of the ruin of wines because a Negro servant was stabbed in a particular room. Here too is the snobbery of a social order: "Gentlemen do not serve wine in pints after dinner," or "the acquisition of a taste for Maderia in middle life is quite fatal to common people." The eighteenth century Tory has never quite died in Philadelphia.

Three years before its publication as a little book, an earlier version of *A Madeira Party* had been rejected by John Brisbane Walker for the *Cosmopolitan* because of the editor's fears that it would offend the prohibitionists. Instead Walker offered $40 for two poems which were promptly rejected by another editor. Mitchell sent the correspondence to Howells with the note that it recorded "a most amusing incident."

In the same year that *Characteristics* appeared, he also published *Little Stories*, a volume of seven tales quite different from his other work. Several of them are essentially fables laid in the Far East. Two are ghost stories, one on the theme that "houses have active memories and may affect, as with a moral malaria, those who live in them." Mitchell's attitude toward the theory is enigmatic; he lets the materialistic physician laugh at it, but events demonstrate it. It is of course quite possible to accept it merely as a tale, but there is a tradition in the Mitchell family of psychic qualities. Certainly Weir was unconvinced by the spiritualists and mediums during the Seybert investigation, but there seems to have been a lurking mystic sense in the man.

Perhaps the most remarkable story in the collection is "The Waters of Oblivion." It is possible to interpret it as an allegory, but it is equally possible to find in it a Freudian study of a man with a sense of sexual guilt which leads to a mental blackout. In any case, it is a more subtle piece of writing than anything else Mitchell ever did. Although lacking in the terror of James in "The Turn of the Screw," it has the same sort of enigmatic quality. If the interpretation of the story as a study of amnesia is correct, it means that Mitchell was a pioneer in recognizing it as a mechanism of the subconscious for escaping unpleasant reality. It was characteristic of him to embody in his fiction ideas, intuitions, and theories which he could not demonstrate adequately for a scientific paper.

The first full-length novel to follow *Characteristics* was *When All the Woods Are Green*, 1894. It is a rather minor piece of work with an almost nonexistent plot, but with several well-drawn characters. As in two conversation novels, there is a good bit of autobiographical material. On one occasion Mitchell stated that the boys in the story gave a picture of his own boyhood with his brothers. Anne Lindsay, the boys' aunt, is, as has been mentioned (p. 67), a portrait of

Mitchell's sister Elizabeth. The setting is the Canadian woods, where the Lindsays have gone for a summer holiday. Part of the plot involves the tepid and long-drawn-out wooing of Rose Lindsay by Fred Carington, a civil engineer. A more interesting element involves a poverty-stricken family who are involved in the theft of a tombstone. The wife, Susan, who is pictured as a backwoods Lady Macbeth, shoots, but of course does not kill, Carington to protect her thieving husband.

As in *Characteristics*, much of the time is taken up with talk about books and ideas. On one occasion Anne states a point of view that is certainly Mitchell's own, for he keeps coming back to it in other works:

I never found any one human being who, at all times and under all stress of needs, was able to give me everything I want of man or woman.

And its corollary:

I think myself that when women—married women—grow wise, they will want their husbands to have women friends.

Mitchell's frequent restatement of this last suggests that he felt a need to make the point, either to his generation or to his wife.

Women friends were becoming increasingly important to him during the nineties. Sophy Irwin wrote: "Your letters are more delightful than I can say and how good you have been and will be." It was to the doctor and not his wife that she reported the Irwins' European trip and spoke of the "things and places that we have longed for you and Mary to see and hear with us." And the revealing close: "My dear love to Mary for whom this is intended as well."

Another woman, Mrs. Amelia Mason, was a correspondent for a quarter of a century. She had first come to Dr. Mitchell as a patient. Beginning in the eighties he sent her volumes of

his poems, wrote of his literary successes, and discussed literature. Probably most important to him were Annis Lee (Mrs.
Caspar) Wister and Sarah Butler (Mrs. Owen) Wister. It
was his habit to read his manuscripts to some charming lady,
listen with deference to her praise and suggestions, then hunt
up some other feminine critic. But from the Mrs. Wisters he
got real criticism. Both proofread his novels, complained of his
inability to spell. Mrs. Caspar Wister would run a pencil
through an unsatisfactory line: "Bad grammar, my dear Weir
—bad grammar! It won't do!" When the de luxe edition of
Hugh Wynne appeared, her brother Howard Horace Furness
wrote her that he had received a copy, but "Of course he'll
reserve No. 1 for you, who as he said to me, always write half
his stories."

At times her comments give glimpses of nineteenth century
womanhood which make more understandable the attitudes
of some of Mitchell's feminine characters. It was an age when
women were brought up to have neurotic fears about their
health, about men, about love. Therefore the rather theatrical
scoundrel, Arthur Wynne, in Mitchell's novel seemed to her
"just an ordinary bad man of society—thousands of whom are
stalking the earth at this hour." And when she heard that a
daughter had been born to John and Anne Mitchell, she wrote
Weir:

I acknowledge to a certain wave of pitiful emotion whenever I
hear that another woman is born into this world.

This sort of emotion is echoed by the more vivid Sarah
Butler Wister, who once wrote to Weir that since she had
been fifteen the longest, strongest wish of her life had been
for death.

Both women had for Mitchell a deep affection. When
Annis Lee Wister had to go away for a period of convales-
cence she wrote Weir:

Yes, there is no pleasure I shall more miss and long for than those dear hours with you, so full of interest and true enjoyment.

From Europe she wrote:

If you could only know, my dear Weir, what joy the letter I have just had from you has given me, you would not grudge the time snatched from crowding engagements . . . I am always your devoted A.L.W.

From Sarah Butler Wister (he insisted on spelling it "Sara") he got informed and sympathetic literary criticism. Her letters justify his statement that she was the most interesting woman he ever met. Well read in the literature of several languages, she could support his views with well-chosen illustrations. She it was who, despite the success of *Hugh Wynne*, argued that really important novels were usually about contemporary events or those within fifty years of the author's life. Not *Esmond* but *Vanity Fair* was Thackeray's best work:

I suppose Fielding wrote the English novel of his day; so perhaps did Richardson; Scott never did.

And in painting, Alma Tadema was an example of the impossibility of catching successfully the spirit of a past age. No, *Hugh Wynne* was not the great American novel.

Not that her criticism was always adverse. Some of his poetry touched her deeply, and one novel, apparently *Constance Trescot*, "seems to me a length beyond, a head above, anything you have written, more convincing, more complete."

Perhaps more important was their affectionate understanding. To her he could talk about family problems. Thus when Langdon became engaged to Marion Lea, a British actress, Weir told of inviting Miss Lea to visit them while they were in France.

Our object was of course to get on easy terms with Marion. I still hold to my conditions: but apart from these, we effected our object and made I fancy a complete captive. After thus knowing

Marion and spending with her many hours quite by ourselves, I am free to say and glad to say that Marion has risen very much in my esteem and Mary's, and that I am much more nearly satisfied than I was. I begin to suspect that quite apart from the stage business Marion may be after all the best kind of wife for Langdon . . .

Sarah Wister in turn could warn him against trying to run his children's lives, and, as the daughter of Fanny Kemble, could explain Marion's return to the stage some years after marriage:

His [Langdon's] ambition must come from you and your people. . . . He sees in writing for the stage his way to the public's ears and hearts, and to fame. Marion offers the masterpiece the interpreter the intermediary and it is the highest and deepest desire of her life to fulfill this office honestly. . . . He has the inestimable good fortune to be married to a woman who can and will second him and whose ambition is one with his.

Not all of their discussions were solemn. Sarah Wister could be satirical, witty, gossipy, or simply charming. At a commencement at "the Harvard Annex" she observed that among the new women were some girls with the "old fashioned startled-fawn style of beauty." And despite Weir's notion that medical study ruined women's charm, she noted that several women M.D.'s had recently captured physician husbands. Or she could be sentimental:

You used to like to come and see me in town at twilight just when after the long days I was most tired; out here [Butler Place, Logan Station] I do not have those days save once a week and if you can drop in any afternoon (after tomorrow) except Friday, between 5 and 6 thirty o'clock, you will find me, and I have some things to tell you, besides the thousands you promised me, to listen to.

It is not strange, then, that Mitchell's women characters are usually more interesting than his men. This is especially true

of *When All the Woods Are Green*. In addition to Anne and
the backwoods "Lady Macbeth," there is the annoying Mrs.
Lindsay, who "liked best the level lowlands of literature." She
could never understand the need that some people felt to be
alone, and she is always upset by her sister-in-law's humor and
irony. Because of Mrs. Lindsay's possessive jealousy about her
children, Anne has to deal with them through their mother.
Once when Jack has been justly punished for a serious offense,
she sneaks up to his room with a comforting snack. She is the
sort of mother Mitchell had lectured in *Doctor and Patient*.

A significant element in the book is the somewhat self-
conscious attention to accurate observation of nature. There
are several discussions of "The growth of the power to see."
Archibald Lindsay mentions that he did not originally have it
but has learned it. Mitchell argues that poets are not so observing as naturalists:

Take Wordsworth; he was a mere child in minute observation
compared to Shakespeare. Tennyson is better too,—oh by far;
and any clever naturalist sees far more than any one of them.

There is discussion of the exact shade of beech trees near-by
and at a distance, of the purple tints of some distant foliage
and of the reflections in the river. This interest in texture and
color was not an important element in Mitchell's earlier novels. But in a manuscript notebook there are descriptions
which, reworked, appear in *When All the Woods Are Green*.
In his sixties Mitchell was consciously trying to add a new
dimension to his art.

Then in 1896 he published his most famous novel. Many
people today recognize his name only because he wrote *Hugh
Wynne*. It became the year's best-seller, and eventually sold
over half a million copies. Among its many editions was one
designed for school use, and its title still appears on high
school reading lists. In its own day it was often compared to

Henry Esmond. Ironically, Mitchell's most enduring monument is far from being his best work; in fact it is not even a good novel.

In preparation for it he spent several years in research, using his small leisure to work in the library of the Historical Society. In 1895 he wrote and discarded a third of the story. Then one day, while he was walking over the Newport Mountain, he thought of the device whereby a man inherits the diary of a friend. Thus he could have Hugh report things he had not known or would not have said about himself. The following summer he wrote the book in six weeks. Then he revised, rewriting almost every important chapter. In fact he rewrote the first four times.

Unfortunately the long research produced one of the chief faults of the story: the mass of antiquarian detail which slows up every action. Mitchell knew exactly what people wore, what they ate (and where), what kind of china they had on their tables. He reproduces the discussions in Friends' meetings, the social gossip; he takes time to tell the changes in place names or what happened to the various historical persons after the time of the story. He has obviously used primary sources: letters, journals, newspapers of the period. As will appear, he also got hints from two earlier novels on Philadelphia during the Revolution. So accurate and careful is he that as history the book has some value.

But as a narrative it is ponderous and the characters are, with one or two exceptions, thoroughly stock types. The story tells the life of Hugh Wynne from boyhood until his marriage on the eve of the war's end. The son of a wealthy Quaker merchant, Hugh finds his father's cold, rigid discipline increasingly distasteful. Partly through the influence of his wealthy, fashionable aunt, an ardent Whig, he turns away from the pacifistic and often loyalist opinions of the Friends. He learns to fence, goes through a brief period of dissipation, joins Washington's army, is captured in the Battle of Germantown, escapes after nearly dying in prison, and then becomes an officer on Washington's staff. In his ability to meet every important person on both sides and to be present at every historic occasion he much resembles Upton Sinclair's Lanny Budd.

Of course there is a love story and a villain who loves and nearly wins the same girl. She is Darthea Penniston, beautiful, flirtatious, and witty—the type of woman who tantalizes the heroes of countless historical romances, and who, after saving their lives, marries them. The villain is Hugh's cousin, a British officer who tries to cheat Hugh's father out of an estate, to win Darthea, and on several occasions to bring about Hugh's death. Of course he is always foiled in his villainous schemes.

Despite all this customary activity in a historical novel, the movement is slow. It takes 225 pages to get to the Battle of Bunker Hill and another sixty to get Hugh into the army. And a hundred pages before the end it has become clear that Darthea is not going to marry the fascinating villain nor her other wooer, Jack Warder—Hugh's best friend. The conclusion is almost as slow as the exposition.

The two characters who have a certain originality are Hugh's charming French mother and his aristocratic Aunt Gainor. This middle-aged spinster is equally clever in a business speculation or at the card table where she baits the British officers and wins their money. After some Hessian officers are quartered in her house, she takes to her bed and summons Dr. Rush. When he is not available, Hugh effects a cure by reporting the unhappy state of certain Quaker worthies who are also unwilling hosts. The lady is a good portrait of a type of grand dame who has never become extinct in Philadelphia society.

Among those Philadelphians who were not admirers of Dr. Mitchell, there were hints that he plagiarized from *The*

Quaker Soldier (1858) by John Richter Jones, and *Pemberton* (1872) by Henry Peterson. This legend, which still persists, rests upon the similarity of theme in all three—Philadelphia in the Revolution—and upon certain obvious borrowings. While Mitchell was working on his novel, Sarah Butler Wister sent him an advertisement of *The Quaker Soldier*. In it there is Caleb Hazelwood, the prototype of Hugh's strict Quaker father. Like the elder Wynne, Caleb turns to a worthless British kinsman and against his own son. Both fathers are suspicious of their sons and overcredulous of the bounder kinsmen. In each book the kinsman prejudices father against son and tries to bring about the son's death.

In *Pemberton* also, the hero is a Quaker who becomes a Revolutionary soldier. As in *Hugh Wynne,* the hero acts as a spy during the British occupation of Philadelphia. In both books the hero is a friend of Major André's. And Hugh Wynne's visit in disguise to the Mischianza to see his beloved is foreshadowed in *Pemberton* by the same exploit of Philip Morris. In each case the girl, although a Tory sympathizer, protects her rash wooer. In both books a character acts as an innocent go-between in carrying letters for Benedict Arnold, and in both the hero appeals to Washington to spare André. Mitchell's Darthea Penniston is much like Peterson's Helen Graham. Both girls are Tory sympathizers; both are passionate, changeable, witty, and daring. But Darthea's charm is more often described than demonstrated.

In a brief comparison these similarities may seem to bulk large; however, in the great mass of *Hugh Wynne* they play a minor part. Most of the events and characters in Mitchell's book have no counterpart in the earlier novels. He is reported to have said that he took some raw material from them and turned it into an artistic creation. That is not an entirely accurate estimate. *Hugh Wynne* has greater unity than either of its predecessors, but each had certain qualities not found in the more famous work. *The Quaker Soldier* has the memorable Polish Jew, Solomon Isaakski, who lends money to the Revolutionary cause. He is probably a fictional version of Haym Salomon, but in the novel he is a complex and unusual person. Nowhere in *Hugh Wynne* is there so moving a statement as that of Isaakski:

Every vere ve Hebrews are treated as brute-beasts, not as mens; ve hab no rights, but de right to make moneys for de appressors. If dis cause succeed ve vill be mens, and citizens, and freemens; den you vill see vat ve Hebrews can be. Oh! mine frends, ve will be like oder mens, if oder mens vill let us . . .

In *Pemberton* there is a much better picture of the Battle of Germantown than in *Hugh Wynne*. Peterson treats the scene as a whole with the British army "stretched like some huge bird of prey . . . four miles from the tip of one huge wing on the New York road to the tip of the other on the Schuylkill"; whereas Mitchell contents himself with the scuffle immediately around his hero. And nothing in Mitchell's novel matches the poignancy of the tragic love story of André and Helen Graham.

Oddly enough, Mitchell is much more bound by the Victorian conventions than is Peterson. Although Hugh and Darthea were schoolmates, they treat each other like partners in a minuet. Even when Darthea accepts Hugh, they apparently do not kiss; whereas the girls in *Pemberton* kiss their lovers with wholesome enthusiasm. Sarah Butler Wister told Mitchell that the passion Hugh Wynne had for Darthea seemed to her "sadly invisible." Mitchell answered by pointing out that the story was told as recollections of Hugh: "How could an old man writing for his children speak of his passion for their mother?" The lady obligingly withdrew her objections. Contemporary readers, however, are apt to wonder if Mitchell's hero reached puberty before the last chapter.

Why, in view of its faults, was *Hugh Wynne* so successful?

Probably in part because of its faults. Stereotyped characters and stock situations always appeal to the uncritical reader. For the more sophisticated reader there was the mass of historical information. Furthermore, the book appeared at a time when historical romances were the rage. The huge success of Churchill's *Richard Carvel* and *The Crisis,* and of Ford's *Janice Meredith* led publishers to suggest historical themes to their novelists. Thus Sara Orne Jewett turned from stories of the Maine coast to *The Tory Lover;* Mary E. Wilkins tried a Virginia historical romance, *The Heart's Highway;* and Mark Twain perpetrated *Recollections of Joan of Arc.*

With the publication of *Hugh Wynne* Mitchell began to develop that vanity for which the classic adjective is "colossal." A mass of fan mail poured in upon him. As he told Mrs. Mason, "Aldrich writes me: 'there are two great American novels "The Scarlet Letter" and "Hugh Wynne." ' By George! Aldrich does not speak lightly; it took me by the throat." And a few days later ". . . Gilder makes a great fuss over the book . . . However, Aldrich and Mabie and Gilder are so wild in their criticism as to give me a queer feeling of dread as to the general opinion, which is after all, the true verdict, or apt to be." To John Hay he wrote, "My wife read me the longer reviews, where a dozen or more of able writers told me that I have written a book in the highest rank of historical novels." Mitchell had become the darling of the critics of the genteel tradition.

He followed *Hugh Wynne* almost immediately with another historical romance, *The Adventures of François.* As a basis he used his short story *A Little More Burgundy,* published two years earlier. Both stories deal with a clever thief who aids in the escape of a noble family during the French Revolution. The first is concerned with hiding in a wine cellar which is found to open into the ancient catacombs of Paris. The longer version uses this as a key incident, but goes back to the childhood of François, his being left as a foundling at the Benedictine Asylum for Orphans, his later picaresque adventures, and his various escapes during the Terror. Although the book was one of Mitchell's favorites, it is pretty thin stuff. It moves faster than *Hugh Wynne*, but François is a kind of light opera thief, a French Robin Hood. Because of Victorian conventions there is no genuine picture of an underworld character. Mitchell has almost no conception of what makes such a person tick. François is essentially a shrewd, mischievous boy with a boy's sense of chivalry. Yet in a cryptic statement in a letter Mitchell wrote that there was more fact in the book than he would ever get credit for until he told the real story—and that he never meant to do.

As a picture of the French Revolution it is even more unsatisfactory. The sympathy is all with the fleeing aristocrats; the Jacobins and citizens are a scurvy lot. Mitchell seems to share Tennyson's notion that the whole thing was simply "the red fool fury of the Seine."

Mitchell's writing during the nineties was not confined to novels. There is a child's story, *Mr. Kris-Kringle*; a verse drama, *Francis Drake* (1893); and *Philip Vernon: a Tale in Prose and Verse* (1895). This last is also laid in Elizabethan times and is in dramatic form. Neither is a full-length play. He sent a copy of *Drake* to Mrs. Mason with the comment, ". . . no one buys it, so the merit is small." However, on occasion he gave readings from it to groups of admiring or polite friends. The blank verse is competent, but uninspired, and the characters go about spouting noble sentiments. As with his earlier attempts of the same kind, they belong to that type of pseudo-Shakespearean drama cultivated by Robert Browning.

Much more important was his address as president of the Congress of Physicians and Surgeons at its Triennial Meeting in Baltimore, 1891. This was *The History of Instrumental Precision in Medicine*, later published as a monograph. It brought together his knowledge of history and of medicine. He and Osler shared an interest in medical history. They searched out first editions and rare medical works for each other and for the library of the College of Physicians. This hobby had borne fruit in 1890 in the Dalton memoir which Billings had inveigled Mitchell into writing. In return, Billings, who had become head of the New York Public Library, put a young man to work looking up material for his friend's monograph on *Instrumental Precision.* Characteristically, Mitchell wrote to find out if the young man needed money. Thirty-eight years after its publication Dr. Logan Clendening wrote that he had found Mitchell's monograph the most valuable treatise he could obtain on the subject.

This is only one of a number of addresses given during this decade. A talk by Mitchell had become almost a standard feature of any medical gathering. In December of the same year he sneaked away to Brown's Mills for a few days to prepare his address for the opening of the Department of Hygiene at the University of Pennsylvania.

This department had grown out of a proposal by Mitchell to the Board of Trustees, of which he was a member. He had then deviled Henry Charles Lea into contributing $25,000 toward the project. Nor did Mitchell's interest cease with his dedicatory address. With the aid of Billings he got a contribution from the Smithsonian Institution and, through his friend Wolcott Gibbs, a promise of money from the Bache Fund. This latter was to be used for a chemical study of bacteria. Mitchell found the new department useful in his own medical work; through its facilities he was able to solve at least one "exceedingly difficult case." He was also enthusiastic over an investigation of potable water, and urged Lea to finance the publication of the findings.

Then as president of the College of Physicians Mitchell led a delegation from that body to warn the mayor of Philadel-

phia of a threatening cholera epidemic. They asked among
other things for the paving of certain slum streets. A frightened
City Council immediately appropriated $400,000—certainly
one of the quickest actions on record for that body. Philadelphia had a tribal memory of terrible epidemics.

That his own medical work and research remained active
is shown by a continuing stream of papers in medical journals: nine in the single year of 1893. These are chiefly neurological and psychiatric, dealing with such topics as hysteria,
sciatica, and sudden mental aberrations. Some of the work belongs to the field now called psychosomatic, the study of
physical ailments of neurotic origin. Thus one of his papers
deals with "Undescribed Form of Skin Disease in Hysteria"
and another with "Erythromelalgia and Raynaud's Malady."
It will be remembered that Mitchell was the first to describe
erythromelalgia (cf. p. 80), a skin trouble of neurotic origin.

The following year he delivered an address which still
echoes in the history of American psychiatry. The Medico-
Psychological Society, an Association of Medical Superintendents of American Institutions for the Insane, invited him
to speak at their fiftieth annual meeting in May 1894. He
replied that if he spoke it would be in criticism rather than
compliment. Nevertheless the committee repeated the invitation. Mitchell then set about gathering ammunition by his
questionnaire method. He told Billings that he had written to
a few of the leading neurologists and consultants in America
asking the following questions:

Do you think the present asylum management of the insane in
America as good as it could be made?
What faults do you find with it?
If you had full freedom to change it, what would you do?

Billings answered that he did not think the management of
asylums was as good as it might be. He believed that the care

of the insane in private institutions was better than that in public ones, and argued that these latter had "contributed very little to advancement in knowledge as to the causes, pathology, and best treatment of the various forms of insanity and as compared with the results obtained in asylums in Europe." The reasons were, he thought, too much political influence, the pressure of mere administrative duties, and insufficient appropriations. He advocated appointment through civil service, a separation of administrative and medical functions, greater inducements for educated young men to undertake clinical work, and a separation of the hopeless from those who might be helped. The chief efforts should be upon the latter.

In contrast to Billings' long discussion, Osler's reply came on a postcard. His suggestions were: emancipation from politics, separation of executive and professional functions, and a staff of assistants trained in modern psychological and pathological methods.

In his address Mitchell used these and other suggestions from the people he had questioned. There is little in his speech that is original with him; what gave it weight was his own reputation and the forthright character of what he said. The responses to his questionnaire make it clear that among physicians and neurologists there was widespread dissatisfaction with the public asylums of the day. On the other hand, Mitchell charged that there was entirely too much smugness on the part of the officials in charge of these institutions. They were, he said, too exclusively concerned with the administrative aspects of their job. It was not enough to make the insane more comfortable. Merely placing a patient behind walls and bars did not cure his disease. Compared to the progress in surgery, medicine of the eye, with the approach to precision all along the line, there had been slight progress by the alienists. They were too much isolated from the rest of the medical profession.

Where, we ask, are your annual reports of scientific study, of the psychology and pathology of your patients? . . . We commonly get as your contributions to science, reports of a case or two, a few useless pages of isolated post-mortem records, and these are sandwiched among incomprehensible statistics and farm balance-sheets. . . . Where indeed are your replies to the questions as to heredity, marriage, the mental disorders of races, the influence of malarial locations, of seasons, of great elevations, all the psychological riddles of a new land, a forming breed, never weary of quickening the pace, of inventing means of hurry—relentless workers?

Then, after attacking political appointments and self-perpetuating boards, he demanded better training for permanent assistants and a higher quality of nurses. The assistants should have hospital training, a knowledge of psychology and of neuropathology. "Then demand of your people original report or product of some kind."

He concluded with a sketch of the ideal type of institution for the possibly curable insane. In this he enlarged upon a suggestion by Dr. H. C. Woods, who in his answer to the questionnaire spoke of a cottage system of housing patients. Mitchell pictured an asylum without barred gates, with "no vast melancholy, unsympathetic parlors." There would be attractive cottages, tennis courts, croquet courts, shops with tools and lathes, a library and reading rooms. "I would have kindergarten methods, and modeling and patterning and embroidery."

Fifty years later many of Mitchell's suggestions are in operation in private institutions, but too often the public asylums are as dismal as those he complained of. It is significant that fifty years after what John C. Whitehorn calls a "historic scolding," a number of contributors to the centenary volume, *One Hundred Years of American Psychiatry*, were still defending their profession against Mitchell's charges.

To what extent his address coincided with or was the cause

of the development of research is a matter of dispute. Its chief weakness is that it did not set the pattern which psychiatric research was to follow. Instead of the neurological and environmental studies that Mitchell suggested, the productive research came largely from the investigations of personal relationships, the psychobiological and psychoanalytic research stimulated by Freud and his followers.

Whatever its faults, the address grew out of two fundamental principles of Mitchell's own work: research and emphasis on the curable patient. It was Mitchell and the other great physicians of his age who introduced into America the European concept of research as the foundation for medical knowledge. And it was, as Henry A. Bunker points out, the neurologists who first concerned themselves with the mentally ill who were not confined to institutions. In fact, Mitchell in his address argued against committing patients to institutions save as a last resort.

Two years later Miss Agnes Irwin persuaded him to address the students at Radcliffe. New England reticence prevented so violent a reaction as that produced by the lecture to asylum superintendents. But much of what he told the young ladies must have been most unpalatable to them, and especially to Miss Irwin. However, she could hardly have been surprised. The two had often clashed in discussions of higher education for women. That she invited him to speak is a testimonial to his charm for women. For some reason they seem to have enjoyed being scolded by the courtly and dynamic physician.

Miss Irwin with characteristic irony wrote:

The preachment at Radcliffe is to be at five o'clock Friday afternoon. Mrs. Agassiz then expects to bear you off to her house and give you a room to rest in . . . and then as you know you are to dine here. I am invited to meet you.

In his talk he repeated his old fallacy that many fewer women than men were able to endure the physical and emotional strain of higher education. And although he paid lip service to the right of women to choose a vocation, he went on to say that "I no more want them to be preachers, lawyers, or platform orators, than I want men to be seamstresses or nurses of children." His ideal of women's education was represented by the École Normale in France. There women learned the household arts, hygiene, the care of children, along with a thorough scientific training.

More interesting and of more universal application were his remarks on scholarship for its own sake: "This hunger after the riddles of learning, this avarice for knowledge only because it is knowledge. . . . It is neither for honest joy nor for real use." If Anglo-Saxon was studied so that one could read the great sea songs of the past, well and good. "That is knowledge for joy, for the sweetening of life, for help of noble company in sorrowful hours . . . but—and this is a large *but*—to know any foreign language to such perfection as to enjoy (not to pretend to enjoy) its poets is, believe me, rare." Nor had he any patience with courses which turned literature into a study of dates, names, and verse forms. The important thing was the training of the imagination. Whatever his prejudices, Mitchell had no love of pedantry.

During the year 1894 he took a hand in another matter. When various libraries in New York were consolidated into a single system, and the great central unit was erected on Forty-Second Street, Mitchell suggested to John Cadwalader that the man to head the library should be John Billings. As head of the Surgeon General's Library in Washington, Billings had done a magnificent job, but his pay as an army officer had not been commensurate with his abilities. After Cadwalader persuaded the directors to select Billings, there was the problem of obtaining his release from the army seven years before retirement age. Mitchell made trips to Washington to lobby for his friend's release. He finally saw President Cleveland, who said that he was loath to let a good man go; early retirements were more properly arranged for the inefficient. Mitchell finally gained his point, however. In his diary he noted:

Oh—this Billings business. Never again will I do anything like it and yet it is right and just and some one must.

In the autumn of 1895 he went to Europe to receive an honorary LL.D. from the University of Edinburgh and to please Mrs. Mitchell and Maria, who wanted to go. Apparently he went under some protest, for he was convinced that he would be miserable in the British climate. He was not disappointed: they experienced real British weather and he ached all over. "When a man becomes a meteorological instrument he is better out of business in life," he wrote in his diary. He called on Whistler, met Thomas Hardy, and looked up English medical friends, such as Lauder-Brunton with whom he had been corresponding, and Paget whom he had met forty-five years before. For despite his host of more recent friends, Mitchell seldom lost an old one except by death. One friendship, however, cooled off, that with the recently knighted Sir Frederick Treves. Mitchell felt that the new title had gone to Sir Frederick's head, and Sir Frederick was deeply offended by the American's eloquent argument in favor of breaking eggs into a glass. Osler, who was also in England, wrote that "Mitchell is here, and a great success." On the return trip the sea was so rough that one night it tossed Mitchell out of his berth.

Back home he and Osler organized a dinner in honor of Dr. Billings, at the time his retirement went into effect. His had not been a lucrative position, yet Billings in preparing the

Index Catalogue of medical works had performed what Dr. Welch regarded as one of the most important American contributions to medical science in the nineteenth century. Mitchell, believing that his friend should receive recognition for this, set about dunning his friends and acquaintances. From 259 contributors in England and America, mostly physicians, he collected a purse of $10,000. At the dinner in Billings' honor, Mitchell in a witty speech of presentation handed the guest of honor a silver box containing the check.

During the nineties Mitchell returned to his old study of snake venoms and in addition made some investigation into the effect of other alkaloids. For this problem of snake venoms and the body's reaction to them is closely related to the whole problem of antitoxin. It was the great research problem of the decade. In 1890 Behring and Kitasato had discovered the antitoxin for diphtheria. But how the body produces an antitoxin or how the antitoxin neutralizes the toxin were mysteries. Ehrlich was working on the problem, and in Belgium Bordet had shown that when red corpuscles of one animal were injected into another, the host generated something which dissolved those corpuscles. It is here that Mitchell's old problem of venoms comes in, for venoms also dissolve corpuscles. Partly through his work it was known that when a man is bitten by a snake, his blood will not clot and his corpuscles change. Mitchell seems to have seen the parallel in Bordet's dissolving corpuscles and the similar phenomena produced by snake venom.

Thus when he read in the New York *World* of a Raymond Ditmars who was experimenting with snakes, he hunted up the young man in New York. Ditmars, who was not yet twenty-one, was much flattered by the visit from the famous sixty-eight-year-old man. They talked a long time about Ditmars' theory of the variable toxicity of venoms. "It's a good point, Mr. Ditmars," Mitchell announced. "It's one that ought to be cleared up, particularly if the antivenom—you know about Calmette's work, of course—is to be successfully standardized." Mitchell carried back to Philadelphia vials of venom presented by Ditmars, and kept up a correspondence with him.

Three years later Mitchell was to start an even more brilliant young man on this problem. In the meantime he and A. H. Stewart worked on it. The year after the visit to Ditmars, Mitchell and Stewart published some of their results in "Contributions to the Study of the Effect of the Venom of Crotatus Adamanteus upon the Blood of Man and Animals."

During the same period Mitchell was experimenting with other alkaloids. Probably his interest was not due to any link between them and snake venom, but because of their effects upon the nervous system. In *Doctor and Patient* he had had much to say on the dangers of drug addiction, and the need for caution by physicians in prescribing opium. In his discussion of the psychological effects of this drug he almost certainly drew upon experiments upon himself. Speaking of an unnamed physician he wrote:

It . . . no longer gives rise to nausea the next day, as it once did. Although it leaves him sufficiently wretched, and he has taken it but rarely, the drug occasionally keeps him wide awake and delightfully indifferent to the passage of time. The striking hours are heard, and that is all. There is none of the ennui of insomnia. He may have taken morphia a dozen times in his life to ease acute pain, but only twice has it made him thus wakeful. On these nights he saw an endless succession of visions, which he did not forget, as one does common dreams. . . .

It was characteristic of Mitchell to experiment on himself— he once froze his own ulnar nerve and, as he told the medico-psychological association, he had himself tried a strait-jacket for a half hour, during which he experienced "a half frantic sense of desire to fight for freedom." Try it yourselves sometime, he advised. Thus he wrote to Brander Matthews asking for "a good lot of the hasheesh they smoke and that they eat [—] also a pipe." And in 1896 William James wrote with considerable irritation to his brother Henry:

I had two days spoiled by a psychological experiment with *mescal*, an intoxicant used by some of our Southwestern Indians in their religious ceremonies, a sort of cactus bud of which the United States Government had distributed a supply to certain medical men, including Weir Mitchell who sent me some to try. He had himself been in "fairyland." It gives the most curious visions of color—every object thought of appears in a jeweled splendor unknown to the natural world. It disturbs the stomach somewhat, but that according to Weir Mitchell was a cheap price, etc. I took one bud three days ago, was violently sick for 24 hours, and had no other symptoms whatever except that and the *Katzenjammer* the following day. I will take the visions on trust!

This was not the only occasion on which James became irritated with Mitchell. Their correspondence had begun in the eighties on a level of mutual esteem. Mitchell had enthusiastically praised an essay by James on the consciousness of lost limbs:

It has exactly what my own older essay lacked, an explanation and statement of the laws such as only a psychologist of your force could have evolved.

A few years later Mitchell had thanked James profusely for two volumes of his work. But when, after a spiritualistic experiment in the presence of both men, Mitchell called it "inconceivable twaddle," James got sore. It was Mitchell who tried to patch things up in a series of letters. He said that he had spoken only of his own impression, and that his experience in the Seybert Commission had made him skeptical. However, he offered to help James get funds for further experiments and to give some of his own time to them. But he wanted a stenographer to take notes. He protested, "My writing now arises solely out of my dislike to have annoyed a man I both like and esteem."

Next he not only offered to have another sitting with the medium, the celebrated Mrs. Piper, but implied a willingness to meet the expense. For, as he stated, "we did find the Spirits costly and as I said they broke us at last." Obviously it was Mitchell and not James who adopted a conciliatory tone. The quarrel is a revealing one; it shows one reason Mitchell was able, despite strong opinions of his own, to keep friends. In this case, however, conciliation failed: James could not forgive the remark about Mrs. Piper.

There were less serious controversies. Secure in his position as a best seller, Mitchell asked Gilder $250 for a poem, "A Magnolia Bud in the American Convent." Gilder offered less; he had paid Stedman only $50 to $150 for poems for the *Century*. Stedman was Gilder's idea of a really good poet. (Gilder had recently turned down some poems by Emily Dickinson.) On the letter there is a note in Mitchell's tremulous hand: "G. accepted my terms a $300 for Magnolia 100 guidarelli." This latter was "Guidarello Guidarelli" which Gilder described as "all that one could wish; a lovely thing, that will always sing in the mind that it has once entered."

The poem was unusual for Mitchell in that he used a trochaic metre. Such a stanza as

> Still one hears our women singing—
> For a love-charm, so 'tis said,—
> "Guidarello Guidarelli!"
> Like a love-mass for the dead.

bears an unmistakable resemblance to Tennyson's "Frater Ave Atque Vale." Taking the poem as a whole, however, one must conclude that Mitchell was overpaid.

This verse writing was a by-product of a trip to Europe in the summer of 1897, during which he hiked up mountains and read Sainte Beuve. For some reason the Philadelphia *Times* reported his death. This he told Langdon was his third demise. His secretary, Mrs. Combs, gave up her trip to the west and wired Dr. John to learn if the rumor was true. Sarah Wister, reading the news, got such a shock that the letter dropped from her hand. To Mitchell this was only another proof of the mendacity of newspapers and of "the calm indifference of the average editor to the consequences of a paragraph . . . an editor is a gossip hag and devours any garbage."

Undoubtedly he was becoming more opinionated during these years of riding the crest of the wave. Even the usually solemn Horace Howard Furness was tempted to try a practical joke on his friend. He wrote, telling the plot of *A Winter's Tale*, describing it as a real incident involving two people he knew. Weir bit. "The sad case of which you write is by no means unique(!) I have known several, and one especially is perfectly clear in all its details to my mind now." Furness had not the heart to confess the trick, but he gleefully related the incident to his sister. He always found it amusing to tease her about Mitchell. The Doctor in turn took delight in manufacturing bogus Shakespearean quotations, but this so upset Furness that Mitchell gave up the sport.

But even at the wave's crest there were recessions. Lowell's death in '91 must have been expected, for Mitchell had known his friend had Bright's disease. But it brought sadness. And in '93 Phillips Brooks went—a real blow. A reporter brought the unexpected news one morning and Mitchell, greatly shaken, went up to tell his wife. On the way back downstairs he had an odd experience: he could see the face of Brooks, larger than life, smiling, and very distinct, yet looking as if it were made of dewy gossamer. When he looked down, the vision disappeared, but for ten days he could see it a little above his head to the left. The strange incident carried his mind back to the mysterious footsteps heard by his father and mother the night of his brother Alexander's death.

Brooks had been one of the two or three friends Mitchell considered really great, and the two men had been very close during Mitchell's lonely years. They had shared memories of the gallant and witty Elizabeth Mitchell. At the time of the publication of Carlyle's letters, Brooks had destroyed those from Elizabeth to avoid any sinister possibility. After his death Weir thought of publishing Brooks' letters to her, but the timid and orthodox friends of the Bishop feared for their idol. The letters showed hesitations and religious doubts; they might "injure Dr. Brooks' reputation." Relatives wanted to "run their eyes over the letters." Mitchell, disgusted with the whole business, said he had burned the letters. In his diary he noted:

The ashes of a dead friendship

and then below the entry:

No, an ever living one.

Holmes had died while the Mitchells were in England. Mitchell noted in his diary that it had affected him more than he had thought possible. His genuine grief was characteristic, but so too was his comment: "Together our example has done much to emancipate the M.D."

But it was in January 1898 that the wave broke in shattering destruction. His daughter, Maria Gouverneur Mitchell, died of diphtheria. It was the disease which years before had wrecked the health of his brother Ned and had taken his first wife. The terrible irony this time was that diphtheria anti-toxin had been discovered seven years before. Mitchell himself had contributed to the knowledge of antitoxins. But physicians had not fully realized the possibilities of this new tool;

they tended to use it either as a treatment or as a preventive only when there were other cases in the family.

At the time of her death Maria was twenty-two. But Mitchell still thought of this child of his middle years as "the little maid." Now he felt that his old man's heart was broken. In his autobiography after the entry:

. . . I have had as I now see it, a prosperous and, as things go, a happy life. I would, I think, be willing to live it over, but tomorrow, I might not.

there is interlined, "No not since Maria died."

Mrs. Mitchell was prostrated. For a time she too wanted to die, but pulled herself together because "the Doctor will need me." At the end of April Mitchell wrote Aldrich that "my wife most heroical of ladies—is still—or rather again in bed, but not this time seriously ill."

The rhythms of his own life were slowly returning. In the same letter he asked about a poem by Sills on the Battle of Lexington, and defended his use of the word *becketing* to express the clatter of an old woman's canes. The editors of the Century Company had complained that it was not English. He regarded their objections as prissy: " 'Tis a fine clattering word." He thought Stevenson had used it somewhere, and in any case refused to give it up.

After taking Mrs. Mitchell to Atlantic City in May, he went fishing on his beloved Cascapedia in June with his brother-in-law, John L. Cadwalader, and Billings. The latter, who had never been salmon-fishing, was impressed by his friend's skill and by the luxurious manner in which the rich provided for their sport. Billings wrote his wife, describing himself and Mitchell in their shirt sleeves, resting after three hours of paddling in a canoe, during which time he had caught a 28-pound salmon and Mitchell two weighing 23 and 27 pounds.

Mr. Cadwalader has just left for New York, so Mitchell and I are alone together for a week. He is much better and fairly cheerful, joining in talk like his old self. It is a beautiful wild river, the shore opposite the little club house rises abruptly in bold hills covered with pine, cedar and beech trees. . . . Mitchell has an universally accomplished coloured man, Daniel, who is an excellent cook, and who looks after us on shore, and two boatmen who take us out in the canoe . . . Day after tomorrow Mitchell and I are going up the river about 14 miles, taking the indispensable Daniel, and camp for three days.

For a man of sixty-nine Mitchell had made quite a recovery. This does not imply that his grief was momentary. The sense of loss remained, but in time he turned it into creative channels.

When late in July Dr. William Pepper died, Mitchell tried to get Osler back to Philadelphia to occupy his chair at the University of Pennsylvania. He insisted that Osler should not say no until the faculty had met, but Osler thought he would be worried to death by practice in Philadelphia. Baltimore had apparently proved more congenial. As Dr. Cushing put it, Philadelphia had not been big enough to hold both Pepper and Osler at one time, with the result that it now had neither of them.

Mrs. Mitchell's recovery was slower than her husband's. Despite a summer spent away from home, she was still ailing in October, so Mitchell took her on an extended trip to Egypt and the Near East. For him it was like stepping into a timeless world. He wished he could go there every winter.

The trip and his own grief made him almost a poet. In Constantinople he saw the Lycian tomb called Les Pleureuses. Niched between Doric columns were eighteen figures representing the same woman in various attitudes of grief. Because of his own recent loss the work spoke to him. The result was his best poem, *Ode on a Lycian Tomb*, which he wrote the following autumn at Bar Harbor. The first draft took three or four mornings, but he reworked it six times until he could scarcely read his manuscript. He told his literary son Langdon that he had been "in that queer mood when one thinks in rhythms and is capable of begetting verse." In doubt about its value he sent the poem to Lany, saying that he could trust his own judgment about novels but not about verse: ". . . for it so sets one vibrating with sense of creative maternity that the mother feeling seems to effect the critical powers." To Mrs. Mason he wrote more confidently that it was a "poem on the higher levels of English verse. . . . Probably this is a great poem?"

He first had it printed privately, vowing never to publish it in a magazine because of its very personal character. But before the year was out he had published it.

There are, as he recognized, a few echoes of Keats' *On a Grecian Urn*, but the language is simpler, the tone more personal. The mood is well sustained throughout the 114 lines. Some of the stanzas are even memorable, for example 4, 11, 12, and 18:

Thou who has wept for many, weep for me,
For surely I, who deepest grief have known,
Share thy stilled sadness, which must ever be
Too changeless, and unending like my own,
Since thine is woe that knows not time's release,
And sorrow that can never compass peace. . . .

Doubtless for thee thy Lycian fields were sweet,
Thy dream of heaven no wiser than my own;
Nature and love, the sound of children's feet,
Home, husbands, friends; what better hast thou known?
What of the gods could ask thy longing prayer
Except again this earth and love to share? . . .

For all in vain with sweet imaginings,
We build of dreams another earth than ours,
And high in thought's thinned atmosphere, with wings

That helpless beat, and mock our futile powers,
Falter and flutter, seeing naught above,
And naught below except the earth we love . . .

There are whom sorrow leaves full-wrecked. The great
Grow in the urgent anguish of defeat,
And with mysterious confidence await
The silent coming of the bearer's feet;
Wherefore this quiet face so proudly set
To front life's duties, but naught to forget.

Despite his seventy years, however, Mitchell was riding a
bicycle daily at Bar Harbor in the company of his "cycle
groom," Parker, a handsome man "with a nose which ought to
be in the peerage." He was delighted at the success of Langdon's first play, *Becky Sharp*, and went down to New York
to see it. As Mrs. Mitchell would never enter a theater, he
asked Langdon for a copy to read to her. His own novel, *Dr.
North and His Friends*, was ready for publication. Apparently
he had written it during his Egyptian trip. It is a wise and
serene book, unclouded with his personal bereavement. He
found it amusing that Gilder and the publishers had difficulty
in classifying it. Mitchell took a certain ironic delight in bait-
ing the conventional Centurians. After having been away
from home for eighteen months, with the exception of six
weeks the preceding fall and four days in June, he was ready
for renewed activity.

VIII

The Sage

1900 - 1909

"Some work of noble note may yet be done."
—TENNYSON, *Ulysses*

AT SEVENTY-ONE Mitchell was very much his old self. In March he visited Boston, where he enjoyed himself immensely. Charles Eliot Norton praised *To a Lycian Tomb* so highly that Mitchell hesitated to quote the phrases lest they had been incorrectly reported. The two men discussed rare books, and Mitchell, after describing some of his own collection, wondered if he and Norton would ever find themselves "on the mighty shelves of the great Master's library of human books worth the keeping."

But his vanity had not made him a stuffed shirt. One cold, rainy Saturday night a servant brought upstairs a wet letter which had been handed him by a man at the door. Mitchell read it and went down to see the caller. It was a young, penniless Japanese, Hideyo Noguchi. He had come to Philadelphia in search of Dr. Simon Flexner, whom he had met in Japan. Flexner, who was new at the University of Pennsylvania, had not been able to help the young man because of a rule against giving positions to foreigners. There was no room for Agassiz at Penn. The Japanese had been told that Mitchell had eyes which could see right through a person. Certainly the keen blue eyes saw, beneath the nervousness and almost cringing timidity, some unusual quality.

On Sunday evenings it was an absolute rule for the Weir Mitchells to dine at Dr. John's or to have the John Mitchells come to their house. The servants were thus assured of a day off. On the evening following Noguchi's call, Mitchell talked enthusiastically of his visitor—a most interesting person. Dr. John laughingly reminded his father that he was given to enthusiasms. Dr. Weir stuck to his opinion: the man had an unusual mind, but of course one could not be sure how successful an oriental would be in an occidental environment.

He discovered a fund which could be called upon to aid a deserving student. It was his own money, but he always gave this explanation, for he believed it was not good for students to feel obligated to an individual. It was a grant for research, not charity. At his bank there was a separate book labeled simply "The fund." Sometimes a grateful patient contributed, but Mitchell himself kept it solvent.

Noguchi remembered that the Doctor patted him on the back and said, "This is not Professor Flexner's boy, but my boy." He set the young man to work on the problem he himself had begun to explore fifty years before—snake venom. The recent discovery of diphtheria antitoxin by Behring and Kitasato had indicated a new direction for the old study. Quite possibly the death of his own daughter had made Mitchell especially aware of the need for further knowledge in this area. Even before Noguchi had turned up, Mitchell had been anxious to initiate this study. He asked Noguchi to resume the study of venom "along the line of the new biological conceptions of toxicology and immunology."

The first batch of rattlesnakes from Florida died, but Mitchell soon got hold of others. Sometimes, after leaving the Orthopaedic Hospital, he dropped in at the laboratory where Noguchi was at work. They talked of the progress of the research and about Japanese art. Mitchell had a collection of Japanese fans. The Mitchells were planning a trip to

Japan, for Mrs. Mitchell had not yet recovered from her loss.

The following November Noguchi was invited to give a demonstration of his work before the National Academy of Science. As his biographer says, "It is good work, but it is Mitchell's theme." Mitchell was of course at the meeting, and in the evening presided at a banquet at the Bellevue Hotel. Noguchi, probably through Mitchell's arrangements, sat next to Dr. Welch of Johns Hopkins. Osler too was there. At the afternoon session Noguchi had been appointed a Bache Fund Fellow—again on Mitchell's recommendation. But the Doctor had further ambitions for his protégé. He wanted to expand the scope of the investigation and to that end got a grant from the Carnegie Institution. As each stage of the study was finished, it was published in the University of Pennsylvania *Medical Bulletin*. Mitchell was of course one of the trustees of the University and on the Medical Committee. And he was also a trustee of the Carnegie Institution, which later published a handsome volume on the whole project.

One day that winter there was a heavy snowstorm and Noguchi left the laboratory because of a cold. Late in the afternoon Mitchell dropped in and found the place empty. Wondering what the trouble was, he sent a note of inquiry to Flexner. Even in 1901 a servant with a note was more common than a telephone call. Perhaps the young man needed money; if Flexner learned of any such need, he was to let Mitchell know. Two days later Mitchell dropped in again. He found Noguchi there and told him not to hide away when he was ill. The Japanese was deeply touched: "I am moved by the warm heart of the doctor. Up to this time I thought him to be only friend of my science and I did not think he wanted to help me also in this body way."

In November Osler visited Philadelphia and found Mitchell "still in harness at the Infirmary for Nervous Diseases, still glad to give freely of the treasures of his ripe and unique experience to whosoever needs them." A month later Mitchell complained to Norton that he had no calm leisure. Even at night there were committees or other engagements:

I used to think of age as a kind of monastery where we older fellows would go about and visit and tell our tales or sad or glad. I think that with me the noise and racket of life increase and what is worst there are the voices of unavoidable duties. I am thinking how to get rid of some of them. But to choose is hard and habit is very insistent.

Habit won out. He wrote to Osler, saying that he was to speak in Baltimore in January and asking Osler to put him up overnight. At Osler's suggestion he was reading Sir Thomas Browne, and he had just got hold of an original pencil sketch of Charles Lamb by George Dance. As usual he was full of enthusiasm.

What a fine fellow is Flexner. I have got him on to snake poisons, and have planted him full of suggestive ideas, for now I am at a time when I can sow and let others reap.

That same January he also spoke in Boston at the dedication of a medical library building. Osler and Billings were with him on the program. He visited Norton and chatted about books before an open fire.

In March he and Mrs. Mitchell sailed for Japan. He told Norton that it seemed "like a wide rift in friendly relations," but he looked "forward to it as a journey into fairyland . . ." He refused to read informative books on the country. During their three and a half months' trip he enjoyed himself exceedingly. In Koyohan a large party of physicians formed a welcoming party in his honor. He was presented at the Emperor's court. Altogether he found the time in Japan "a most agreeable stay." He estimated the cost at $5 a day for their party. On the ship coming home he helped another physician during a long appendectomy, and suffered a painful headache from ether. Because of various delays he was not home in time to go salmon fishing.

On their return in July he found his brother-in-law, John C. Cadwalader, dangerously ill with pneumonia. J. P. Morgan offered his yacht, *Corsair*, to take the ill man to Bar Harbor. With two other physicians, one of them Billings, and two nurses they went to Mitchell's cottage, which was turned into a hospital. For Mitchell it meant the loss of much of a summer, but he boasted to Mrs. Mason, ". . . we literally pulled a most valuable man out of the jaws of death. I am well rewarded for a summer well lost for I helped to save my dearest friend."

There were minor annoyances: taking a walk with Miss Minot he strayed from the path. In his diary he noted the result: ". . . sat on a yellow jacket nest. Eheu!" And shortly before Cadwalader went home, Mitchell jotted down: "All nurses are more or less curses, useful and disagreeable." Then Theodore Roosevelt refused to confirm the appointment to Annapolis which McKinley had promised to a nephew of Mitchell's. He sputtered:

Why are my services less than those of this or that admiral. They differ in kind—have involved quite as much peril.

It particularly annoyed him that at his age the worst of getting one's face slapped was that "time leaves . . . so small a margin for retributive justice."

Despite a harried summer he had become enthusiastic about the recent poetry of William Vaughan Moody and Kipling's *Kim*. As he once told Norton, Kipling always refreshed him so that he would have wished to like the man personally, but could not. "He was very ill mannered to me once and I imagine him brutal on some sides and self full." He had also been reading Byron's letters. Byron both fascinated and repelled him. As a boy he had coveted the brasses from the poet's gondola—a treasure Dr. John had stated would never be his.

Then in 1898 a Mrs. Spencer had sent them to him. They took their place among his most cherished treasures.

Somehow he also found time by September first to finish the revision of his novel *Circumstance*, which he had written largely during the preceding summer. In many ways it was an advance over his earlier fiction.

The theme is the effect of environment or circumstance upon character. It is a densely populated novel with an unusual number of complex people. There are the two orphan cousins, Kitty Morrow and Mary Fairthorne, who live with their aged uncle John Fairthorne. Mary, a reserved, statuesque girl of twenty-three, "was engaged in the construction of character out of strong but not very plastic material. The cousin known to her intimates as Kitty was as nearly an instinctive creature as evolutionary forces and education training permit a young woman of her class to be."

At Bar Harbor Kitty comes under the influence of a Mrs. Hunter, an adventuress in the tradition of Becky Sharp. She too is a penetrating psychological study. Completely unscrupulous, she flatters the featherweight Kitty into revealing the family situation and inviting her to Philadelphia. There through her cleverness and handsome figure she intrigues old John Fairthorne so that he makes her his secretary and chief adviser. Fairthorne, once an able, selfish man of wealth, has become a querulous semi-invalid, sure that his nieces are neglecting him. The study of his gradual mental and moral decay is superbly done.

But Mrs. Hunter has two weaknesses: she is foolishly fond of her worthless younger brother Lionel Craig, and she has a sadistic love of inflicting pain. The latter quality leads her to persecute and humiliate Mary Fairthorne, who runs the household, and to make an enemy of Fairthorne's physician, Sidney Archer.

Archer is a projection of Mitchell himself, the preternatu-

rally wise physician with an extreme code of honor. He is too
good to be true. More interesting are three other men, all, like
Archer, in their forties. There is Tom Masters, who longs for
"another good, honest war, where you cannot have a doubt as
to which side to take." He is bored with club life, with hunt-
ing and fishing. For him life ended with the Civil War. The
Reverend Cyril Knellwood is much more complex. As a chap-
lain in the war he had called it horrible, but loved the battle
line. Now through prayer and fasting he is trying to subdue
the natural urges of an athletic body. Because of very high-
church convictions he has vowed himself to celibacy; yet
Kitty Morrow's physical appeal tortures him. She is attracted
to him for the same reason; her instincts responded to his
athletic body. Mitchell is startlingly explicit on the nature of
the attraction between them. Of Knellwood he writes: "He
was sinning against nature, thinking to serve God, and nearly
lost self-control." At another point Knellwood in answer to a
remark of Kitty's says, "I cannot think what verse of St. Paul
could apply to me." Mitchell's comment is, "He might have
thought of more than one"—obviously a reference to "It is
better to marry than to burn."

Mrs. Hunter for all her cleverness cannot quite understand
the fascination between Knellwood and Kitty.

Herself cold and passionless, she could not fully apprehend the
influence which this self-indulgent beauty exercised over so many
men. It was the force which in all ages has mocked the rivalry of
every other feminine influence—mere bodily perfection, with the
animal instinct of desire to capture. It is apt in the end to make
passionate surrender to some coarse athlete, or at least to fall
sense-awakened before some man of athletic build.

A third tortured celibate is Roger Grace, a self-made millionaire. Keenly aware of his lack of social skills, Grace rather
timidly tries to break into the Philadelphia society of exclusive
clubs and the hallowed Assembly. But periodically every two

or three years he has an ungovernable compulsion to go on a prolonged drunk. At such times he goes to a small hotel in Carlisle where for a week or two he can drink himself into insensibility. Mitchell's handling of Grace is most sympathetic. The man is pictured as a really noble person, generous and high-minded. The Reverend Cyril Knellwood is powerless to help him, but Mitchell suggests that the physician, Archer, might be able to do so. In the end, Grace becomes engaged to an understanding woman. Mitchell leaves the clear implication that a happy marriage will solve Grace's problem.

Two minor but well-drawn characters are Mary's sister, Madge Swanwick, and her lawyer husband, Harry. Harry is a pleasant, honest man of mediocre ability. It is the petite Madge who skilfully runs his household, governs the children, and thinks out his law cases. But so subtle is her technique that her devoted husband hardly realizes that she is the abler member of the team.

The story is long and involved, but worked out in terms of the psychological forces involved. As the foregoing account indicates, Mitchell has used his psychiatric experience to a greater extent than in any previous novel. He has explored—even if reticently—the effects of sexual repression. No novelist of his time other than Henry James has delved so deeply into this area of life.

As in the Dr. North novels there are many passing and sometimes epigrammatic comments on life. Thus certain people of no importance disturb the lives of others, and have "the confusing effect of displaced punctuation marks." Or "all doctors ought to have a bout of several educational diseases." And "If one could go from bed to bed, and simply be the technical engineer of human machines, it would be easy; but these machines have mothers and wives, and notions. One has to listen and prescribe for anxieties, and splint broken hopes." When old John Fairthorne once remarked to Mary that human beings were more or less well-trained animals, "She replied, being then of the age of sixteen, that she was not an animal, he advised her to adjourn opinion until she was a mother, which sent her away reflective." Then too there is Mitchell's discussion of the fact that for a man turned loose from jail there are agencies to rehabilitate him, whereas there are no places for an honest workman discharged from a hospital to recuperate.

Yet despite an unusual gallery of vividly drawn characters, a good plot, and much thoughtful observation of life, the book is not quite successful. At the moments of potentially high drama, Mitchell is inclined to pull his punches. Kitty never actually seduces Knellwood; the dangerously wounded Luke Pilgrim recovers; Mrs. Hunter hesitates long enough in her attempt to poison John Fairthorne to permit him to die naturally of a heart attack. Another serious weakness is the use of the sentimental love-story convention of the period. It appears in the tepid romance between Roger Grace and Clementine Markham and again in the coy hesitations of the otherwise straightforward Mary Fairthorne before she accepts Dr. Archer. When some hours after they have become engaged he asks for his "honorarium" and says, "I want those dear lips to speak to me, to mine," "she blushed red, under the masking darkness of the night, but paid him honestly." Perhaps even worse was her reaction to the proposal by Luke Pilgrim, Mrs. Hunter's much abused ex-husband, who had wooed Mary before Archer appeared on the scene:

She had replied that whether or not she cared enough for a man to be willing to marry him his divorce would be an insurmountable objection. Yes, she knew him blameless, but this she could never face. It was a matter of sentiment rather than of principle.

And

He, too, had the sad conviction being as sensitive as she, that to marry a divorced woman with a husband alive would have been as horrible to him.

Thus he accepted defeat and "went his manly way through a lonely life of distinction and usefulness."

As Henry James said of the novel of his day, "there is a traditional difference between that which people know and that which they agree to admit that they know, that which they see and that which they speak of, that which they feel to be a part of life and that which they allow to enter into literature." In *Circumstance* Mitchell had shown clearly that he knew a great deal more about life than did his contemporaries, but he accepted their prejudices. Even worse, he seems to have shared them. Yet despite these prejudices he has more fully explored human nature in *Circumstance* than in any of his earlier novels. Both in his use of upper-class society and in his psychological insight he is nearer to Henry James than was any other contemporary novelist.

Oddly enough, Mitchell did not care for James's novels. The reason seems to have been James' complex and often tortured style. Mitchell himself was penetrating, but rarely subtle. For one thing, he had as long ago as the Turner's Lane days developed a clear, expository style. But it was a style without nuances and shadings. As he wrote to Dr. J. William White, he found James' style exasperating. "However, I am too old to learn a new language and still struggle to write my own with clearness."

He must have expressed similar views to Owen Wister, who answered with a long and brilliant analysis of James. Among other things he said:

I explain to myself his bewildering style thus: he is attempting the impossible with it—a certain very particular form of the impossible, namely, to produce upon the reader, as a painting produces upon the gazer, a number of superimposed, simultaneous impressions. He would like to put several sentences on top of each other so that you could read them all at once, and get all at once the various shadings and complexities, instead of getting them consecutively as the mechanical nature of his medium compels. . . . He does not undertake to tell a story but to deal with a situation, a single situation. Beginning . . . at the center of this situation, he works outward, intricately and exhaustively, spinning his web around every part of the situation, every little necessary part no matter how slight, until he gradually presents to you the organic whole, worked out.

However, despite Mitchell's dislike of James' style, he invited him in 1904 for a visit at Bar Harbor. Before he left England, James declined the Bar Harbor invitation, but said he expected to see Mitchell in Philadelphia. When James reached America, Mitchell wrote again, offering one of his books and extending an invitation to his home in Philadelphia. James again declined the invitation, but condescended to accept the book and to find an appropriate hour for reading it. Both Dr. White and Sarah Butler Wister had the two men to dinner within a week. Of the second, Mitchell wrote, "Dine at Sara W's with Hy James of the inscrutable and not over pleasing face."

The same year that he published *Circumstance*, Mitchell had a lesson to demonstrate James' belief that people were unwilling to see in print all that they knew. He sent to Gilder a short story "The Sins of the Fathers." In it an Englishman returned from Africa tells his friend, Captain Marston, of redeeming from slavery a young halfbreed who had borne a beating with extreme fortitude. The lad had reminded his rescuer a bit of Marston because of an unusual lock of white hair over the temple. Marston, who had been in Africa about fourteen years before, has the awful realization that the youth was his own son. Gilder reacted with a horrified, "It's awful . . . lots of heads of families would think it gross in suggestion." When the *Century* thus refused it, Mitchell sent it to

Lippincott's Magazine, which printed it. In a marginal note
on Gilder's letter Mitchell wrote:

Interesting because we differed as to the propriety of printing the
little story of the Sins of the Fathers. Finally Mr. G. decided
against it and it was left out, but printed later by Lippincotts
Mag. and restored to its place in the book of little stories. It was
considered by some editors as highly improper. Never was I more
glad to say a bold word.

Only nine years before, Howells had argued that "a faithful record of life in far the greater extent could be made to
the exclusion of guilty love and all its circumstances and consequences." So great was the prurience of the times that he
stated that an author who even "hints the slightest hope of
the smallest potential naughtiness . . . holds all readers in his
hand." When such influential critics as Gilder and Howells
were so squeamish, it is remarkable not that *Circumstance* is
reticent, but that it is so outspoken. As far back as 1895
Mitchell, after a visit to the *Century* office, had indulged in a
rare Rabelaisian remark: "The monthly [sic.] are getting so
lady-like that naturally they will soon menstruate."

In 1902 Andrew Carnegie founded the Carnegie Institution
of Washington with an endowment of $10,000,000. Mitchell
was one of the trustees, and the chairman of the Advisory
Committee on Physiology. During the first five years of the
Foundation he did not miss a single annual meeting. These
were held at the New Willard Hotel in November or December. Mitchell's committee, which included Bowditch of
Harvard and W. H. Howells, submitted a report pointing to
the great increase in knowledge in bacteriology and advocat-
ing the establishment of a laboratory for the study of nutrition. In fact, nutrition became one of Mitchell's interests
during these years. He had a theory that in milk there was
some substance or quality little understood in the nutritive

process. In an age preoccupied with calories, his hunch had led him to the threshold of the theory of vitamins.

In the year of its foundation the Carnegie Institution gave $50,000 to the Library of the College of Physicians in Philadelphia. Here again Mitchell's hand is evident, for this library was one of his enthusiasms. Always he was on the lookout for rare volumes on medical history. It was a subject on which he was an authority, witness his *History of Instrumental Precision in Medicine* (p. 145) and his "Historical Notes on Benjamin Rush" (1903). Osler, Welch, and Billings shared this interest; it is one of the things which characterize the great physicians of this period. It gave their knowledge a breadth and depth sometimes lacking in the scientific specialist of a generation later.

Much more important, however, was the revival of the *Index Medicus*. This had suspended publication in 1895 with the withdrawal of the Congressional subsidy. At a meeting of the A. M. A., Osler's appeal for voluntary subscriptions had produced only thirty subscribers at $250 a year, which had not been enough to save this most valuable reference work. Mitchell had tried to get the College of Physicians to underwrite it, but this too had not materialized. Therefore one of his first acts as director of the Carnegie Institution was to urge that body to finance the publication. In this he was supported by his friend of forty years' standing, John S. Billings. The Institution's policy was to leave medical and public health interests to the Rockefeller Foundation, but Mitchell with a project in mind was a hard man to resist. The *Index Medicus* resumed publication in 1903, financed by the Carnegie Institution.

It was this sort of interest in medical history and medical literature that led Osler to tell the British Medical Association:

Medicine is seen at its best in men whose faculties have had the highest and most harmonious culture . . . Morgan, Shippen, Red-

man, Rush, Coxe, the elder Wood, the elder Pepper, and the elder
Mitchell of Philadelphia—Brahmins all, in the language of the
greatest Brahmin among them, Oliver Wendell Holmes—these and
men like unto them have been the leaven which has raised our
profession above the dead level of a business.

Twenty years later he could have included his own biographer, Dr. Harvey Cushing. Possibly Cushing owed something of his own culture to such men as Osler and Mitchell.
He met Mitchell in 1902. To the thirty-three-year-old physician, Mitchell appeared "powerful old." Dr. Mills had asked
the younger man to hear his paper on brain tumors. After the
meeting where it was read, Mitchell, always on the alert for
promising young men, waylaid Cushing and invited him to
go along for a smoke and chat. W. W. Keen and John K.
Mitchell were also going to what Cushing called a "memorable midnight session":

Mitchell's study or office at his home on Walnut Street was a
delight. It was a capacious room dominated by two portraits—
copies of the Reynold's Hunter and Janssen's Harvey . . . I remember his pointing out how clearly J. had portrayed Harvey's
arthritic knuckles. Then there was a beautiful coloured bust of
Dante, Keats' death mask, and in a glass case the head, recumbent,
of a Roman, as I learned, who had been killed in battle some eons
ago outside the walls of Ravenna. M. said it was of Guidarello
Guidarelli and when he first saw the original in the museum of
Ravenna he made a request of the Curator that he be permitted to
have a copy made of the face . . . "Jack," he said, "I once wrote
some verses on Guidarelli." Whereupon Jack got out a volume of
his father's poems from the shelves which lined the wall and read
the verses aloud. I have always liked this best of M's verses perhaps due to this association. He subsequently gave me a copy of
the book . . . adding that the publishers had never been able to
dispose of them. . . .

There was much more about books after this and I recall Rob't.
Burns copy of Pope, a presentation copy of Robinson Crusoe;
and something brought up Mrs. Piozzi, whereupon Jack got down
a copy of her Johnson which had in it a Ms. letter about a New

Year's sermon. The copy I think had belonged to Horace Walpole and later to Thackeray and M. chided Jack on his removing from its place an old foxed paper marker saying Horace had probably put it where it was and there it should remain. There were many other interesting association books—one of them a Harvey with a presentation note in H's script.

We must have lingered on from about eleven to three A.M., Dr. M. meanwhile smoking a succession of heavy cigars and he finally got out some old Madeira with a history of three times around the Horn. I saw him many times in later years. Once he stayed with us in Baltimore. It must have been in 1909 at the dedication of Osler Hall which accounts for my having come to possess his manuscript. The night before in looking over my few books he came upon the copy of his "Lycian Tomb" which I had put in covers from the *Century Magazine* and he solemnly remarked, "Charles Eliot Norton told me this poem was the high tide of American verse." Mitchell was vain but he had much to be vain about. He eagerly lapt up adulation . . . He was probably the most picturesque and many-sided physician of his time—and knew it . . .

No one has painted a better portrait of Weir Mitchell in his seventies.

Cushing's account suggests also the extent to which Mitchell was a diner-out, a being who had few of his roots in purely domestic life. This is evident also in his addiction to clubs, especially those centering around good food: the Biological, the Mahogany Tree, the Triplets, the Charaka Club of New York (devoted to discussion of medical history) and the Franklin Inn, which he helped to found. Part of this was the heritage of his years as a widower, part the result of Mrs. Mitchell's reluctance to go out after the death of her daughter. Thus Mitchell when asking for a copy of his son's play *Becky Sharp* told him that Mrs. Mitchell would never enter a theater. She did, however, continue to hold an annual Christmas party for children despite the fact that as Mitchell told Norton, this was a "grim anniversary in this household for just after it the

blow fell in '98—which left us alone. We are really brave I
think to have a tree and gather all the children we know and
give them gifts and unwholesome diets, and so forgetting, do
remember best." Mitchell had expected his wife to give up
the custom; when it was not abandoned, he remarked, like the
true Victorian he was, that "good women are ever amazing
things to us of the coarser sex."

Certainly he had a deep love and respect for his wife, but
he seems to have found his intellectual life increasingly outside
his home—and to a large extent his emotional life. Throughout
his later novels is the repetition of the idea that a man needs
women friends and that a wise wife recognizes this need. In
his moments of leisure he wrote to many women, discussing
with them his ideas, telling them of his literary ambitions,
triumphs, and defeats. The letters to Mrs. Amelia Mason cover
nearly two decades. And it was to Mitchell that Sophie Irwin
confided her theory that "Every life has a back gate in it." Of
course she felt it necessary to add in another letter, "My dear
love to Mary for whom this is intended as well." And at Bar
Harbor he read aloud to various admiring women his manuscripts, and basked in their admiration. His literary debt to
the two Mrs. Wisters has been noted.

There is not the slightest implication of scandal in all this.
As his novels show, he knew the power of sex, especially in
women. His patients felt the immense sexual attraction of the
man. But in the latter decades of the nineteenth century and
the first two of the twentieth, Maderia and terrapin often substituted for a woman, and a literary flirtation for a love affair.

All this has bearing on the psychiatric theories of the time.
American mores made it almost impossible for psychiatrists
to study the part that sex plays in the psyche. Mitchell's friend
and colleague, Charles Kasner Mills, in his lectures was so
reticent about discussing sex that he took care not to bring
before his classes patients who might shock them. Mills was a

much younger man than Mitchell. It is not strange then that Mitchell made fun of the new psychiatric theories of Freud and his followers. Yet if an American physician of his time was ready for Freud, it should have been Mitchell. More often than scientists are willing to admit, their conclusions grow out of their social milieu.

As the famous anecdote of his threat to get into bed with a recalcitrant patient (p. 83) illustrates, the mere suggestion of sex was enough to produce a legend in the latter part of the nineteenth century. Changed attitudes have permeated the field of psychiatry to a degree which makes it difficult to understand the older cultural milieu in which Mitchell lived and worked. Often he speaks of the confessions patients thrust upon him. But as the squeamishness of Mills indicates, even the medical profession would have been shocked at a frank discussion of such material.

Yet as far back as 1877, the year of Mitchell's *Fat and Blood*, Dr. A. J. Ingersoll had published *In Health*, a book stressing the sexual factors in neuroses. Ingersoll believed that "we cannot look with condemnatory spirit upon any part of our organization, without creating disease in that part." He also stated that intemperance was due to a restlessness which had its origin in overrestraint of the sexual drive. Mitchell hinted at this in his portrait of Roger Grace, and implied that a happy marriage was the solution of his difficulty.

Ingersoll's book is an interesting social document, for it gives a horrendous picture of an age tortured by religious teachings that all sexual desire was sin. A series of case histories brings forward a procession of men and women physically and mentally sick because of this teaching. Even married people tried to root out of their lives the desire they had been taught was bestial. Ingersoll's approach is, however, far from that of the modern psychiatrist. He ties up all his teaching with a theological point of view: "I think with all Christians

that sexual lust is sinful, and unless we look to Christ to re-
deem it, we shall be lost."

Perhaps that is the only way his theories could be presented
to the people of that era, but it is possible that the evangel-
istic theology somewhat discredited the scientific teachings.
Mitchell was religious, but he would have been repelled by
the revivalist tone of much of *In Health*.

Early in the twentieth century psychoanalytic doctrines
had able exponents in Brill, Frink, Jelliffe, and White. But to
most American physicians and psychiatrists these matters remained a topic for cloakroom wisecracks until after World
War. I. Certainly Mitchell was not a pioneer in psychiatric
thinking during the first decade of the century, but neither
was he a mossback. As his novels show, he was somewhat
ahead of rather than behind the thought of most of his contemporary American colleagues. But like most of them, he
found sex shocking. He borrowed from the College of Physicians library a work on Freud. After reading for a while he
sputtered, "Where did this filthy thing come from?" and
threw the book in the fire. His nephew, Dr. William B. Cadwalader, rescued it. It all adds up to the fact that most American psychiatrists of Mitchell's time refused to believe what
they knew. The case histories of Ingersoll and those of
Mitchell had provided evidence which was so contrary to the
mores of the time that it could not be fitted into any accept-
able social theory. Ingersoll's somewhat farfetched attempt
to link his sexual knowledge to the teachings of Jesus and
Paul is a symptom. An acceptance of the implications of the
new psychiatric thinking involved a complete revision of
American mores, at least of the official mores. There was no
place for the new theories in the chivalric code which all
Mitchell's novels preached. It was not merely the problem of
a new psychiatric theory; it was the necessity for a revalua-

tion of American life which Mitchell and most of his contemporary psychiatrists could not face.

The neurotic capacity of Mitchell's contemporaries to be shocked again revealed itself in the response to his work on George Washington. He started on the subject in 1902, asking John Hay to have a State Department clerk find out if there was a catalogue of Washington's papers. He was looking especially for letters. He told Billings that he had worked six hours one day on the subject of Braddock's defeat. On February 22, 1903, he gave a talk at the University of Pennsylvania on "Washington in his Letters." As he told Norton, he made the discovery that Washington had revealed himself with extraordinary frankness in his letters—never in his diaries. After going carefully through the fourteen volumes of correspondence edited by Paul Leicester Ford, Mitchell became so much interested in the subject that he began to put together an autobiographical statement from the man's own account of himself. Then Mitchell the novelist stepped in. He pictured Washington a year or two before his death going over his diaries and papers in order to write an autobiography. These he pictured as bringing to the old man's mind memories of the events which had called forth the letters.

This resulted finally in my supposing him to have written for his own interest as an old man a record of his life up to the close of Braddock's defeat. This became at once for me as I went a mosaic of bits from his letters, autobiographical in character, but also scenes and acts from the point of view of the writer of fiction and of course according with the character of the persons involved and who to some extent were in and modified the life of young Washington. It enabled me to draw what I think is a good portrait of his friend and helper Lord Fairfax, of his brothers and more or less of the Virginia life of his day. I have also frankly written in letters from London ladies to Fairfax, letters of Washington's brother from the siege of Cartagena, and even letters of Franklin.

He had had the whole thing printed (but not published) during the summer of 1902 and had revised it extensively during the year following. Nothing he had done before had so much pleased and interested him. He was troubled, however, by a problem of literary ethics: could he properly call it *An Autobiography of George Washington to the Close of Braddock's Defeat*, edited by S. Weir Mitchell? He knew of other fictitious autobiographies, one of Sir Thomas More's daughter. The Washington was in part fact and in part fiction. Did Norton see any objection, ethical or literary, to the use of the term "autobiography"?

Whatever the answer was, Mitchell published the work under the title *The Youth of Washington*. It ran in the *Century* as a serial from April to October, and then appeared as a book. The extent of his revisions before publication is shown by the fact that he printed from a fifth copy.

His fears were only too well grounded. People objected to the use of the autobiographical form and were shocked by the realistic portrayal of Washington's mother as a querulous, dissatisfied woman.

On the whole it is a good portrait of the young Washington. Mitchell makes no attempt to paint him as a man of wit or imagination; instead he shows his common sense, courage, and honesty. Mitchell's own rather formal style makes it easy for him to catch the eighteenth-century formality of the people he writes of. There is no artificial quaintness. The pictures of the hard-drinking, cock-fighting Virginia gentlemen and the even harder-drinking British officers are well done. The details of Braddock's defeat are vivid, but as in *Hugh Wynne* the panorama of a battle is not too well handled.

At times Mitchell's pet ideas creep in, such as ". . . no action ever grew out of only one motive. . . ." And Washington's opinion that the army officers of distinction came from north of the Mason and Dixon line is one of Mitchell's dinner-table dictums, one which recent historians support. Even these, however, give a vitality to the book which is often lacking in other accounts of Washington. He was the sort of man a Philadelphian could understand—noble without being a prig or a stuffed shirt; able without being scintillating. And Mitchell was enough the novelist to tell the story well.

The research and writing involved in this might suggest that he had largely given up scientific work and medical practice. However, a letterhead of 1904 shows that he kept consultation hours in his office from 9 A.M. to 1 P.M. except on Fridays and Sundays. A year later he was writing to Billings, "As I have had a fearful morning in the office and have more letters than I can possibly get through with, I ask my secretary to sign this." And at seventy-eight, "I am horribly busy as John is away." Also he was still working at the Infirmary for Nervous Diseases. And although the medical papers were becoming fewer, they continued to appear. In 1902 there was one on "Muscular Factors Concerned in Ankle Clonus," a further contribution to his lifelong study of nerve lesions. The next year he published "Historical Notes on Dr. Benjamin Rush," and in 1906 another paper on medical history and one, with W. A. Spiller, on "A Case of Uncomplicated Hysteria in the Male." The next year he published "Ailurophobia: the Power to Be Conscious of the Cat When Unseen and Unheard." As he had done before, he got much of his data from a questionnaire. He used also an experience of his father's, which had indicated that it was possible for persons to sense the presence of an unseen cat. In his study he ruled out those persons subject to cat asthma. His findings led him to the conclusion that certain persons had a sense of smell so keen that even unconsciously they could detect the presence of a cat. Even at eighty he published a study: "Motor Ataxia from Emotion."

This last, of course, grew out of his practice rather than

from special research. It would seem, however, that the diminished flow of scientific papers during this decade is due less to age than to increased literary production. In 1905, the year after *The Youth of Washington*, he published another novel, and for the years 1906-08, *The Readers Guide* contains eighteen entries of his poems, essays, and still another novel.

One article he wanted to write, however, never appeared. It was to be a discussion of the excesses of college athletics, especially football. His friend Dr. J. William White had written for the *Saturday Evening Post* two long papers praising the sport, arguing that Samson, though he lacked discretion, was a judge in Israel. This was the period of "the strenuous life" when Theodore Roosevelt interested himself in setting up uniform eligibility rules. The University of Pennsylvania introduced summer training on Long Island, and there were charges of professionalism in various colleges. Charles Eliot Norton annoyed White with the remark that football was the chief industry of the University of Pennsylvania. Mitchell talked over his proposed paper with White, who dissuaded him on the grounds that it might hurt the campaign for funds for a gymnasium. Mitchell approved the gymnasium, but warned White that a revolt in college management was imminent. At an alumni dinner in New York he spoke some of the criticisms which would probably have gone into the abandoned article. In his day the college hero had not been the captain of a team but the honor man. "We loved Thackeray and Tennyson. Some of us were enthusiastic over Socrates. Do college men talk of Socrates in these days?" As his autobiography shows, not all of his contemporaries at college talked of Socrates, but as a university trustee he had good reason to be perturbed about overemphasis on football. Samson was not perhaps the ideal college man nor judge in Israel.

The novel published in 1905, when he was seventy-six, was *Constance Trescot*. He had intended to call it *The Vendetta*

until he read a novel of that name by Marie Corelli. "No
shilling dreadful could be as stupid," he told Sarah Wister. He
was right in believing *Constance Trescot* his best novel. In
fact it can stand comparison with any of its American contemporaries, including those by Henry James. It is a memorable portrait of a possessive woman who becomes a
monomaniac, and of a social order—the postbellum South.
Constance would be a remarkable portrait in any era; she is
especially so in an American novel of 1905. She is described as

... one of those rare women who, for good or ill, attract because
of some inexplicable quality of sex. Incapable of analysis, it
accounts for divorces and ruined households, even for suicides or
murders. It may be faithful to a great passion, and be modified
by character and education, and even by religion but it is felt,
whether the woman wishes it or not, and she who has it instinc-
tively knows its power.

To the rather restrained George Trescot, who becomes
engaged to her on a two weeks' acquaintance, she is rather
startling. On his return from a week's absence she flings her
arms joyously around him. "Conscious that the embrace was
as much hers as his, he cast an uneasy glance about him, fearful of profane eyes, of which she was, to appearance, heed-
less." After their marriage she is completely possessive. When
her sister Susan presents George with an encyclopedia, Constance is annoyed; she wanted to give it herself. Trescot
"knew little of women, and nothing of the woman who desires to absorb, so to speak, all the thoughts and feelings of one
man, and who as time goes on, becomes jealous of his friends,
and even of his work, and, at last, of every hour not given
to her."
It is she who arranges for their marriage a year before
George had planned it. She did it by persuading her fuddy-
duddy uncle and guardian to appoint Trescot as his agent in

St. Ann, a southern town in which the uncle owned valuable, contested property.

This uncle, Rufus Hood, is also a well-drawn character. Wealthy by inheritance, he is convinced of his own firmness of purpose and business acumen. In reality he is easily dominated by his strong-minded nieces and is a pompous fool in business.

In St. Ann, Trescot finds sectional feeling strong against the northern millionaire, Hood, who is insistent on dispossessing some ex-Confederate squatters at the same time that he is involved in a suit over a valuable river-front property. Through sympathetic and honorable dealing, Trescot, though a former Union soldier, wins the respect of the community.

Pitted against him in the lawsuit is John Greyhurst, an able but unstable lawyer. Greyhurst, whose evil temper has caused him trouble in the Confederate army and has cost him a divorce, tries to inflame the community and later the jury against Trescot. During the trial Trescot demolishes Greyhurst's case. The latter calls Constance Trescot as a witness, to his own discomfiture. Angered and in danger of financial ruin, he taunts Trescot into what amounts to a challenge for a duel. Trescot, although opposed to dueling and suffering from a war-damaged arm, has no choice under the Southern code. Then Greyhurst, pretending to believe Trescot was drawing a weapon, shoots him down on the street. A local jury acquits him.

The tragedy was an inevitable product of the forces involved: community feeling and southern mores, Greyhurst's ungovernable temper and Rufus Hood's meddling in a dangerous situation. But this is only half of the book. Constance, in her agonized grief over her husband's death, loses her unborn child. On her recovery she dedicates her life to the destruction of Greyhurst. With a devilish ingenuity she haunts the man, ruining him financially and breaking up a love affair.

What had been a passionate love becomes an equally passionate and unscrupulous hate. The tragedy is essentially modern rather than Greek; it is not the product of an outside fate, but of psychological forces. It is in the tradition of *Macbeth* and *King Lear*, but its setting is thoroughly American. Compared to James' *The American* it is a much more penetrating study of our national types.

In its psychological insight it does resemble James, but it lacks his ignorance of passionate emotion and his involuted style. Therefore it has been less appealing to a certain type of intellectual.

Like other novels of Mitchell's, it has penetrating comments on human nature. Thus ". . . when Uncle Rufus pinches you [figuratively of course] or me, it is because some one whom he cannot pinch has been pinching him." Or of the doctor:

He had, however, a fund of pitiful charity, kept full by sad personal experiences and by the physician's vast explanatory knowledge of the lives of men and women, which accepts heredity, education, and environment as matters not to be left out of the consideration of disease or of the motives of men's actions.

Among all of Mitchell's books, *Constance Trescot* has the greatest unity and vigor.

The same year of its publication Mitchell became involved in a controversy with Gilder over the price of a poem called "Indian Summer." Mitchell asked $200. Gilder answered that a poem by Tennyson or Longfellow (both safely dead) would bring a high price because the mere announcement would be "a business asset." As a clinching argument he said that his own best work brought only $50 from *Scribner's*.

This was the second time Mitchell and Gilder had haggled over prices. Eight years before, Gilder had backed down and paid the price asked. This time he turned down "Indian Summer" as too expensive. It is not a very good poem, but it was the sort of thing Gilder liked. Mitchell promptly presented it to the *Century*, and vowed never again to accept money for verse. A note on this correspondence in his own hand states that he stuck to his resolution. In another hand, apparently a secretary's, there is a note which seems to be a comment of Mitchell's:

I trust when these letters are used that one may be free to state frankly this kind of correspondence and that the volumes will not be over edited to the destruction of interest.

It is likely that this was added at the time Mitchell turned the letters over to Mrs. Gilder after her husband's death.

Much better than "Indian Summer" was another poem published the next year. This was Mitchell's verse-rendering of the fourteenth-century poem, *The Pearl*. Its attraction for him is understandable: it is a lament by a father for a lost daughter. In his preface Mitchell freely acknowledged his debt to Israel Gollancz, who had translated the poem into unrhymed metrical stanzas. Furthermore, he omitted about half of the original, on the grounds that certain stanzas had little value or dealt with uninteresting theological discussion. He made little effort to preserve the alliteration of the original, but he did use its twelve-line stanza and octosyllabic meter. At times he used archaic words such as *pleasance* and *smoothen*. He told Howells: "I have done for it (modestly speaking!) what Fitzgerald did for Omar Khayyam's poem...."

In that opinion he was mistaken. On the whole, however, he handled the material with considerable skill and charm. A comparison of the Gollancz rendering of stanza VIII with Mitchell's will indicate the latter's free use of his source:

(Gollancz)
'Mid the magic of these wondrous hills
my spirit soon forgot all grief;
flavors of fruit so fresh were there,

as food full well they gave me strength;
birds in the wood together flew,
of flaming hues, both small and great;
nor citole-string no cithesner
could e'er re-tell their goodly glee;
    for when those birds did beat their wings,
    they sang with such a sweet accord,
    no rapture could so stir a man
    as to hear and see that wonderment.

(Mitchell)

My spirit there forgot its woe,
So wondrous were those charmed hills.
Rare flavoured fruits thereon did grow,
Fit food to cure all human ills.
In fair accord the birds flew by
Like winged flames, both great and small,
Nor cittern string nor minstrelsy
Might hope to match their joyous call:
For when the air their red wings beat,
Full choir sang they rapturously.
Nor greater joy a man could greet
Than this to hear, and that to see.

Mitchell's own feeling blends with that of the fourteenth-century poet in such stanzas as XIII and XIV:

What wonder more did daunt my sight?
I saw beyond that mystic mere
A shining cliff of crystal bright,
With royal rays, as morning clear.
At foot there sat a little maid—
A maid of grace, and debonair;
In glistening white was she arrayed,
Well known ere I saw her there.
More radiant than refined gold,
She stood in sunshine on the shore.
Long did my sight that vision hold,
And more I knew her, more and more.

Long feasted I on her dear face,
The lissome curves her figure wore,
Until the gladness of her grace
My heart's guest was as ne'er before.
Her gentle name I fain had called,
But stayed was I with wonderment,
So strange the place I stood appalled,
My eager gaze upon her bent.
Then turned me on her visage fair,—
As ivory white the face she wore.
Heart-struck was I to see her there,
And still I loved her more and more.

Mitchell's reworking of *The Pearl* is not a great poem, but Gollancz is right in calling it a "charming version."

In the same year he published *A Diplomatic Adventure*, a novelette of the *Monsieur Beaucaire* genre. The scene is laid in France. A Mme. Bellegrade picks up some papers showing France's intention of intervening in the American Civil War. The daredevil Captain Merton and an embassy attaché (who tells the story) manage to steal them from her house under the noses of the police and get them to Charles Francis Adams in London. It is cloak-and-sword romance laid in a later period than usual. The melodrama is rather cleverly handled, but the story is more noteworthy for zest than for profundity.

A year later, in 1907, Mitchell returned to the *Hugh Wynne* pattern in a historical novel of Philadelphia during Washington's presidency, *The Red City*. In fact, some of the characters carry over from the earlier novel: Hugh Wynne himself and Aunt Gainor—obviously a great favorite of Mitchell's.

The hero is a French emigré, Vicomte René De Courval; the villain a Jacobin who had caused the death of René's father during the Terror. The heroine is a type Mitchell often used: a beautiful, clever girl with a mind of her own. She is not unlike Mrs. Westerley of *In War Time*, Anne Vincent of

Dr. North, or Darthea Penniston of *Hugh Wynne.* The romance is the standardized one of a hundred historical novels.

What gives the novel some weight is the carefully drawn background: the feud between the Federalists and the Democrats, with the complications caused by the French in American politics. Mitchell, very much the Federalist, pictures Jefferson as a fox. There is also a rather vivid picture of the yellow fever epidemic. It is very much a Philadelphia novel, full of local color and good food. The gourmet, Savarin, discovers with enthusiasm reedbirds, terrapin, canvasback ducks.

Mitchell described his work thus:

The "Red City," like many of my novels, simmered in my head for some three or four years, and for it, slowly at intervals, I collected material. At first I called it "René Vicomte de Courval" but changed the title to "The Red City." In the first chapter a French emigré, approaching Philadelphia, observed its general color, for then it was almost entirely built of brick. Except Amsterdam, it is the only thoroughly red city known to me.

I was tempted to use this period because of the material furnished by the French emigré and the savage party strife, as well as by the interest of the historical characters involved. It was made possible to me by a free use of the diary of Elizabeth Drinker, which covers this period and far more. This Quaker lady seems to have attracted many of her intelligence and education, and in her diary I found ample material, which I used with the freedom of a writer of fiction. The episode of Edmund Randolph's supposed treachery was difficult to deal with but enabled me to make out of it the quite romantic episode of what is known as Dispatch No. 10.

On the whole the book is no better or worse than *Hugh Wynne,* but because it deals with less thoroughly worked-over ground, it has a certain interest that the older work lacks. But there are few of those penetrating remarks which make even Mitchell's duller novels come alive. One, however, stands out for its prophetic anticipation of more recent thought:

"Only in the loneliness of great spaces am I able to feel eternity; for space is time."

That same year he ran afoul of the taboos of the *Ladies' Home Journal*. Edward Bok bought the story, "A Christmas Venture," but sent back the proofs with the request that all references to drinking be deleted . . . "it is absolutely necessary that there should be no mention of drinking in our magazine." Mitchell returned the proof with only minor corrections, saying:

I accept the consequences of the sale of my story—but I will not personally sin against my own beliefs and habits nor will I violate my sense of literary fitness—cut out as it seems best to you. It will quite ruin the final scene.

Why, when you first read the story did you not tell me of this limitation—and if drinking is *never* to be *mentioned*, not even a temperance essay is possible! You could not have printed "Hugh Wynne" and yet I have had letters telling me of lives saved from drunkenness by the earlier scenes of that book.

When you send me the other proof vinously emasculated, let me have the manuscript, because when we make of it a little book I shall want to replace those vinous allusions to the ways of another day.

Thus for the second time in his eighth decade Mitchell had found himself too free-spoken for the magazines of the time. Even dinner partners sometimes found him startling. One lady who sat next to the elderly man at a dinner asked, "But, Doctor, you don't drink champagne, do you?" His eyes twinkled as he answered: "For breakfast, dinner, and supper." In fact, the diary for these years occasionally records a bad morning with the comment, "Too much champagne."

To many people he might seem a benevolent opinionated olympian untouched by age or trouble. But as his diary shows he was frequently troubled with severe eczema, especially, as he noted, in times of stress. His deafness, with accompanying head noises, was increasingly annoying. In fact he worried a

good bit about his health. "This fractional decay is unpleasant," he jotted down after one of his inventories of his physical condition. It surprised him to find his mind apparently
increasing in vigor at a time when his other powers were
obviously failing.

There were also financial and family problems. He lost
$32,000 on some Lake Superior stock just at a time when
Langdon again got into financial difficulties. Even a check for
$10,000 from his long-time patient, J. K. Vanderbilt, did not
make it possible for him to bail his son out of his difficulties.
Lany sold Reculver to his brother John, but this did not solve
his problems. Finally Dr. Weir had to take the bitter step of
altering his will so that Lany's inheritance would be left in
trust. Fond as he was of his son, he desired to protect Marion
and the children. In his diary he noted:

It is bitter but needful. . . . He has spent like the heir of Linn.
Now he makes over to Marion his house and farm on which I
hold an unsatisfied mortgage to protect those prodigal wood birds.

Two years later, at the time he was working on *The Red
City*, there were more serious troubles. How the book ever
got written at all is a mystery. He told Mrs. Mason that working on it had kept him from dwelling on his troubles. In June
of 1905 he was ill during his annual fishing trip to the Cascapedia. The "painful belly" he complained of proved to be
gallstones. Then while he was slowly recuperating at Bar
Harbor in August, the news came that the Real Estate Trust
Company had failed under particularly unsavory circumstances. The president committed suicide; the treasurer and
assistant treasurer were arrested. Huge sums had been loaned
to a promoter (also arrested) on poor securities. The total
indebtedness was at first estimated at $7,000,000.

Mitchell told Dr. J. W. White, ". . . while I was the color
of a bad lemon and could have quoted Beppo—this damn trust

had to go and bust." As one of the directors he felt keenly
the bitter attacks of the newspapers. True, the president had
destroyed warning letters to the directors from the state bank-
ing commissioner, but the *Philadelphia Press* was certainly not
libelous in describing them as an "easy-going board of directors." Mitchell's somewhat querulous complaints about the
newspaper handling of the board lost some of their force in
view of the fact that the same *Press* which attacked the board
never mentioned him by name.

At first some of the directors, such as John H. Converse
and John F. Betz, both described as multimillionaires, declared
that they would not voluntarily hold themselves liable. There
is a tradition that Mitchell dramatically announced at a board
meeting: "I am putting half of my fortune at the disposal of
the Trust Company, and I expect you gentlemen to do the
same." However, according to contemporary news accounts,
it was George H. Earle who devised the plan under which
the directors subscribed $2,500,000 so that the bank might
reopen. Smaller depositors were paid in full; those with $300
or more were given one-third in cash and two-thirds in preferred stock. Earle's statement that the directors were making
virtually a gift is not quite accurate; they were to be repaid
after the bank's original capital of $1,500,000 had been re-
stored and dividends of 8% paid.

Mitchell wrote to Norton that the papers, which had been
critical, now described the directors as angels. He added, "I
assure you the wings were costly." To Billings he wrote that
the worry had slowed his recovery, but that the financial situation was going to turn out better than expected. To Lany he
spoke of the usefulness of his "side career," literature, in helping him to raise the money. The $12,000 which the *Century*
paid in advance for the serial rights to *The Red City* was a
godsend. Even so he had to sell his Pennsylvania Railroad
stock to raise the $50,000 he put up toward the rehabilitation

of the trust company. What worried him most was that he was forced to live partially upon his wife's income.

For him the saving feature of the disaster was the generous response of his friends. John Cadwalader cabled an offer of unlimited aid. One man wrote offering half of a large estate, and a rich woman traveled a long way to say, "Whatever sum you require for whatever period you need to see you through, is yours." Five other people offered loans. To Norton he wrote:

As dear to me are letters like yours, and I have had many, so that I have been ingeniously questioning myself to know how I have come to win so much affection from so many people. Certainly the bread comes back on the water big loaves indeed.

On the whole Mitchell took considerable pride in his part in the matter. For although the directors had under existing law no legal responsibility, ". . . our action was simply in obedience to a code of honor, rare under like circumstances." It was a code of honor Mitchell had preached in his novels. Behind it were the teachings of his Virginia-born father and of eighteenth-century Philadelphia. In this case bitter newspaper condemnation had had a part in sharpening the directors' moral sense. But an American then reading of the graft in the building of the state capitol at Harrisburg and the revelations of Steffens, Tarbell, and Baker, found the action of the directors somewhat amazing.

As if illness and financial disaster were not enough for a man of seventy-seven, Mitchell lost two friends in accidents. In August Ed Coles, "a very lovable man," was killed by a runaway horse, and on Thanksgiving word came that "my much loved friend Philip Schuyler was killed with Mr. Spencer F. Fisher in a rear end collision near Lynchburg." Two weeks later there was more bad news: his sister, Sarah Neilson, had died in England. To Norton he wrote that death for her was a welcome release, but it left but two of the original nine brothers and sisters who had formed the close-knit family of sixty years before.

At the start of 1906 he had written in his diary:

What have you in your closed hand oh silent child of time.

On December 31st, he added:

Alas—it has been cruel.

But neither the disasters and heartaches of Mitchell's eighth decade, his extensive literary work, nor his medical practice could keep him from other activities. Some of his work on the Carnegie Foundation has already been mentioned. Membership on boards and committees was almost never perfunctory. Thus, after a meeting in Washington, he continued the discussion in a letter to Billings. They were in agreement that the Carnegie Foundation should not support an arctic expedition in 1904, partly because there were no funds available, partly because it lacked scientific explorers with the exception of Peary. The following year, after going to the meeting at Washington, Mitchell got in touch with his friend Augustus Saint-Gaudens to arrange for having a Carnegie seal made. Saint-Gaudens referred him to a man in Paris.

Saint-Gaudens had once made a bronze relief of Mitchell as a standing figure, but was never satisfied with the work. On the death of Maria, Mitchell had asked his friend to make a bas-relief. Saint-Gaudens had refused, saying he was overwhelmed with work. Then Mrs. Mitchell wrote a letter she never showed her husband. Saint-Gaudens dropped all other work and made the bas-relief, "The Angel of Purity," which was put in St. Stephen's Church. "I never knew a man of greater sweetness of character . . . more gentle, more magnanimous," wrote Mitchell in his autobiography.

Mitchell carried into his committee work his genius for friendship. Equally remarkable was his catholicity of interests.

At the same time that he was discussing arctic explorations with Billings, he was corresponding with Professor Corson of Cornell and Professor Thomas Lounsbury of Yale about a Chaucer dictionary financed by the Carnegie Institution. To the latter he wrote:

The two people who are most responsible for Flügel and his Chaucer dictionary are you and myself. Certainly without your support Billings and I never would have been able to support so formidable an enterprise . . .

Two weeks later Mitchell was sending a book of Lounsbury's to John Fox (author of *The Trail of the Lonesome Pine*) and calling the Yale professor's attention to Fox's handling of the dialect of Eastern Kentucky.

Two years later he wrote Norton that he had persuaded his fellow members on the Carnegie board to give $2,000 a year for three years to Professor Sommer to finance a rendering of the complete Arthurian legend. He added:

I am also rather proud about Flügel's Chaucer Dictionary—a matter of which I took the responsibility. This will cost us $50,000 or more—and will give what is practically a full mid. English Dictionary to scholars at cost.

With Lounsbury he also discussed a grant for a study of *The Ring and the Book*. Mitchell felt that the Foundation had done so much for physical science that it ought if possible to give more attention to literature. However, he had understandable doubts about the value of the proposed Browning study:

Whether the work is worth doing or not I am just a little in doubt perhaps for some lack of enthusiasm about the "Ring and the Book," a personal difficulty against which I feel I must guard in order to be just.

Another organization which occupied much of his time was the College of Physicians. He was a prime mover in raising

money for a new building. After he had raised $44,000 for it,
he agitated for a move to a new location on Twenty-second
Street. The arguments were stormy. At last in 1904 he noted:

200 M. D.'s decided by 96-62 to move to 22st. . . . The Pa. Hosp
men were as usual stay still folk. There is a local infection there
of unenterprize . . . great election work.

He felt it was no more than just that he should have had his
way. Two years later he was able to announce that he had
received from Carnegie a gift of $50,000 for the College. And
in January of 1910, when Edward T. Stotesbury gave $75,000
he concluded, "Thus ends my 7 year struggle. Thank God."

He found time also to take a hand in all sorts of matters.
Not only did he help to found a literary club in Philadelphia,
but he successfully worked to get it named as he wished—not
"the Authors," but "The Franklin Inn." He sat for his portrait to John Singer Sargent. To John Hay he wrote suggesting that the body of John Paul Jones be brought to America.
He took an active interest in having markers put at historical
places in Philadelphia and in Virginia. To Earl Grey, Governor General of Canada, he sent a novel of Owen Wister's and
Macaulay's *Marginal Notes* with some marginal notes of his
own. From time to time he also sent Grey a case of California
wine. And when Grey visited Philadelphia, Mitchell took him
on a tour of historic spots. Even in that disastrous year of
1906, Mitchell introduced Grey to Judge Ben Lindsey—
whether in person or as a writer is not clear. And when Grey
asked for a copy of *George Dedlow* to give to a paralyzed
friend, Mitchell sent twelve volumes of his works. Grey was
a fishing companion during the summers.

When in 1905 the University of Pennsylvania gave an
honorary degree to President Theodore Roosevelt, Mitchell,
despite his protests, was chosen to present him. He thoroughly
disliked Roosevelt, partly for political reasons, partly because

the President had once turned down a request by Mitchell to appoint a young protégé to Annapolis. Mitchell therefore found it difficult to compose a suitable speech of presentation for the degree. Finally Mrs. Mitchell wrote some remarks which had a certain cryptic flavor. Her husband used them with much satisfaction:

On the 4th of July, 1783, the University of Pennsylvania conferred the Degree of Doctor of Laws upon the first President of the United States. The Trustees of the same University do now, after one hundred and twenty-two years, request the Provost to honor with the same degree you—our latest President. Comment is needless.

On that occasion the Mitchells had a dinner for some of the distinguished guests who were to receive degrees. He wrote to John Hay to find out who should have precedence if both the English and German ambassadors accepted the invitation. And who should take Mrs. Mitchell in to dinner, and who should sit at her right? He wanted to do the thing exactly right.

He himself received honorary degrees, one from Princeton in 1906 and another from Toronto in 1907. The following year the Royal Society made him a foreign fellow. Osler cabled the news and wrote that the choice had been between Ehrlich and Mitchell. It is likely that Osler had worked for the election of his old friend. On receiving his diploma Mitchell promptly sent it back to have a correction made in the spelling of his name. It was Osler who told him that Jenner's inkstand could be bought for £30. Mitchell bought it and used it on his own desk. For one night he placed his F. R. S. diploma in front of it: "There was noble company."

In the spring of 1909 Osler was honored at the dedication of Osler Hall of the Maryland Medical and Chirurgical Faculty. He came from England for the occasion. Mitchell, who gave the principal address, spoke on the subject near his heart:

the building of a medical library collection. In fact, at eighty he was engaged in trying to raise an additional $4,500 for his beloved Philadelphia College of Physicians. In his address he proposed that a medical library should have not only the great works in medical history and the contemporary authorities, but also the quacks and eccentrics: lay theorists, anti-vivisectionists, and Mary Baker Eddy. He told anecdotes from his own experience: a seven-year search for a book by Sanctorius which was not in the British Museum and which had been lost by the Bibliothèque Nationale. Finally Quaritch had found it for him just in time for use in something he was writing. Another anecdote was even more characteristic. One night he had gone to the College of Physicians in search of a book he particularly wanted. Getting a candle from the janitor, he went searching through the stacks. The candle went out. Suddenly he felt himself in a vast burial place where eighty thousand books were "tombs with inscriptive titles to which the living years continually gave the lie." A sense of the immense vanity and futility of all this effort came over him: the failures, the anemic theories, the wordy wars. Then his mood changed. Here was the record of a vast army forever winning or losing, forever recruited. What books would one ask for after two hundred years? His answer was prophetic:

In that day a professor will say to his class it is needless to tell of yellow fever or plague because there are no such maladies now. Then shall cancer be a defeated foe, and tubercule a lightly regarded disorder, and typhoid a curio of hospital records.

Osler, who was also a collector of medical history, surely applauded both the prescription for a medical library and the prophetic vision. Mitchell took his old friend back to Philadelphia for a reunion.

In May, Mitchell gave an address at Chicago before the American Neurological Association, of which he was president. It was a long talk filled not with anecdotes but with suggestions for further research in half a dozen fields. He stated that asylum care was to be used only as a last resort or when poverty or extreme peril left no other resource. This is in accord with his lifelong practice of treating the ambulatory patient, of regarding the mental patient as someone to be restored to a useful place in society. He reported on his own as yet unpublished study of exophthalmic goiter which showed that it was extremely rare in Negroes. He threw out suggestions for further studies of the Negro to determine why he was relatively immune to chorea, migraine, yellow fever, and malaria. Was there any possibility of using Negro blood as a serum for the two latter diseases? And might not the study of reinforced reflexes aid spastics?

The bulk of the talk, however, was devoted to a discussion of the nature of nerve energy. The study of plants might shed some light. But his discussions with Professor Macfarlane and a young graduate student, E. B. Ulrich, had shaken his belief in the theory of nerves in plants. That, he said, was a problem for the laboratory.

He and Osler had discovered that even in a spinal fracture which apparently had isolated the brain from the lower cord it was possible for the patient to reinforce the knee jerk. This led him to a suggestion that ". . . strong exercise of the upper limbs will remedially aid to keep in condition lower centers when these are partially insulated by disease." Thirty years later a President of the United States demonstrated the validity of this theory.

The whole address is a looking forward. A man of over eighty had outlined a program of research which forty years later has not yet been fully developed.

All this activity, however, did not prevent him from being alert for new people and ideas. A young man from Virginia came to Philadelphia to study medicine. This was Beverley R.

Tucker, whose grandparents Mitchell had visited as a child. When the young man called, Dr. Mitchell took him into his office for a long chat about Virginia, about the visitor's medical preparation and views on various topics. He produced cigars and rang for brandy. When Tucker accepted these, his host looked at him quizzically and said, "I'm glad to see you have some petty vices. I hope you have no great ones. I am usually afraid of a man who has no petty vices."

Apparently young Tucker made a good impression, for the Doctor promised to obtain for him a hospital appointment. Tucker questioned his own fitness for work on nervous diseases. Mitchell, who was standing by the fire with his elbow on the mantel, looked down sternly: "Never fail to accept any opportunity which will broaden your horizon." But the real sign of the young man's acceptance was that Mitchell offered him a seat in his pew at St. Stephen's. This, said the Doctor with a smile, was the greatest courtesy a Philadelphian could offer a stranger.

This kind of interest in promising young men was typical. As we have seen, Mitchell extended the same sort of hospitality to Dr. Harvey Cushing on his first visit to Philadelphia. On another occasion he heard that a graduate student at the University of Pennsylvania was experimenting with leaf movements in plants. This was E. B. Ulrich, who one afternoon found the keen blue eyes looking at the apparatus he had designed. The famous seventy-eight-year-old man engaged the student in conversation, then took him home to the celebrated study where they argued for half an hour about the possibility of nerves in plants. Mitchell had subscribed to the old theory of the Bartrams and Dr. Rush that plants had nerves. The young man was finding otherwise in his experiments. As we have seen, Mitchell modified his ideas in accordance with the young man's discoveries, and used some of the material in his address before the Neurological Society.

Mitchell continued to interest himself in Noguchi's work after Flexner had taken the Japanese to the Rockefeller Institute. In 1903 Mitchell had wangled a grant for his protégé from the Carnegie Foundation. Three years later he sent Elihu Root a letter of Noguchi's on antidotes for snake venom. Root suggested that a supply might be useful in American politics.

It was characteristic of Mitchell to invite his wife's nephew, Dr. William B. Cadwalader, into a consultation so that the young physician might learn how specialists conducted such a matter. And it was equally characteristic of him to give advice and encouragement to a young drug clerk in Proctor's Pharmacy—a boy whose parents had named him S. Weir Newmayer in honor of the famous physician. The young man became an eminent physician in his own right. Mitchell had an almost psychic insight which enabled him to spot people of ability.

Mitchell's eighth decade was on the whole a fruitful and happy one. Yet running through his letters is a threnody for passing friends. In 1908 alone he lost three of his most intimate circle: Charles Eliot Norton, Sarah Butler Wister, and Annis Lee Wister. The year before Charles Eliot Norton's death Mitchell had written him that although he had many friends, those who were men of distinction had come down to a small count of veterans: Henry Charles Lea, Horace Furness, William Doane, John Shaw Billings, and Norton. Osler had left for England in 1905.

Mitchell had told him that he was "wisely counselled to go." But

Selfishly speaking I am filled with the most honest regret. One by one the older men who shared with me the fates of war and the contests of peace, have died. I have picked up new friends—the younger ones, men and women—and among the best, you—and is it twenty years indeed? When I read your letter to my wife she said isn't it splendid? And I—isn't it sorrowful?—for of course this does take you out of my life, and at 74 the arithmetic of opportunity is easily summed up and made out . . . very soon you will be saying raily for really . . . and you will say Gawd for God.

However, Osler did not go out of Mitchell's life entirely. They corresponded often, and as we have seen, had a reunion in 1909.

The friendship with Norton had been largely "a letter friendship." Mitchell had been in his house not more than three times, and had once or twice entertained the Bostonian in Philadelphia. But he had greatly valued Norton's literary opinions, especially the one expressed at a Franklin Inn dinner that the *Ode on a Lycian Tomb* was "the high tide of American verse"—an opinion he could not get Norton to repeat in print.

The loss of the two Mrs. Wisters was much more personal. He described Mrs. Sarah Wister as "the brilliant kinswoman . . . gipsy Kemble cross on the Irish aristocratic Butlers . . . the most interesting woman I have ever known." Mrs. Caspar Wister he "loved with a difference." For many years she had listened to his reading of manuscripts, had criticized his grammar and spelling. To her he sent Number One of de luxe editions of his novels. As he said to Norton's daughter a few weeks before his eightieth birthday: ". . . these losses begin to make one realize that fear of what may be the arctic loneliness of too prolonged life."

Perhaps the most satisfying friendship of this period was one which had endured since the Civil War, that with John Shaw Billings. After Billings went to New York to head the Public Library, Mitchell kept sending him questions on medical history. Both men were founders of the Charaka Club, devoted to the study of this subject. Mitchell not only attended meetings of this club, but often dined with his friend at the Round Table. They met also at the Carnegie Institution in Washington, at which times Billings usually stopped off in

Philadelphia. A friend recalled seeing them driving about Washington in a ramshackle buggy with an indifferent-looking nag, Billings holding the reins.

On Mitchell's seventy-fifth birthday Billings sent a letter which reveals the man and epitomizes the friendship:

My dear Weir:

Schuyler tells me that to-morrow is your birthday. This being St. Valentine's day I think it not improper to send you a little love letter by way of expressing my feelings.

One by one of the majority of my old friends have passed away, but so long as you remain life is still worth living for me. I do not need to give reasons for my affection for you—there are many of them, but the essential thing is that I have it, and that when I think of you it is not as a great physician—or as a poet— or as a leader in science—but as, "Weir"—just, "Weir." And I have a comfortable cardiac (or free cardiac) sensation in the thought that I have the right to call you "Weir." May you live long to enjoy life as you do, and when the time comes—may it be painless and prompt. I mean by this the end of this life—for I don't think that will be the end for you—but rather that it will be a new beginning. I suppose you have had beginnings before the nineteenth Century—probably Philip Sidney may have been one of your trial trips.

Be that as it may you have been mine in a sense for forty years now—not exclusively "mine"—but mine in a rather special way. And you know, that I am yours—also in a special way—don't you?

If you don't—there is no use in telling you—nevertheless I am

Yours

J. S. Billings

Once at a reception at the Carnegie Institution, Mitchell told a friend: "I have known two great men in my life; one was Wendell Phillips [almost certainly a misquotation for Phillips Brooks]; the other John Billings."

It was to Billings that Mitchell first hinted that his multiple activities were becoming a burden. At seventy-nine he mourned the passing of summer and disliked the thought of leaving the quiet of Bar Harbor "for the jostling labor of what is called civilization."

More and more his son, Dr. John, quietly shouldered the burdens of his father's practice. He even checked up on prescriptions to make sure that age and forgetfulness had not led to errors. Even so, the elder man was the more vivid personality. A woman patient, in contrasting them, said that to have Weir Mitchell enter a sickroom was to have a highly charged electric current started through the dormant mental and physical being. In fact, the stimulation of his intense personality was so great as sometimes to leave the patient intensely weary. This was especially likely to be the case on those occasions when he sat by the bedside and for an hour read aloud in his odd, penetrating voice. On the other hand Dr. John, with his lower voice and quiet manner, left the patient soothed and relaxed.

The elder man thrived on activity. When in 1902 he gave up his Friday clinics at the Orthopaedic Hospital, he missed them. And when he had few patients in the office, he found himself annoyed at the implication that he was regarded as aged. A new rush of patients would produce a cheerful note in the diary. Thus at seventy-eight he noted with pleasure that at a home clinic there had been many patients from a variety of places: Pennsylvania, Ohio, Canada, New York, Florida, and Georgia. "This rush of work acts as a tonic on me." And at eighty he noted, "crowded office."

Shortly before this latter entry he had entertained at his home President Taft and the presidential party. He had even overcome his prejudice against motor cars sufficiently to borrow one so that he might take the President sightseeing. They visited points of historic interest and M. Carey Thomas of Bryn Mawr. Mitchell was in such an expansive mood that he was able to meet his "old antagonist . . . with reasonable friendliness." Taft's own unfailing good humor was evidently contagious; certainly Mitchell found him a charming person, and one he respected. The two-day visit, the banquets, speeches, and late hours were wearing but delightful.

A month later he went with the trustees of the University to lobby at Harrisburg. Here he saw the new capitol, which he thought vulgar. Its two-ton gold chandeliers and countless brass spittoons did not appeal to his eighteenth-century taste. And the return to Philadelphia by motor car at sixty miles an hour did not please him.

As usual, in June he went to Canada for the fishing. A severe "belly ache" warned him to lessen his diet. But there were still occasions when he would note that he had indulged in too much champagne. Life was still full and interesting.

IX

Coda

1910 - 1914

I cannot rest from travel. I will drink
Life to the lees.

—TENNYSON, *Ulysses*

AT EIGHTY-ONE Mitchell was still operating under full steam. True, increasing deafness annoyed him, and his hands trembled with palsy. A friend, seeing him on the New York train, noted how the old man's hands shook as he corrected proof. For he was publishing another novel, one on which he had worked for three summers. His winters were still too busy to allow time for writing. That of 1909-10 had been especially filled. His son John had been made vice-president of the American Neurological Association, and this meant absences during which Weir had to carry the whole burden of their practice. However, as he wrote to Miss Louisa Minot, "If labor was a curse to Adam, I have no doubt that before he died, he grew to like it, and with me it has become a necessity."

He was reading with great interest the life and works of Robert Burns. And he had been invited to a meeting of his brother's old regiment, the Sixth Pennsylvania Cavalry. Here he got into a long argument about placing Lee's statue in the Hall of Fame. Mitchell thought it should be there, but in a Confederate uniform. He found, however, that the hundred or so old men didn't get his meaning when he said the question had become academic. So he told them it was time that "the dog on top quit barking." They got the point and made him an honorary member of the regiment.

In April he went to Washington for a meeting of the Carnegie Institution. Here he announced his intention of resigning from the board at the end of the year. The next day he attended a meeting of the National Academy of Sciences. That afternoon he went driving with Mrs. Bayard in Rock Creek Park, where he had an accident which might have been serious. A boy batted a baseball which struck Mitchell on the back of the head. His derby broke the force of the blow so that he escaped with a headache and a sore scalp. After talking to the boys, he laughed off the incident, and went to call on Mrs. Taft (who was out), and then to dinner with friends. Here he got into an argument with a "raging suffragette." Then he decided to go home and nurse his headache instead of going to a reception. As he felt fine the next day, he attended the Academy dinner, where he had a pleasant talk with Alexander Graham Bell.

In Philadelphia he continued to visit the Orthopaedic Hospital, where his son was also on the staff. Dr. Tom B. Throckmorton, who came there as an interne in 1910, has given a portrait of the elder Mitchell at that time. A few weeks after beginning his interneship, Dr. Throckmorton was notified by the porter that Dr. Mitchell was present and wished to see him. With the head nurse they visited a patient of Dr. John's. According to custom the interne and nurse should have waited outside the patient's door while the visiting physician paid his call, but Dr. Mitchell insisted that the young man come along in. When the nurse introduced them to the patient, the lady sat up in bed with an incredulous expression:

"Surely this is not Dr. S. Weir Mitchell?" The great man's eyes twinkled: "Yes, madam, this is the real Dr. Mitchell."

After examining the patient and going over her history,

Dr. Mitchell turned to the interne and asked what treatment he would recommend. The flabbergasted young man managed to make a few suggestions. Mitchell nodded approval and had the orders written on the chart.

When the famous man was ready to leave, the interne helped him on with the big overcoat with its long attached cape. Dr. Mitchell offered a big black cigar, which the young man declined. Mitchell asked where he was from. The young man said Iowa. Mitchell ran his fingers through his beard looking the other in the eye, stated one of his favorite dictums: "Young man, I am always suspicious of one who has none of the outer evidences of the lesser vices."

During his year as interne, Dr. Throckmorton, like so many others, developed an almost superstitious awe of the uncanny precision with which Mitchell could sum up a situation. No one else could notice so many details in such a short time. At the end of his service the young man was summoned to the office at 1524 Walnut Street. He climbed the marble steps, and was ushered into the reception room. After an interval he was admitted to the office where Mitchell, in a velvet coat, received him cordially. He praised Throckmorton's work at the hospital, and after a long chat, asked about his plans. Then he offered advice: specialization should not come too soon; Dr. John had engaged in general practice for ten years; he himself had not specialized until he had had a long experience in general medicine. Earlier in the year Dr. Throckmorton had asked for a photograph, which had been promised on condition that his work was good. When the young man mentioned it, Dr. Mitchell took one from his desk and autographed it.

If there was a touch of histrionics in the noblesse oblige, there was also a genuine kindness and interest. Dr. Throckmorton of Iowa had not come, like young Beverley Tucker, from an old Virginia family with links of kinship to the

Mitchells. Yet his reception was much the same. A promising young man was always encouraged. Dr. Mitchell had none of the sort of provincialism shown by a learned and stately Philadelphian who, confined to the hospital, refused the services of an interne with the remark, "No man from Kansas is going to examine my bladder."

Despite his work at the Orthopaedic and his other activities, Dr. Mitchell was anxious to get away to the woods. In May he wrote:

Every green thing I see lures me, and in the city at this season [May] the dust is intolerably death laden and I long to get away from it. If I had been in the country, I should have long ago shaken off the consequences of my influenza.

It is not strange therefore that the novel he finished during the summer is filled with forest scenery. His notebooks in later life show his increasing attention to color, odor, and texture. This carries over into his novels. For instance, dawn in a Maine forest is described thus:

. . . of a sudden long lines of light flashed through the forest maze, girdling the trees with golden light and leaving here and there untouched in shadow the trunks of delicate purple.

John Sherwood is not an old man's book; it is filled with zest: the morning plunge in 56° surf, trout fishing, sailing in rough water, sleeping in a tent during a lashing gale, and, as always with Mitchell, good food. The colored man Dodo, reminiscent of Mitchell's cook on the Cascapedia, prepares a camp supper of chowder, baked lobster, broiled chicken, and clam omelette—all superbly cooked.

The theme of the story is Wordsworthian: the regeneration of a man's character through the appreciation of nature. John Sherwood, left an orphan at three, is put to work as an adolescent in the ironworks owned by his two hard-shelled uncles. They are described by a cousin as being like two dried-up peas. By the time young Sherwood inherits the business he is well on the way to become like them: merely an efficient machine for making money. He has had no youth, nothing to touch his sympathy or his imagination, merely a life of getting to the ironworks at six in summer, seven in winter, and driving himself all day.

At thirty-four he finds himself worn out and with incipient tuberculosis. At his doctor's command he takes a rest, but insists upon doing it in his own way. Having read Weir Mitchell's *Camp Cure*, he sets up a camp in Maine where, with Dodo to cook, he spends an eventful summer. First there is the gradual recovery of physical vigor, then the gradual discovery of natural beauty and of human relationships among his neighbors.

Among them in the recluse Hapgood, whom Sherwood recognizes as the Reverend Benedict Norman. Upon inquiry he learns that Norman, after trying to kill his wife, had been put in an insane asylum, from which he had escaped. As Mitchell told Osler, the character is a study of paranoia. Sherwood, the layman, sees Norman only as a tortured soul, possibly on the road to recovery. But Sherwood's cousin Dr. Heath, recognizes the danger; the man is like a stick of dynamite.

The plot builds up to a melodramatic climax with the appearance of Mrs. Norman, the attempted murder of Heath, and Norman's own violent death. Up to that point the story has been well developed and alive. The last fifty-odd pages bog down into Victorian mush. Although Sherwood is in love with Mrs. Norman and although she had been away from her husband for two years before his death, another two years must elapse before he declares his love. In the meantime she has given all of Norman's money, $250,000, to two of his aunts, who hate her. Then Sherwood discovers a will of Norman's which accuses his wife of adultery with Heath and bequeaths his estate to the same aunts and a Baltimore hospital. The charges are obviously those of an insane man. But Sherwood feels honor-bound to show the will to Mrs. Norman and she to give most of her remaining fortune to the hospital. In this Sherwood anticipates her with an anonymous gift to the institution. Honor becomes so fine-spun and quixotic as to be absurd.

As always in Mitchell's novels there are provocative ideas such as the need for evolutionary change in religious creeds, the unity of mind and body, the relation of a man's individual nature to his ailments, and the statement about "little corner closets of delusion . . . sedulously kept locked by men whose lives seem commonpalce." There is much speculation about the cause of paranoia and the extent to which the patient can control his fantasies. Dr. Heath states, "Sometimes we can trace a delusion back to an apparently inadequate cause . . ."

Mitchell has patently identified himself with large areas of Sherwood's experience. There are the childhood memories of keeping an imaginary bull terrier and of seeing a gilded coach. Sherwood's intense love of the sea, the pine woods, the Maine storms, is obviously Mitchell's. So too in all probability is Sherwood's wish that he had had a chance to test his courage in the Civil War, as well as his feeling that he had been useful behind the lines.

John Sherwood is not a great novel, but it is certainly more adult reading than is, for instance, the much more famous *Virginian* published six years before by Mitchell's young kinsman, Owen Wister. Mitchell did not expect his novel to be popular, largely because of its study of insanity. His statement to Osler about the book as a portrait of a paranoid suggests that this element in the story was for him its distinguishing feature. It is probably most significant for the modern reader. To Katharine Hunt he wrote:

My publishers warned me that it was a book that would have no great sale such as had the idiotic sentimentality of books, we will say like the Rosary for example, or the yellow covered literature, but then I said, "I am sorry that you will not make so much, but I am relatively indifferent and if I can be repaid in the coin of perfect sympathetic touch with people, then that will satisfy me."

After all, the Century Company had no real complaint. Over a period of twenty years the sale of Mitchell's books was great enough to bring him an average royalty of $10,000 a year. "Not many have done better," he noted with satisfaction.

In addition to finishing *John Sherwood*, he was working on William Harvey. He wrote to Osler suggesting that there might be a good deal of manuscript material in court records of Harvey's long lawsuit with the heirs of Lord Lumley. By the end of the year Mitchell was writing Osler once a month on the subject. What evidence was there of Harvey's having taken poison? And how could such a story "have been invented without the aid of a newspaper reporter?" At the same time he was also corresponding with Sir D'Arcy Power on Harvey.

Mitchell's lifelong feud with newspapers flared up in a letter to the *Public Ledger*. He suggested that the editor discharge a reporter who had credited him with the statements that he called neurasthenia "anesthesias" and that he had never seen a case of neurasthenia in which no anesthetic had been used. Next time would the editor please send someone to a meeting of the College who knew his business. In another letter to a newspaper he pointed out that he was not an Englishman and did not live in a palatial residence on the Wissahickon.

In April there was a dinner in honor of William Welch at the Belvedere Hotel in Baltimore, with five hundred guests. Flexner and Leonard Wood made addresses, and Mitchell read a poem. He wrote to Osler with some satisfaction that Johns Hopkins did "not seem to be so exultantly and alarmingly prosperous as they used to be."

That same year the Jefferson Medical School, which had many years before twice refused him a position, now gave him an honorary degree.

He went fishing as usual in June and then to Bar Harbor. Osler, who was again traveling in America, visited his old friend there. On his return to England he wrote that he wished his son Revere could have a few lessons in fishing from S. W. M.

Mitchell wrote back an anecdote about Ehrlich who, so the story went, had wanted to repay John D. Rockefeller for his financial help in research, and had hit upon the idea of sending the philanthropist one thousand doses of 606. Mitchell said that he had no doubt of the truth of the story, as it came from either Flexner or Welch. But more important was the news that Noguchi had found a way of cultivating in some preparation of the liver the specific organism of syphilis. Mitchell was enthusiastic:

This would be the final triumph in the chain of wonderful discovery. I think this is calculated to produce enormous influence upon the civilization of the world, on the efficiency of armies and navies, and on the hygiene of the next generation or two.

And to Billings he wrote praising the work on starches by Edward Reichert, who thirty years before had been a collaborator in the study of snake venom. Mitchell rarely lost touch with a friend. He suggested that because of this work and that on crystallography of the blood, Reichert might be nominated for honors. Mitchell was planning to attend the Round Table dinner in New York.

With his old friend, Horace Furness, he got into a discussion of a pun of Sir John Harrington's on the name "Jacques"

(Jakes). Mitchell couldn't at first get the point of the anecdote of the maid who refuses to introduce a character by that name, preferring to use the word *Privy*. After looking it up, he found that *jakes* was an ancient word for *privy*. Then he discovered in an old book by Ramozzini, Professor of Physics at Padua, dated 1705 and called *A Treatise on Diseases of Tradesmen*, a chapter on "The Diseases of the Cleaners of Jakes." Obviously Mitchell was continuing his habit of wide reading.

To Osler he wrote of a research problem on which he was embarked. It was to determine whether or not odors could be detected electrically. If the experiments succeeded, he believed that a new line of physical inquiry would be opened. The experiments would be costly and troublesome, but the professors of physics at Johns Hopkins had agreed to work on the problem. According to Mitchell they regarded it as "one of the most important scientific enterprises undertaken within recent times."

He added some jibes about England, which seemed to him to be undergoing a revolution. The House of Lords, having failed to pass some social legislation, was further restricted in its powers of vote. George V at the behest of Asquith had forced the Lords to accept this limitation on their power. Mitchell said plaintively:

I want the House of Lords preserved. I want the big old houses preserved, and I want some of the old things guarded for enjoyment of the American of this later day. As for your Mr. Asquith, it seems to me he has the characteristic political morals of a ward politician.

Mitchell, with a rare burst of modesty, added that one could of course make mistakes in judging the politics of another country. The letter represents less the conservatism of an old man than it does the point of view of a lifetime: a Philadelphia Brahmin's point of view.

In January of 1911 he told Osler of his resignation from the Board of Trustees of the University of Pennsylvania after thirty-five years of service. He was tired of the "usual constant hot water in the Faculty." Why was it that this was always the situation when doctors were associated in teaching positions? The resignation relieved him from university committees. It seemed to him he did nothing but attend committee meetings. He told his wife that if he died she was to put on his tombstone, "Committeed to the grave."

That spring he went as usual to Cascapedia. To Osler in a thoroughly characteristic letter he boasted of his prowess as a fisherman:

Tell your son that I killed a 45 pound salmon last week, and two days before three, 40, 39, 29 lbs. Of less importance is it that you are a Bart. What is that to me, for whom you are long ago high in the peerage of friendship. A lessening number of survivors, four, only four. Time has terribly dealt with that splendid peerage, Lowell, Holmes, Alex. Agassiz, Brooks, and last Ch. Norton and Aldrich, and I am the last of nine children and one sister. Therefore please to take care of the new Baronet. . . . Keep an eye on any Harvey things for me and quit writing me those half-page scraps of letters. I have seven queries to put about Harvey I spare you. Could I learn at the Heraldry Office when Wm. H. got arms? I hear you cuss.

In August he was writing to Osler from Bar Harbor telling of a dozen schemes for medical papers of the sort they both liked to write. However, he lacked time because he was working on another novel, a project which he had begun the summer before, and which would probably take a third summer to finish. It was to be a story laid in the time of Buchanan's administration and the war. No one, he thought, had sufficiently put on paper the bitterness of party and of family divisions during that period. It was a theme he had started to develop in an abortive novel many years before.

As he told Osler, he had to fill his vacant hours. What did

people do with their time at a resort like this? He did not play bridge, and although he hiked in the afternoons in the company of "some pleasant young women," he found the long hours of the morning a burden.

Dr. Thayer of Johns Hopkins found the energy of the old man amazing. "It is impossible to tire Weir Mitchell at eighty-two." Even young people found his conversation fascinating.

He was also busy with a project to place bronze markers on the Gettysburg battlefield wherever physicians had been killed or wounded.

On his return to "the horrid conditions of city life" he experienced his usual autumn depression of spirits. The same thing happened when he left for the woods in the summer. It was a psychological phenomenon he could not explain, but one which had grown more acute with the years. With it came an oversensitiveness about the welfare and health of friends and family.

But once back home he plunged as usual into varied activity. He was studying the medical treatment of epilepsy. To Osler he wrote, "It is an abominable thing one is not twins —in fact I should like to be numerous."

In February he went to Baltimore to receive a degree from Johns Hopkins—an honor he had twice refused. But for him Johns Hopkins had "destroyed the charm of Baltimore."

The terrapins used to wallow on the front steps, canvas back ducks to fly down at call in back yards, and the madeira to flow like the springs of the Promised Land. The young people did know madeira from cider, and the women were beautiful and the men delightfully ignorant, and there was no intellect in Baltimore, but the charm of a highly refined society.

In March, because of Mrs. Mitchell's rheumatism, he took her to Bermuda where he enjoyed two weeks of warmth and flowers, and a sea of "translucent turquoise, turning emerald

Mitchell at Bar Harbor

over the shoals or ruddy above a reef." The trip, however, was a mistake; it made his wife's rheumatism worse.

He came back to resume his practice. To Mrs. Mason's inquiry he answered that he was certainly not tired of sick women; they were doubly interesting. His mornings were spent in the office. One or two afternoons a week his carriage would come to take him to visit a hospital, usually the Orthopaedic. Then at five he would take a "nap"—a period he used for reading proof and correcting manuscripts. He dined at eight and went to bed early except on occasions when there was a club dinner or official function. One of his favorite social activities was the Franklin Inn Club, of which he was president.

In February of 1913 he went to Chicago to deliver an address before the Physicians' Club. His talk on the Medical Department of the Civil War gives a vivid picture of the methods of practice used in the army hospitals. From England Osler wrote that he had heard reports of the lecture and that it was a successful one.

In March came a severe blow: the death of Billings. As Mitchell told Osler, the monthly meetings of the Carnegie Trust had brought Billings and himself together so often that they were not separated as busy men are apt to be. Billings' death was therefore not merely the loss of a friend of fifty years standing; it was a break in a living relationship. Mitchell wrote Osler:

. . . this last loss was a far more serious calamity to me than would seem likely to hardened old age. The sentence is bad but will be clear to you. I grow not less but more sensitive as time goes on . . . I have always dreaded the Arctic loneliness of age and now alas!

His gloom was somewhat relieved by a visit from Osler in April on his way to Baltimore. Mitchell got together a group of old friends for a dinner. At Mitchell's urging, Osler visited Philadelphia again in May and found his friend aging but as mentally keen as ever. From the steamer he wrote that it was good to see his old associate in such fine form. He had never heard Mitchell speak more clearly and to the point than at the Billings memorial meeting. "How I wish I could see you on the river tackling a salmon!" As long as Mitchell could do that, it was nonsense to talk of old age. "You have done more in the past twenty years than many an active-minded man in a lifetime." It was the sort of flattery Mitchell loved, and oddly enough it was also true.

From time to time, as he had done for fifteen years, he noted in his diary the sign of his physical decay, especially his deafness and accompanying head noises. But despite occasional melancholy thoughts and various aches and pains he retained his basic optimism. To Mrs. Mason he wrote in 1912:

I was afraid of death when I was young; I have no fear of it now. I think it merely a station in some larger life; we get off the train, we do not know the name of the town where we alight, but there a new existence awaits us.

As usual Mitchell went to the Cascapedia Club for salmon fishing, and as usual packed some of his prize catches in ice to send with accompanying notes to his friends.

Before he went, however, he finished up another novel. It was one he had begun about 1866 and laid aside. In 1911 he had taken it up again and worked on it during his long summer vacations. Shortly after his eighty-fourth birthday it was ready for the publisher. In the very shaky hand characteristic of his later years, he wrote the editor of the Century Company, asking if they would print it by autumn. "I am too old to wait a year for the birth to occur." Four days later his secretary wrote saying that Dr. Mitchell was taking the eleven o'clock train on Friday and would bring his novel to the

Century office shortly after one. By November Osler had
received and read the book.

Like Mitchell's earliest novels, this one, *Westways*, is a
story of the Civil War. There are links to *In War Time* and
Roland Blake in the battle scenes and in the whole attitude
toward war.

. . . war is a disgustingly dirty business. You don't realize that
in history, in fiction, or in pictures. It's filthy.

and John Penhallow says:

I used to dream of the romance of war when I was a boy. There
is very little romance in it, and much dirt, awful horrors of the
dead and wounded, of battles lost or won, and waste beyond
conception.

There are vivid pictures of Gettysburg and the Wilderness
campaign. Mitchell tells of the screams of horses and mules
and of the wounded. There are the ambulance trains, and a
baker's wagon wiped out by a bursting shell. And there is
"that strange complex odour which rises from a battlefield."
It affected him as horrible and unlike any other unpleasant
smell.

There are scenes too of soldiers laughing at an officer being
knocked off a pontoon bridge by a wagon, of the army post-
office marking letters "not found—missing—and so on."
There is an excellent picture of an army in motion.

Mitchell was of course drawing partly from his own memories of Gettysburg, but as his Chicago address shows, he
had questioned army officers for details of the behavior of
men in battle. To refresh his own recollections he had in May
of 1912 spent two days at Gettysburg. No doubt also he had
drawn extensively upon John Billings' experiences in the
Wilderness campaign.

At one point in the story, two characters from another war
novel, Roland Blake and Philip Francis, appear briefly. This

was a favorite device of Mitchell's: to link his novels by having characters appear in more than one.

The book as a whole, however, is closer to his later work in style and ideas than to his early novels. As his letters and diaries show, it is principally the work of his summers between 1911 and 1913. Like many of his novels, *Westways* lacks compactness of form, but it is a more mature piece of work than *Roland Blake*. Certain ideas are similar to those in *Dr. North*, such as the one that a man must have both men and women friends or he will miss "what the double intimacies alone can give." As in the "Dr. North novels" there are pseudo-quotations from oriental sources such as "In the inn of decision there is rest."

The theme, but not the plot or the characters, is that of Mitchell's abortive novel of many years before: the bitterness of family controversy during the Civil War. It was a theme which Mitchell knew first hand both as a Philadelphian and as a man whose father had been a Virginian.

Squire James Penhallow, an ironmaster, goes into the Union army. His wife, Ann, is of Southern family and sympathy. Both are represented as fine people: country aristocrats of the old school, who look after their tenants and dependents in a paternalistic fashion. But because they do not talk out their differences of opinion, Ann goes through a fainting spell and gets herself into a hysterical condition. Mitchell knew enough of the more recent theories of neurosis to say, "She had been living in a state of unwholesome suppression."

James Penhallow suffers a head wound which gradually transforms his whose character until he becomes self-centered and psychotic. An operation finally restores him to his true self. It is a case history skilfully woven into fiction.

The love story of young John Penhallow and Leila Gray is in Mitchell's usual sentimental tradition. On one occasion Leila writes a tender letter to John, who is in the army, but tears it up and sends a colder one. The author's comment is significant.

> The nobler woman instinct is apt to be armed by nature for defensive warfare. If she has imagination, she has in hours of doubt some sense of humiliation in the vast surrender of marriage. This accounts for certain of the cases of celibate women, who miss the complete life and have no ready traitor within the guarded fortress to open the way to love.

It is small wonder that in a social order where marriage meant "surrender" and where love could only be admitted as a kind of traitor to refined instincts that the psychiatrists of the time found their offices filled with neurotic women.

On the whole, *Westways* is far from being Mitchell's poorest work. There are a number of well-drawn minor characters, many effective scenes, and a sense of reality about the whole thing. It is a better piece of work than the Civil War novel *Roland Blake* written twenty-seven years earlier. It gives no indication of being the work of an aged man.

At seventy-five he had told Osler:

> The mind is something more than the grey matter—even if that be needed for manifestation. Why is it that my brain at 75 is still improving when all else of me is too clearly failing.

Perhaps at eighty-four his mind had ceased to improve but, as *Westways* shows, it was as keen as ever.

Later that summer the Mitchells went to Hot Springs, presumably because Mrs. Mitchell suffered less there from rheumatism than at Bar Harbor. Her husband as usual was bored at resorts. He bombarded Osler with questions about rare books he was seeking and about some letters of William Harvey. He also started work on a dramatic poem, *Barabas*. He got in touch with Dr. Solis-Cohen to ask help in finding material on Hebrew lore, methods of recording time, etc. Dr. Solis-Cohen enlisted the aid of scholars at Dropsie College.

Then Dr. John Mitchell suffered a fall from a horse, and his father had to take over the whole practice. Mitchell wrote to Howells that for the winter he was heavily loaded with work. At times he took veronal to sleep, but found it caused him to dream and made him dreamy during the day. He added a note of complaint. A sale catalogue of the library of the poet laureate listed a volume of Mitchell's verse—uncut. His only consolation was that a copy of George Meredith's poems was also uncut.

Around Christmastime Mitchell came down with influenza. Apparently he did not consider himself seriously ill, for he lay in bed reading proof of *Barabas*. When his nephew, Dr. William B. Cadwalader, called, Mitchell sent him across the street with the proof sheets to show Dr. Solis-Cohen and to ask if anything in the poem might offend the Jews.

But age and a winter of hard work had left him no recuperative strength. His sons and their wives were summoned to the bedside. In his delirium he imagined himself at Gettysburg, operating on the wounded. He died on January 4, 1914. Had he lived until February 15, he would have been eighty-five. On January 6 he was buried in Woodlawn Cemetery. Two weeks later Mrs. Mitchell was laid beside him.

Osler heard the news in a cablegram from Dr. John Mitchell. In a copy of an *Ode on a Lycian Tomb* he noted the date and added, "one of my dearest friends—had I been a son he could not have been kinder to me during the five years of my life in Philadelphia."

Writing for the *British Medical Journal* he summed up:

Of no man I have known are Walter Savage Landor's words more true: "I warmed both hands before the fire of life." We have to go to other centuries to find a parallel to his career. . . . And of Mitchell Dr. Johnson's remark of Meade is equally true: "No man ever lived more in the sunshine of life."

X

The Man

Tho' much is taken, much abides.

—TENNYSON, *Ulysses*

How GREAT a man was Weir Mitchell? The answer involves an evaluation of his work as a scientist, physician, and writer. To a large extent the foregoing chapters have suggested this evaluation, but perhaps these suggestions should be synthesized into a more positive statement.

It is clear from any account of the man's work that he was an important figure in his time—which in his case means a half-century. From *Gunshot Wounds* in 1864 to *Westways* in 1913, Weir Mitchell was doing significant work. The first was a medical landmark; the last was praised by the literary critics of the time. W. S. Braithwaite in the Boston *Transcript* called it "certainly one of the best books Dr. Mitchell has ever written. . . . It is more real than *Hugh Wynne*." The *New York Times*, also comparing it to *Hugh Wynne*, spoke of "an even finer art, a surer touch" in *Westways*. If only for the extent of his work he would be an amazing figure. Few men in history have been intellectual forces during so many years of their lives.

The two works just cited are examples of the immense versatility of the man. As Dr. Osler recognized, it was necessary to go back to the eighteenth century to find parallels. His own contemporaries most often compared Mitchell to Franklin. Certainly there are similarities, not only in their versatility, their zest for life, their harmony with the times in which they lived, but also in their limitations. Neither man left us any world-shaking discovery, any unique philosophy, any single great classic of literature.

As a scientist Mitchell's work in snake venoms was valuable, but he left no landmark as did Pasteur, Lister, or Koch. He was only one of many research workers who remade medicine during the nineteenth century. Many lesser men did research work as significant as this.

In neurology his work is probably more important. Two publications growing out of his Civil War hospital work, *Reflex Paralysis* and *Gunshot Wounds*, insure him a place in the history of medicine. Most commentators agree that Mitchell was the outstanding member of the trio which produced them. Morehouse never attained the stature of the other two; Keen was at the time a very young man more or less under the tutelage of Mitchell. It was Mitchell who persuaded Surgeon General Hammond to appoint Keen to the staff at Turner's Lane Hospital. But there is sufficient glory for all three. Nearly eighty years after its first publication, *Reflex Paralysis* was reprinted by the Yale University School of Medicine with an introduction by John F. Fulton, who points out that Mitchell clearly recognized the presence of motor centers in the forebrain which controlled musculature on the opposite side of the body. And even more important, these men gave a clear-cut description of what are now called primary and secondary shock. Furthermore, they recognized the syndrome which is now called "primary blast," that is, collapse from proximity to an explosion without sign of an external injury. Dr. Fulton sums up thus:

The book on gun-shot wounds and the Circular which preceded it thus stand as one of the great milestones in the history of American neurology and American clinical medicine.

Similarly in *A Short History of Psychiatric Achievement* (New York, 1941) Nolan D. Lewis places Mitchell among the great neurologists of the nineteenth century:

> In historical retrospect some fifty or sixty years ago, Hughlings Jackson, Charcot, Erb, Strumpel, Weir Mitchell, Segiun, and Spitzka were active establishing clinical forms and especially revealing the pathologies-anatomical basis of disease. They were the shining lights of their time and their efforts in necessary and fundamental research constitute an era of usefulness and importance, the extensions of which are noted even today.

Despite all this and despite Professor Carlson's statement that Mitchell was great primarily as a physiologist, it is rather his work as a pioneer psychiatrist for which he is remembered. This is true even though much of his purely psychiatric work is now outmoded. *Fat and Blood*, for all its common sense, and the celebrated Rest Cure are outside the main channel of modern psychiatry. A less important man, A. J. Ingersoll, whose book *In Health* came out the same year as *Fat and Blood*, is in the main stream. Brill wrote about Ingersoll as "An American Precursor of Freud." Why then is Mitchell important as a psychiatrist and what were his methods?

If he did nothing else he took psychiatry out of the madhouse and brought it into everyday life. It became respectable to be treated for mental illness. The Rest Cure was designed to restore neurotics to normal life. *Fat and Blood*, written to explain the method to physicians, is easily read by laymen. Despite the controversy it created, the rest treatment gained wide acceptance. Weir Mitchell institutes appeared in France; Dr. William Playfair, among others, used the method in England; Dr. Sigmund Freud in Vienna adopted a modification of it.

Freud stated that he combined what he called "the Weir Mitchell rest cure" with his own psychoanalytic therapy. Thus on the one hand he prevented the disturbing intrusion of new psychic impressions during therapy; on the other he avoided the monotony of the rest treatment. Freud believed that his method kept the patient from falling into harmful reverie.

Despite the controversy over the Rest Cure, it was less shocking to the people of its time than the theories of psychoanalysis. Nineteenth-century America was not ready for a Freud.

Some idea of the difficulties of psychiatry in Mitchell's day can be illustrated by his experience with a patient who came to him after trying numberless forms of treatment. A woman of thirty-three, she was pale and feeble, and had dropped in weight from 125 to 95 pounds. She had become morbid, at last giving way to utter despair. Under treatment she regained health of mind and body. However, her mother, a wealthy New England woman, wrote Mitchell in great indignation because he had prescribed champagne and had recommended a lady's maid. The alarmed mother, a prohibitionist, condemned the prescription and stated that a properly instructed New England husband was quite capable of helping his wife dress. She warned that her daughter might be purchasing bodily comfort and ease, health, and enjoyment at the cost of her immortal soul.

A more informed and less intolerant age may find the undoubted effectiveness of Mitchell's now outmoded psychiatric methods hard to understand. Apart from rest, massage, and a general physical toning up, just what were these methods? First of all, he had one premise which is still regarded as sound: the interrelationship of mind and body. Today psychiatrists are likely to treat physical ills by curing those of the mind; Mitchell reversed the process by trying to heal the mind through first restoring the body to health. That is the whole basis of the Rest Cure.

Late in life he attacked the psychoanalytic theories on the

basis that they held "that neurasthenia is always a disease of the mind alone—a psychogenesis." His own belief was that "a goodly proportion of neurasthenia . . . has no more psychic origin than has a colic." Today, of course, even the source of a colic would be sought in the mind.

Yet, as Mitchell himself recognized in talking about physicians of the past, a faulty theory may go along with sound practice. In his day psychiatry was in a position not unlike that of medicine a century before: there was a dearth of sound theory about the basic causes of disease. Under such conditions, treatment is based on trial and error. Mitchell's father had often amused social gatherings with demonstrations of hypnotism; Weir frequently used it in the treatment of his patients, especially those with hysteric symptoms. The results were often disappointing; but one man afflicted with a hysteric pendulum motion of the arm could be relieved for a time at least by hypnotic suggestion.

However, neither hypnotism nor the Rest Cure is the secret of Mitchell's effectiveness with neurotic patients. Two other factors were more important: training the patient in self-control, and the personality of the physician. After building up the patient's general health, Mitchell told her that control of hysteric or neurotic symptoms was like learning to control temper.

It is not hard to open this point of view to a clever woman. You urge the idea from day to day; you ask her to try your way. She says I have done so, and then you point out that with ill health success was out of the question, while with rising health it might be easy. At last you get her to promise to fight every desire to cry, or twitch, or grow excited.

Above all, you teach her the priceless lesson for a woman of the value of moods, of the ease with which she can get herself into a state of dangerous tension, of the necessity of learning not how to bear a thing, but how to approach the idea of bearing it in a state of calm. It is a long sermon—it is always apt to win with a woman of intelligence, and fools are to be dealt with by other moral drugs than these, or the honest pill must be gilded with timely flattery or such better motives as may help it to find a woman's conscience, if that is to be stirred at all.

Similarly in his discussions of education, he stressed the need to train in self-control. The over-indulgent mother always came in for attack.

Often his methods were merely applied common sense. To an overly religious park guard who worried over his evil thoughts, Mitchell stated that everybody had such thoughts. Far from being evil, the man was basically good, for it was only good people who worried about such things. The man's real trouble was that as a park guard he had too much time to brood over his thoughts. Dwelling on them was like scratching a mosquito bite; it made things worse. Even to the uneducated, Mitchell tried to give an understanding of their reactions. To the "queer fellow" who reported that the devil was always tempting him, Mitchell said, "Tell him to go to hell."

Behind all his methods was the man himself: urbane, interesting, self-assured, and with a strange personal magnetism. A granddaughter says half his woman patients were in love with him. Some of their letters and reminiscences certainly show a gratitude bordering on idolatry. The real answer seems to be that in Mitchell women found a man who seemed to understand them. In an age contemptuous of women's neurotic ailments, here was a man who took them seriously. Without using the psychoanalytic technique, he achieved certain of its effects: the transfer of a burden to the physician. (And as Mitchell's remarks show, patients often poured out "confessions"). He gave the patient faith in his or her own ability to overcome the difficulty. And without a theory in the matter he produced both the hostility of patient toward the analyst (witness the famous anecdote of threatening to get into bed with a woman) and the emotional drive toward the analyst.

He was modern in at least two particulars: he recognized that a nervous ailment had deep roots. Dr. Guy Hinsdale, who worked under him, stated, "Mitchell was remarkable among his contemporaries for his attentions to the entire life of his neurasthenic patients, realizing that the local manifestations were symptoms of a deeper cause." Secondly, as shown by his own remarks quoted above, he endeavored to give a patient insight into his own condition. This is fundamental to modern practice.

Throughout his life he was interested in the problem of epilepsy. As has been noted, he never ceased to mourn Morehouse's loss of the notes made at Turner's Lane on rare types of epileptics. His own handling of cases involved both neurological and psychiatric methods. Using his knowledge of the localization of brain function, he carefully noted what parts of the body of an epileptic were first affected in a seizure. Like his contemporaries he treated these patients with lithium bromide, a salt no longer used because of the discovery of acetanilide and modern barbituates. If the patient could afford it and was physically able to go, Mitchell sent him to the seashore or on a fishing trip under the care of a physician. Camp cure was the treatment Mitchell had used on himself when he had gone through a period of neurasthenia, and which throughout his life he regarded as the best possible mental hygiene. All his methods are a mixture of insight and pragmatism. Perhaps most important was his belief that patients could be helped, a belief which led him to take immense pains, to try one thing after another. For Mitchell, medicine was an art, not merely a scientific routine of tests, injections, and vitamin pills. And if he failed to develop a master theory of neuroses, he also avoided the trap of theories. He was never the slave of a single system—not even of his own Rest Cure.

Few men of science have ever written with more clarity. From the notes on patients at Turner's Lane in the sixties to

his "Motor Ataxy from Emotion" written at eighty, he uses
a nontechnical expository style comprehensible alike to specialist and layman. He had a distaste for jargon. When the
young eye specialist, Dr. George E. DeSchweinitz, sent a long
technical report on a patient, Mitchell wrote back, "Thanks.
What I want to know is: Does the woman need glasses?"

As a poet and novelist Mitchell is less secure in his reputation than as a physician. His verse, with the exception of one
or two lyrics and the *Ode on a Lycian Tomb*, is thoroughly
undistinguished. But as has been suggested in the discussion
of individual novels, there are several of considerable merit.
In War Time, parts of *Roland Blake*, *Dr. North*, *Circumstance*, *Westways*, and above all *Constance Trescot* are still
worth reading. In a period when American novels were chiefly
designed for hammock reading, Mitchell's have an intellectual
quality which is rare among his contemporary writers. The
comparisons which most often come to mind are Oliver Wendell Holmes and Henry James. All three were interested in
abnormal psychology. Unlike Melville, they made no attempt
to solve the riddles of the universe, the problem of evil. They
were psychologists, not metaphysicians. Their characters
move in an accepted universe. Such problems as they have
are the problems of adapting themselves to that universe. Of
the three, James is of course the greatest. But Mitchell, using a
similar social milieu, has a health which James lacks. Mitchell's
characters enjoy good food and drink; they fall in love and
marry; they beget children. So often the world of Henry
James is an old man's world. Strether in *The Ambassadors* is
a thoroughly typical character. James' people are the literary
ancestors of Eliot's Prufrocks and Gerontions. Mitchell, on
the other hand, tends to write of men and women between
twenty-five and forty-five—people at the height of their
powers and with a zest for life. Even the maladjusted characters are alive: Octopia Darnell tries to dominate those around

her; Mr. Norman, the paranoid, attempts to murder his wife and her fancied lover; Roger Grace, the self-made millionaire, goes on extended binges; Constance Trescot hounds her husband's murderer to his destruction. There is none of the old-maidish resignation of Caroline Spencer in James' *Four Meetings* or the frustration of a Daisy Miller. James wrote of the ineffectuals, the people in the backwaters of life; Mitchell chose men and women battered by war, financial trouble, or imbued with plain cussedness. It is perhaps a commentary on our times that the anemic neuroses of James' men and women are regarded as more significant than the forceful neurotics of Mitchell's books. Certainly it is a commentary on this age that Mitchell's studies in abnormal psychology should seem more important than his more normal characters such as the intelligent men and women of *Dr. North* or the charming Alice Westerley of *In War Time*.

What then keeps Mitchell from being first-rate? Certainly he is more adult than Winston Churchill, Owen Wister, Marion Crawford, or F. Hopkinson Smith. He has more grace than William Dean Howells, a deeper understanding of psychology. There is more history, especially historical detail, in his *Hugh Wynne* than in most of the thirty-two historical romances written during the six years from 1896 to 1902. George Washington swears at Monmouth and gets merry over his wine. In the probing into the bypaths of psychology, the only contemporary who did as much was Henry James.

Part of the answer is Philadelphia. Mitchell never threw off its reticences, its social mores, its emphasis on class and family. He could help to support Walt Whitman, but he could never forget that Walt was not a gentleman. He was a friend of Carnegie's and he put Xerxes Crofter, the malefactor of great wealth, into his books, yet he has no conception of the America of *The Pit* and *The Octopus*. His people are the absentee owners of coal lands, the Philadelphia aristocracy of bankers and lawyers for inherited estates. In their unchallenged position they could afford generous charities, fine distinctions of business honor, and a discriminating taste in Madeira. They had not become the timid George Appleys and H. M. Pulhams of a later day. Mitchell was almost as unconscious of the proletariat as was Henry James.

A more serious fault is his adherence to the love-story convention of his time. With few exceptions there is always the pure, clever, strong-minded girl who refuses to acknowledge to herself that she is in love until the last page. If she is a widow she puts up an even longer battle before she "surrenders." She appears in the stories of Stanley Weyman, of Owen Wister, of Winston Churchill—yes, even in Henry James and Frank Norris. One is forced to believe she must have existed—if only in imitation of a literary fashion. Between 1885 and 1915 she was as ubiquitous as the modern clever career woman who in contemporary novels sleeps with a series of wrong partners before finding love. In Mitchell's day the heroine merely flirted with the wrong man throughout the book, only to marry the hero at last.

As Mitchell demonstrated in *Roland Blake* and *Constance Trescot*, he could draw other types. In fact the adventuress, Mrs. Hunter, in *Circumstances* is an American Becky Sharp. But for the most part he is content to follow convention. At a number of places he hints at the baleful effects of sexual repression, but none of his "good" characters ever violates the strictest propriety or questions the Elsie Dinsmore code. This, combined with the need for happy endings, produces a rather high mortality among rascally or psychotic husbands. In Mitchell's novels unpleasant husbands were not a good insurance risk.

In medicine Mitchell was often in advance of his age; on most social and economic questions he was behind it. He deplores the fact that ailing workmen must be discharged from hospitals without means of support, but his only solution is a rest home supported by charity. Despite his own voluntary sacrifice of a fortune to aid small depositors of a bank in which he was a director, he shows no glimpse of the effect of panics on the worker. His social order is paternalistic; it revolves around the dinner tables of the wealthy. Even the American Revolution becomes an affair of Philadelphia drawing rooms.

As a physician and neurologist Mitchell was able to put much into novels that his contemporaries could not. His fiction has an intellectual quality unusual in his day. Certainly he deserves to be restored to the canon of American literature. Despite the faults of his novels (and they were faults of the time) his work has the flavor of an unusual man. But except in *Constance Trescot* he never let himself go. He never wrote anything which might offend a Philadelphian.

In fact he once boasted that he never wrote a line which might cause a young girl to blush. At a time when even so ardent a feminist as his friend Agnes Irwin could advise a college girl that at seventeen she was too young to read Fielding and Smollett, this point of view had obvious limitations for the novelist who would present a serious picture of life. Certainly Mitchell's statement gives the lie to Howells' contention that the Young Girl (Howells' own capitals) had not sealed "the lips of Fiction with a touch of her finger."

It was this same tendency to conform to the mores of a highly conservative community which perhaps kept him from entertaining more daring theories of psychiatry. There is some point to Emerson's aphorism: "Whoso would be a man must be a nonconformist." Certainly the original thinker or artist must on occasion be something of a nonconformist: he must see beyond the prejudices and limitations of his contemporaries. This habit of conformity is perhaps the chief reason why Mitchell is not regarded as one of the very great. Only in old age did he seriously question childhood beliefs. (Cf. p. 279.) He was a regular churchgoer: St. Stephen's usually, but Christ Church on Easter. His friend Talcott Williams could say: "the winds of criticism and doubts of the day passed him by; he retained through all his life that simple and sincere faith he had early known and seen . . ." It is one thing to win faith through doubt; it is often a sign of limitation to be untouched by doubt. Few intellectual leaders have achieved greatness without first seeing through the shams and stupidities of their times. Mitchell was a great man in his era; he did not transcend it.

What of Weir Mitchell's inner life? Despite a mass of personal letters, an autobiography, and diaries for the years 1894 to 1912, it is a difficult question to answer. He was a reticent man even with himself. Thus in 1904, after a visit to Reculver where he had wooed his first wife, he noted:

A wonderful cold autumn day and glad with the voices of children and at evening the old hymns. But alas Reculver memories of joy, of pain—none could dare tell all of his life.

And three years later, in noting the anniversary of his father's death, he added: "No man can reveal his whole life. No man dare. The wisest are the most silent."

It seems unlikely that he was hinting at any dark scandal in his past; more probably he was thinking of his love for the wife of his young manhood. It would have been like him never to hint of it lest it pain Mary.

Of his love for the companion of his mature years there is no doubt. The diaries abound in affectionate references to "M," "Polly," "Poll"—he used the last most often. Especially in the two or three years following Maria's death, he was deeply concerned about Poll's welfare, and he admired her quiet courage.

Ah dear lady, if I could tell you all of my life as honour forbids, you would know what you are and have been to me and my later life.

But always in the diary and in his letters to her, there is a restraint; there is nothing of the lover-like longing to be with her such as that in his father's letters to "Darling Matilda." Part of it is, of course, that Weir's are the emotions of an older man. But part of it seems to have grown out of the restraint of Mrs. Mitchell's nature. In fact, after the death of Maria, Weir found his wife's repressed emotion hard to bear. He would have preferred to talk about their "little maid."

References to Mary by her friends suggest friendship rather than warm affection. Over and over some correspondent of Weir's will say "Give my love to Mary," or "thank Mary for her letter." The affectionate friendships were with Weir. Thus Sarah Butler Wister wrote him that

Within a fortnight I have twice tried to storm Mary's defense, but she "sported her oak." I was tempted to renew my delightful alley gate visit to you, but the first was an accident and I thought to do it deliberately would be high life below stairs . . .

And after Maria's death, Mrs. Wister wrote to Weir: "At length I have ventured to write Mary . . . when I think of your stricken face, I can hardly see to write."

Perhaps Sarah Butler Wister and Weir Mitchell were more than half in love with each other. Certainly their letters abound with assurances of love and affection. Thus, when he got a letter from her while he was salmon fishing:

I gave my rod to my man and forgot the beauty of hill and stream for awhile in the pleasant company of a friend more dear to me than most, even of the many I love.

One thing is clear: Weir Mitchell was an affectionate man. His youthful letters from Paris to his parents and to his brothers and sisters are warm and intimate. So, too, are those of twenty years later to Lizzie, Letitia, and Chap. As has been pointed out, he was a devoted father. Every new publication of Lany's brought an enthusiastic letter from his father and was proudly noted in the diary. John and his wife, Anne, were ever in Weir Mitchell's thoughts; he worried over their every ailment or disappointment. As the years went on, John and his father were very close. "No one could have been a better son to me," Weir once wrote.

His friendships show the same warmth. Those with Holmes, Brooks, and Billings have been recounted. A dozen years after Brooks' death, Mitchell reread some of the letters; "with sense of what refreshment it is to know that he loved me and was my friend." When his friend Ed Coles was killed by a runaway horse, Mitchell noted in his diary, "A very lovable man, a great loss to us all." Of Augustus Saint-Gaudens, "I know no one of whom I saw so little for whom I had so great an affection." And when his brother-in-law, John Cadwalader, was ailing, the eighty-year-old Mitchell spoke of having for him "the strongest male affection I have ever known outside of my family."

Along with this affectionate quality in the man, there went another characteristic not usually associated with outgoing personalities: he was an introspective person. The diaries record many inventories of his physical and mental powers. When nearly eighty he noted:

My own youth in imagination amazes me. I should be failing in mind. I am not and as a poet I am rising steadily.

And a few weeks later:

I sometimes think I am really three or four distinct people when I am M. D.—art—scientific—thinker—novelist. Poet—of this I am the most sure. I mean that my temperament changes as I vary my mental uses.

During his later years he discovered in himself an increasing irritability over trifles and a tendency to fret about the welfare of his loved ones. He also believed that he had a growing tendency to hoard money, but this did not appear in his actions. He was forever giving money to worthy causes or to members of his family. Langdon needed help from time to time. And to Langdon's son, Weir, his grandfather gave an allowance of $500 annually. Nearly a year after the crash of the Real Estate Trust Company, Mitchell made a resolution to get out of debt. He listed his chief obligations:

> $4000 to College of Physicians
> 1000 to Hospital
> 12000 to Stables
> 2000 my salmon folly

The last item apparently refers to the expenses of his membership in the Restigouche Salmon Club, and his annual fishing trip. At the same time he noted:

Small things irritate and worry me—especially papering—house changes. I ask what use at 77 [he was 78] to decorate.

But he continued to give money, to buy rare books, and to go fishing each June.

Allied to Mitchell's introspective bent was an intense esthetic appreciation of nature and of beautiful women. Though he was an erratic diarist, he never failed to note the date of the first crocus each spring. On a train to Colorado in 1907, he was struck by the view, the "Wonder of gold on horizon line of corn stalks." *Westways*, the novel he finished at eighty-four, is filled with descriptions of forest and sea. On a trip to Bermuda at eighty-three, he spent much time hiking about the island. Of one walk to the sea he wrote, "wonder of blue and green," and at the aquarium he noted, "green eyes of fish, gold and silver iridescence." A few months later in Canada: "Long walk with the living and my dead," the "silence of the

wood." And a few weeks after that: "Went up Salmon River
. . . mosaic of bottom—timber water yellow, green, black;
wild rapids; black spruce wonderful."

And when at eighty-two he went to the Assembly, where
he stayed until two, he observed "numberless pretty girls.
Men lack carriage, etc. In England it is reversed." All these
are marks of the same Weir Mitchell who in his teens liked to
lie for hours in a boat on the Schuylkill, watching the river
and sky, and who as a young man in Paris wrote home of the
grace of the French girls.

Always he had an immense zest for life, and an unflagging
curiosity. As we have seen, he experimented upon himself
with drugs, a strait-jacket, and freezing of a nerve. On a trip
abroad in 1891 he attended a bullfight. At the age of sixty-six
he began taking lessons in bicycle riding. For a time he had to
give it up, but despite worries about what it would do to his
prostate gland, he tried again three years later—and learned
to ride. At sixty-eight he wrote in his diary:

I repent of many things done in life but regret only 2 left undone
ie   that I was never up in a balloon and never saw a battle. I have
been under fire in Paris in 52.

He took great delight in his grandchildren, going hiking
with Lany's son Weir, and taking John's daughters regularly
to the zoo. There he would insist that the keeper of the snake
cages should get out reptiles for the little girls to handle. Even
at seventy-four, having a little free time in New York, he
went to the zoo alone.

Despite his nineteenth-century notions of propriety, he
could enjoy himself at a risqué play. Thus:

. . . with Marion & Lany to theatre. . . . It was vulgar and funny.
I feel a certain shame as at one's enjoyment of the real wit of a
smutty tale.

So too he could relish Howells' anecdote of introducing Aldrich to Whitman, who said, "Aldrich, yes, yes, I've heard your little sheep bell tinkle." And despite strong prejudices in literature, he continued to find new enthusiasms such as Kipling (as a writer, not as the disagreeable person he once met) and Shaw. The two books he wished he had written were *Vanity Fair* and *The Ordeal of Richard Feverel*.

This same zest appears in all sorts of comments. Thus:

This night I have done Hugh Wynne and revised it— It has been a pleasure past belief.

And a month later after a trip up the Hudson and to Boston:

Impossible to render the joy of this week the morn'g quiet for work the afternoon talk & walk with Hy Holt & . . . Mrs. Holt.

A few months before his eightieth birthday he attended the Hippodrome, "vulgar and amusing," and an Army-Navy game, a "splendid sight."

It is true that he became opinionated and irascible in later years. Thus when he found on Chestnut Street a storeroom in which some ladies had set up a chamber of horrors to exhibit the alleged cruelty of vivisection, he snorted, "It's all lies," and stamped out to demand that the police close it up. His vanity he freely admitted. Thus Sarah Butler Wister could tease him by writing that in addition to salmon fishing, "You have besides your unsated literary appetite, your unabated literary powers, and you have your vanity which finds perpetual incense."

He was fond of telling anecdotes about himself. Perhaps his favorite was the one of his visit to the great neurologist, Charcot. Mitchell, who had not announced his name, presented himself as a patient, and gave an account of various symptoms of the neurasthenic syndrome. Charcot, learning that the supposed patient was soon to return to the United

States, recommended that he see Dr. Weir Mitchell, who "knew more about those troubles than anyone else." The incident must have occurred in 1873, for Weir in a letter of that date to his sister spoke of visiting Charcot. Mitchell's lifelong pride in the incident was undoubtedly due in part to its early testimony to his reputation in Europe.

Although he was not noted for his sense of humor, he could see a joke on himself. Throughout his life he was addicted to puns, most of them painful. But when someone called Philadelphia City Hall a "vision of beauty," he answered, "No, a division of booty." It was characteristic that he should record his remark in his diary.

Many people envied him; some of the younger men thought his reputation overinflated, his manner pompous. In committee meetings he usually got his own way, as when he bulldozed the College of Physicians into moving into a new building. To a large extent he raised the money for it, and took full credit. Friends and detractors alike recognized him as a personality and force. He became a legend in his own time, the subject of countless anecdotes. Weir Mitchell was quite a person.

It is the flavor of his personality which gives life even to his less-inspired novels; and it was the force and charm of the man which filled neurotic patients with hope and confidence. That he became fearfully conceited is undeniable. But despite wealth, conceit, and absurd adulation, he never became a stuffed shirt. Until the end of his life he remained alert for promising young men, and started them on the road to success. What his lifelong friend Dr. W. W. Keen called his "yeasty mind" continued to work on new problems, to throw off suggestions for others to follow. No man ever had a greater gift for friendship, whether for his famous elders like Holmes, his contemporaries like Phillips Brooks and Billings, his colleagues like Keen and Osler, or rising young men like Noguchi

and Cushing. He left his mark on three generations of physicians and scientists. He had a happy family life; his two sons
both achieved distinction, one in medicine, the other in literature. Dozens of people from Noguchi to Walt Whitman were
in his debt, and hundreds of patients regarded him with emotions of awe and affection. Osler was right: few men have
lived so fully in the sunshine of life. His own lines sum it up:

> I know the night is near at hand,
> The mists lie low on hill and bay.
> The autumn leaves are drifting by,
> But I have had the day.
>
> Yes, I have had, dear Lord, the day.
> When at Thy call I have the night,
> Brief be the twilight as I pass
> From light to dark, from dark to light.

Notes

Page references for novels are to the
"Author's Definitive Edition," New York, 1915

I. *Philadelphia Boyhood*

Page 2: on fevers: Fielding H. Garrison, *John Shaw Billings,* New York, 1915, p. 164.

Welch called it "the work of a great medical prophet," ms letter to S.W.M., May 19, 1896. (Trent collection.)

Holmes: Letter from O. W. Holmes.

Anna Robeson Burr, *Weir Mitchell, His Life and Letters,* New York, 1929, p. 80.

ether in child birth: S. W. Mitchell, ms *Autobiography* (also in Burr, p. 45).

Page 3: asepsis: Richard H. Shryock, *The Development of Modern Medicine,* New York, 1947, p. 119.

Meigs preferred to attribute the many deaths "to accident or providence."

Eleanor M. Tilton, *Amiable Autocrat,* New York, 1947, p. 174.

"Oh, fly," etc., Burr, p. 21.

letter from Richmond, Burr, p. 24.

Page 4: voyage to China: S. W. Mitchell, ms *Autobiography* (Burr says 4 times, p. 7).

Page 5: letter to Matilda Henry: Burr, pp. 11-12.

Page 6: "among gentlemen": *Autobiography* (also Burr, p. 7).

description of J.K.M.: S. W. Mitchell, *A History of Two Families,* Philadelphia, 1912, p. 16 (privately printed).

Page 7: letter from Richmond: Burr, p. 24.

Page 8: skating accident: S.W.M. to his sister, Jan. 14, 1849, Burr, pp. 50-51.

golden chariot: Charles W. Burr, *S. Weir Mitchell, Physician, Man of Letters, Man of Affairs,* Address before College of Physicians, Nov. 19, 1919, Philadelphia, 1920.

Page   8:   pink elephant: *Autobiography* (also in A. R. Burr, p. 28).

warning to parents: Charles W. Burr, *op. cit.*

Page   9:   *Midshipman Easy:* Talcott Williams, Address in *Memorial Addresses,* Philadelphia, 1914.

Sarah on J.K.M.: Sarah Mitchell Neilson, "Recollections of Mrs. Neilson" ms Family Papers.

Page   10:   books and reading: *Autobiography* (also in Burr, p. 36).

Page   11:   threatened with tuberculosis: *ibid.* (also Burr, pp. 41-42).

accident in laboratory: *ibid.* (also Burr, p. 29).

Page   12:   schooling: Talcott Williams, Address, in *Memorial Addresses and Resolutions,* Philadelphia, 1914.

Page   13:   *Autobiography* (also Burr, pp. 36-38).

drunkards: *Autobiography.*

1100 Walnut St.: Neilson, *Reminiscences,* Family Papers. *Autobiography.*

Page   14:   botanizing: Edward Sculley Bradley, *Henry Charles Lea,* Philadelphia, 1931, p. 48.

summer activities: *Autobiography* (also Burr, p. 27).

Cape May food: S.W.M., *Roland Blake,* p. 228.

visits to Virginia: Beverley Tucker, *S. Weir Mitchell,* Boston, 1914, pp. 42-43.

Page   15:   composition: ms Mitchell family papers.

buys boat: *Autobiography* (part in Burr, pp. 41-42).

Page   16:   fishing and sailing: *ibid.*

college life: *ibid.* (also Burr, p. 40).

Page   17:   oratorical contest and college: ms Mitchell family papers.

Page   18:   plans for career: *Autobiography* (also Burr, pp. 43-44).

Jefferson Medical College: *ibid.* (also Burr, pp. 44-45).

Page   19:   Welch on medical schools: Simon Flexner and James Thomas Flexner, *William Welch and the Heroic Age of American Medicine,* New York, 1941, p. 87.

New York College of Physicians: *ibid.,* p. 111.

Billings: Fielding H. Garrison, *John Shaw Billings,* New York, 1915, p. 12.

Page 19: Osler: Harvey Cushing, *The Life of Sir William Osler*, Oxford, 1925, I, 284.
Welch and microscope: Flexner, *Welch*, p. 118.
Eliot: Simon Flexner, *A Half Century of American Medicine*, Address, University of Louisville, p. 7.

Page 20: Mitchell's preparation: Burr, p. 44.
Huxley: Flexner, *A Half Century*, p. 12.
Preceptorial system, *ibid.*, p. 6.
Billings: Garrison, *Billings*, p. 14.
jaundice: Burr, p. 46.
Miss Chapman: Burr, p. 49.

Page 21: works in drug store: William H. Welch, "Weir Mitchell, Physician and Man of Science," in *Memorial Addresses*, Philadelphia, 1914, p. 102.

II. *Wanderyear*

Page 23: et seq.: Life in Paris: mss. letters, family papers.
Page 25: dinner with Robin: *Autobiography*.
Page 26: Claude Bernard's work: Richard H. Shryock, *The Development of Modern Medicine*, New York, 1947, pp. 202, 309.
Page 31: Hiram Powers, 1805-1873. His Greek Slave, 1843, caused much controversy.

III. *The Young Doctor*

Page 34: Pennsylvania Hospital: Mitchell was even refused permission to take books from the hospital library. *Autobiography*.
Page 35: Keen: W. W. Keen, "Silas Weir Mitchell (1829-1914) Personal Recollections," *Proceedings of the American Academy of Arts and Sciences*, Vol. 59, No. 17 (Jan. 1925), p. 649.
laboratory work: *Autobiography*.
Page 36: Hammond: *Autobiography*.
Page 37: Mitchell on mental process: Burr, pp. 75-77.
Page 38: incident of the door mat: *Autobiography* (also in Burr, p. 77).
adventure with snake, Beverley R. Tucker, *S. Weir Mitchell*, Boston, 1914, pp. 57-58.
Page 39: Holmes' letter: ms letter, Feb. 25, 1861, Trent Collection (cf. Burr, 78).

Page 39:   sends poem to Holmes: Burr, pp. 81-82.

writes Holmes about project: ms letters March 23, 1859 (Houghton Library, Dec. 21, 1874) Harvard University.

Holmes on diet: *The Autocrat of the Breakfast Table.*

Page 40:   letter to Dr. Warren: ms letter, Massachusetts Historical Society.

Parkman: ms letter Dec. 9, 1885, Massachusetts Historical Society.

Lowell: letter to S.W.M., July 15, 1888. With a notation in Mitchell's hand, Houghton Library.

Meredith: letter July 27, 1885, Yale Library (quoted Burr, p. 213).

Page 41:   courts Mary Elwyn: Burr, pp. 88-90.

Page 42:   Elizabeth on "coarse woman": ms letter, Sunday, Feb. 20 (1853?) Family papers.

Elizabeth's letter: ms letter Aug. 8, 1856. Family papers.

income: *Autobiography* (quoted, Burr, p. 91).

Page 43:   resigns from St. Joseph's: *ibid.* (cf. Burr, p. 138).

schools for nursing: Charles Burr, *S. Weir Mitchell,* Philadelphia, 1919, pp. 22-23.

dislike of lecturing: A. R. Burr, p. 69.

portrait of sister: *Autobiography* (quoted Burr, p. 41).

Page 44:   Walsh in Panama: ms letters Walsh to Weir, Family Papers (cf. Burr, p. 95).

Keen: W. W. Keen, "S. Weir Mitchell, M.D., LL.D., F.R.S." in *Memorial Address and Resolutions,* Philadelphia, 1914, p. 14.

Brooks: Burr, pp. 97-98.

IV. *The War Years*

Page 46:   letter to sister: Burr, p. 110.

abortive novel: Clements C. Fry Collection, Yale Historical Medical Library

letter to Osler: ms letter (Received at Oxford, Aug. 3, 1911), Trent Collection.

Page 47: Mitchell Henry: Burr, pp. 100-2.
Chapman's commission: autograph letter to sister, n.d. Family papers. (cf. Burr, p. 111).
terror at newsboy's cry: *In War Time*, p. 268.
work as brigade surgeon: S.W.M., "Recollections of the Civil War," address, Apr. 5, 1905. Reprinted from *Transactions of the College of Physicians of Philadelphia*, 1905, p. 5.

Page 48: Billings: Garrison, *Billings* (Quoting *Tr. Col. Phys.*, Phila. 1905) pp. 111-17.
Turner's Lane: *Autobiography* (cf. Burr, pp. 104-5).
Fifty-three years later, Dr. Harvey Cushing cited to Surgeon General Gorgas the work of Mitchell, Morehouse, and Keen as a pattern for the establishment of base hospitals.
John F. Fulton, *Harvey Cushing, a Biography*, Springfield, Ill., 1946, p. 413.

Page 49: Notes on cases: ms in library, Philadelphia College of Physicians.
morphia and atropine: S.W.M., "On the Antagonism of Morphia and Atropia," 1865.

Page 50: lay on field twenty-four hours: One man is reported as lying six days.
Yale reprint of *Reflex Paralysis:* John F. Fulton, Introduction to *Reflex Paralysis*, New Haven, 1941.

Page 51: *Gunshot Wounds: ibid.* and Fielding H. Garrison, *An Introduction to the History of Medicine* (4th ed.), Philadelphia, 1929, pp. 504, 645.
Keen ascribes papers to Mitchell: W. W. Keen, "Personal Recollections," p. 647.
malingerers: Albert Deutsch, "Military Psychiatry," in *One Hundred Years of American Psychiatry*, New York, 1944, pp. 371-73.
Morehouse: Keen, "Personal Recollections."

Page 52: Mitchell on loss of papers: S. Weir Mitchell, "The Medical Department of Civil War," p. 16.
Keen on Mitchell: "Personal Recollections," p. 647.
Medical and Surgical History: Shryock, 181-82.

Page 53: Lytton Strachey, *Florence Nightingale*.
Turner's Lane: *In War Time*, pp. 2, 9.

Page 53: hospital gangrene: S.W.M., "Med. Dept. in the Civil War," p. 7.

Page 54: "Camp Cure": (cf. also *John Sherwood*).
Mitchell on research: Burr, p. 125.
letter about anniversary: ms letter to sister, summer, 1863. Family papers.

Page 55: financial problems: Burr, p. 125.
salary as surgeon: ms in Fry Collection, and *In War Time*, p. 231.
saves $1,500: ms letter to sister, Aug. 1, 1863, Family papers.
Wally in scrape: Mrs. John K. Mitchell, Letter to Lizzie, n.d., Family papers.
Mitchell on Billings: S.W.M., "Memoir of John Shaw Billings," *Science*, XXXVIII (Dec. 12, 1913), p. 831.

Page 56: Billings' reputation in Europe: Garrison, *Billings*, p. 337.
Welch on *Index Catalogue, ibid.*, p. 339.
Mitchell to Lounsbury: ms letter, Apr. 4, 1911, Yale Library.
Date of pass: Burr, p. 107.
Care of wounded: S.W.M., "Med. Dept. in Civil War," p. 10.
horrible memory: *When All the Woods Are Green*, p. 87.
unpleasant smell: *Westways*, p. 381.
last novel: *Westways*, p. 414.

Page 57: carload of wounded: letter to Osler, Aug. 3, 1911, Trent Collection.
Fort Delaware: letters to sister, July 26, 1863, Aug. 1, 1863, Family papers. (Some of this in Burr, pp. 112-13.)
fancy dress ball: S.W.M., "Med. Dept. in Civil War."
Confederate surgeons: Burr, pp. 106, 112. In the *Autobiography*, Mitchell says: "I found that the reports spread by the copperheads . . . were entirely untrue. They were well fed and great pains were taken even to bring water from the Brandywine in tugs."

Page 58: health breaks down: Burr, p. 113.

Page 58: hostility to North: *Autobiography* (cf. Burr, p. 107).
Kearsarge and *Alabama*, Burr, pp. 107-9.
Holmes writes Agassiz and Wyman: ms letters, Mar.
3, 1863, and Apr. 16, 1863, Trent Collection.

Page 59: Wyman letter: ms letter to S.W.M., Mar. 6, 1863,
Trent Collection.
clergyman, doctors, creditors, relatives: letter in
Medical Times, May 30, 1874. Dated Philadelphia,
May 10, 1874, and signed Mat. Med. Among Mitchell
clippings and apparently by Mitchell.
"vile path to preferment": *loc. cit.*
"set of apes": Burr, p. 118.
Carlson: A. J. Carlson, "Silas Weir Mitchell," *Science*, Vol. 87 (May 27, 1938), p. 475.
Clough: S.W.M. letter to his son. Burr, p. 165.
Agassiz: ms letter, Trent Collection. (Quoted, Burr,
p. 119.)

Page 60: "unreconstructed Northerner": S.W.M. to Thomas
Lounsbury, Apr. 4, 1911, Yale Library.
Holmes' letter: Burr, p. 120.
"let in the pigs": John T. Morse, Life and Letters of
Oliver Wendell Holmes, Cambridge, 1896, II, 15.

Page 61: faculty representation: letter to *Med. Times.*
Sanitary Fair: Talcott Williams in *Memorial Addresses*, Philadelphia, 1914, p. 90; *Fuz-Buz the Fly*,
Philadelphia, 1866.
George Dedlow: Autobiography (cf. Burr, pp.
125-26).

Page 62: Holmes on Allibone: ms letter, March 20, 1862,
Trent Collection.

Page 63: family doctor into physiologist: Dr. W. N. Howell,
quoted by A. J. Carlson, "Mitchell," p. 477.
no period more interesting: *In War Time*, p. 97.

V. *Recognition*

Page 64: new ideas for study: Burr, p. 387.
letter to Mrs. Mason: Oct. 27, 1901, Family Papers
(cf. Burr, p. 273).
Anne's remark: *When All the Woods Are Green*,
p. 96.

Page 65: Brooks as Mitchells' house dog: Burr, p. 229.
Brooks's later conservatism: Alexander G. V. Allen, *Phillips Brooks, 1835-1893*, New York, 1931, 226-28.
"Rain in Camp": S.W.M., *Collected Poems*, p. 316.

Page 66: "despair is nearest": *ibid.*, p. 323.
"O Little Town of Bethlehem": Burr, p. 229.
death-bed remark: *Doctor and Patient*, 1904 (Fourth ed.), p. 88.

Page 67: Brooks on Boston and Philadelphia: Allen, *Brooks*, pp. 229, 244.
Brooks and Elizabeth Mitchell: Burr, pp. 229, 230.

Page 68: *The Black Crook:* Elizabeth Mitchell to John K. Mitchell, Family Papers.
terror for own children: Burr, p. 224.
insurance policy, Burr, p. 141.
Walsh's "moral degredation": Burr, p. 148.

Page 69: troubled with insomnia: ms Fry Collection.
visit to Holmes: Burr, p. 146.
advice to son: Burr, p. 161.

Page 70: letters from Europe: Family Papers.
Page 72: ". . . leaf and flower": Burr, p. 165.
Fanny Kemble: Burr, p. 132.
Sarah Butler Wister: *ibid.*, p. 283.
Mrs. Caspar Wister: H. H. F. Jayne, *Letters of Horace Howard Furness*, Cambridge, 1922, I, 350 *et passim.*

Page 73: "gray old scalp": Burr, p. 129.
"family made thoroughbred": Burr, p. 147.

Page 74: meets Mary Cadwalader: *ibid.*, pp. 129-30.
marriage: *ibid.*, pp. 176-77.
honeymoon: family anecdote.
scolded too much: Family Papers.
Mrs. Mitchell: Family Papers.

Page 75: John at Harvard: *ibid.*
letter on venereal disease: S.W.M. to J.K.M., Oct. 29 (?), Family Papers.

Page 76: "share your trouble": S.W.M. to J.K.M., n.d., *ibid.*
horseback riding: S.W.M. to J.K.M., Nov. 1877, *ibid.*
appointment to Orthopaedic: Burr says 1870 (p. 139); Tucker, 1872 (p. 14).

Page 76: relationship between bodily deformity and nervous disease:
Warren Sinkler, "The Philadelphia Orthopaedic Hospital and Infirmary for Nervous Diseases," *Founders' Week Memorial Volume,* ed. by Frederick P. Henry, Philadelphia, 1909, p. 798.

Page 77: "... were the patients millionaires": *Autobiography.*
physiology of cerebellum: Cecilia C. Mettler, *History of Medicine,* Philadelphia, 1947, p. 159.

Page 78: World War I: Burr, p. 122 n.
George Dedlow: in volume with *Autobiography of a Quack,* p. 96.
Holmes' letters: Burr, pp. 143-44, Morse, II, 12-15.
mental fatigue: *Wear and Tear,* pp. 12-13.

Page 79: mental friction: *ibid.,* pp. 18-19.
women unfit: *ibid.,* p. 40.

Page 80: apoplexy and tetanus: *ibid.,* pp. 22, 25.
headaches and eyestrain: Garrison, *Hist. of Med.,* p. 612.
amputation stumps: *ibid.,* p. 645.
"Relation of Pain to Weather": *American Journal of Medical Science,* Apr. 1877. Cf. also Lauder-Brunton, "Dr. Weir Mitchell," *Nature,* Jan. 8, 1914.
"Weir Mitchell's disease": Tucker, pp. 19-20; Garrison, *Hist. of Med.,* p. 645.

Page 81: Rest Cure: S.W.M., "The Evolution of the Rest Treatment," *Journal of Nervous and Mental Disease,* June 1904 (Quoted in *One Hundred Years of American Psychiatry,* p. 371).
Mitchell's account to Osler: Cushing, *Osler,* p. 288-89.
Keen's account: Burr, p. 154.
electrical treatments added: Tucker, p. 18.

Page 82: editions of *Fat and Blood:* Burr, p. 180.
"... incessant feebleness": *Fat and Blood,* Philadelphia, 1877, pp. 27-28.

Page 83: "... nothing less will answer": *ibid.,* p. 30.
anecdote about getting into bed: Burr, p. 184.

Page 84: "... higher sphere of a doctor's duties ...": *Fat and Blood,* p. 43.

Page 85:   ". . . method of using them": *Fat and Blood*, Philadelphia, 1902, p. 61.

"How to deprive rest of its evils . . .": *Fat and Blood*, 1877, p. 51.

Mills: William B. Cadwalader, "The Association of Dr. Mills with Dr. S. Weir Mitchell," reprinted with changes from *The Archives of Neurology and Psychiatry*, Vol. 28 (Dec. 1932), p. 19.

hundreds of autopsies: Shyrock, p. 361.

Page 86:   psychoses with no demonstrable somatic pathology: Shyrock, p. 361.

good or bad mental health: *Doctor and Patient*.

first to treat non-institutional cases: H. A. Bunker, "Psychiatry as a Specialty," in *One Hundred Years of American Psychiatry*, pp. 495-96.

aids C. K. Mills: Cadwalader, p. 19.

Page 87:   satiric novel: Harriet Boyer, *North of Market Street*, Philadelphia, 1896, pp. 51-52.

Page 88:   Mitchell's home and office: Tucker, pp. 63-65 (cf. photograph of office, facing p. 88).

Newport: Burr, p. 133.

James on Newport: *The American Scene*, New York, 1946, pp. 484, 490.

rides with Bancroft: Burr, p. 133.

Page 89:   on roses: S.W.M. to George Bancroft, Mar. 2, 1879, Mass. Hist. Soc.

Brooks: Allen, *Brooks*, p. 331.

Billings: Garrison, *Billings*, pp. 337, 343; and Mitchell, "Memoir of John Shaw Billings."

Page 90:   ". . . owed me a few hundreds . . .": ms letter, 1833 Walnut St., n.d., Billings Papers, New York Public Library.

dislike of war talk: Garrison, *Billings*, p. 133.

letter to Parkman: June 9, 1878, Mass. Hist. Soc.

Page 91:   gay dinners: Burr, p. 136.

VI. *A New Career*

Page 92:   Flexner: Simon Flexner, *A Half Century of American Medicine*, Founders Day Address, University of Louisville, Apr. 3, 1937.

Page 92: Cushing: Harvey Cushing, *The Life of William Osler*, Oxford, 1925, Introduction.
Holmes: Burr, pp. 78-79.

Page 93: ". . . amuse myself": Burr, 127.

Page 94: "fear not God would frown": *Hephzibah Guinnes*, p. 140.
skating scene: *ibid.*, p. 183.

Page 95: remark to Radcliffe students: Burr, p. 233.
Thoreau: *ibid.*, p. 123.
reading in other languages: Talcott Williams, *Memorial Address*.
dislike of games: Burr, p. 127
atmosphere of Newport: ms letter to Henry Charles Lea, July 17, 1883, Lea Library, University of Pennsylvania.
intestinal neuralgia: Letter to Lea, Aug. 11 (1883), Lea Library.
unfinished manuscript: Fry Collection, Yale Medical Library.

Page 96: letter to Aldrich: Aug. 2, 188-, Houghton Library, Harvard University.
"A less imaginative man . . .": *In War Time*, p. 18.
pipe breaks: *ibid.*, p. 17.

Page 97: ". . . amiability so common to selfish people": Almost the same phrase Mitchell used to describe Fannie Kemble's husband, Pierce Butler. *Autobiography*, quoted, Burr, p. 131.

Page 98: effect of Civil War on medicine: *In War Time*, pp. 43-44.
Colonel Fox: *ibid.*, p. 127.
Arthur Morton on war: *ibid.*, p. 226.
"success in medicine": *ibid.*, p. 30.

Page 99: "tender and yet decided": *ibid.*, p. 363.
"no recognition of individualities": *ibid.*, p. 54
Howells' suggestion: letter to S.W.M., Nov. 3, 1872, University of Pennsylvania Library.
Howells on novel: "Decency and the American Novel" (1892).
"I like nearness to life . . .": Howells to S.W.M., October 20, 1885, University of Pennsylvania.

Page 100:   letter from Meredith: Meredith to S.W.M., Apr. 2, 1885. Yale Library. Quoted Burr, pp. 212-13.

Meredith on *Roland Blake:* Letter to S.W.M., June 23, 1898. Yale Library. Quoted, Burr, p. 214. *Autobiography* (quoted, Burr, p. 128).

For a study of the revisions of *Roland Blake,* see Lyon N. Richardson, "S. Weir Mitchell at Work," *American Literature,* XI, No. 1, pp. 58-65 (March 1939). However, Richardson's statement that "In essence, *Roland Blake* is the author's earlier novelette, *Hephzibah Guinnes,* elaborated, seems hardly accurate. The two works use different characters and completely different periods of time.

More important is the study of Mitchell's methods of revision. For instance, Mitchell had printed six large-paper copies of an early version. He gave two copies to critics, and used two in making revisions. Originally the first five chapters described the Olivia-Octopia-Mrs. Wynne relationship. On the suggestion of a critic that he begin with Roland Blake, he made these Chapters IV to VIII in the final version.

This would support the present biographer's belief that for Mitchell, as for the modern reader, the study of neurotic personality was more interesting than the romantic hero. The reverse seems to have been true of the critic and also of George Meredith.

Richardson shows that the final addition was a page of conversation in which Blake tries to persuade the scoundrel, Darnell, not to commit suicide. The Victorian hero "must never, even in a thoughtless moment, be so much as remotely to blame for any unsocial action." Richardson, p. 64.

It is obvious that an author in the latter part of the nineteenth century labored under a heavy weight of tradition and taboo.

source of title: Burr, pp. 194-95.

"Her life was absorbed by Octopia . . .": *Roland Blake,* p. 51.

Page 101:   effect upon Olivia: *ibid.,* pp. 11-12.

Page 101: ". . . duller sound on limb or trunk of man": *ibid.*,
p. 80.
battlefield after charge: *ibid.*, p. 83.
". . . I hated it": *ibid.*, p. 297.
"Character . . . in women": *ibid.*, p. 112.
breaking strain of materials: *ibid.*, pp. 181-82.
Page 102: ". . . criminal psychology": *ibid.*, p. 345.
Page 103: children as complex personalities: *Far in the Forest*,
p. 202.
"The friendship of a man and a woman . . .": *ibid.*,
p. 213.
Page 104: ". . . does not know women": *Doctor and Patient*,
Philadelphia, 1888, pp. 10-11.
Page 105: ". . . so utterly unsatisfactory": *ibid.*, p. 74.
drink of rattlesnake venom: *ibid.*, p. 73.
Page 106: ". . . fortunate woman who does not add alcohol-
ism . . .": *ibid.*, p. 95
Coleridge and De Quincey: *ibid.*, p. 96.
Schneider on *Kubla Kahn*: Elisabeth Schneider, "The
Dream of Kubla Khan," *P.M.L.A.* LX, 784-801, 1945.
on mothers of sick children: *Doctor and Patient*,
p. 111.
Page 107: train girls like boys: *ibid.*, p. 141.
woman's physiological disqualifications: *ibid.*, p. 153.
Page 108: monograph: *The History of Instrumental Precision
in Medicine*.
Poignant lyric: S.W.M., "E.D.M." (1889) *Complete
Poems*, p. 270.
Page 109: discovery more important than Noguchi's: Gustav
Eckstein, *Noguchi*, New York, 1931, p. 97.
Holmes on rattlesnakes: Letters to S.W.M., Mar. 1,
1883 and Mar. 15, 1883. Morse, I, 261-62.
Page 110: Holmes on riddle, Oct. 4, 1882: *ibid.*, I, 352.
Seybert Commission: Furness *Letters*, I, 199, and Sey-
bert Commission, *Preliminary Report*, etc., Philadel-
phia, 1887, p. 5.
Page 111: ". . . a medium worth more than a chicken": *Pre-
liminary Report*, pp. 126-27.
Furness refuses to pass verdict: *ibid.*, p. 159.
Page 112: atmosphere of Philadelphia: *ibid.*, p. 7.
Osler tosses coin: Cushing, I, 220.

Page 112:   cherry pie: *ibid.*, I, 222.
            ". . . has every social need": *ibid.*, I, 223.
Page 113:   madeira and terrapin: *ibid.*, I, 244.
            Osler's jokes: Burr, p. 189.
            Mitchell gives Osler consultation work: Cushing, I, 254.
            interest in rare books: *ibid.*, I, 277.
            ". . . high place among American neurologists: *ibid.*, I, pp. 291-92.
            "had I been a son . . .": *ibid.*, II, p. 392.
            tendency to nepotism: Dr. Howard A. Kelley, quoted Cushing, I, 236.
Page 114:   Dr. Maurice Bucke: *ibid.*, I, 264-66.
            Scribners rejects Whitman: Horace Traubel, *Walt Whitman in Camden*, New York, 1915, I, 184.
            Whitman on Stedman: Traubel, I, 170.
            Furness to Mrs. Wister: Furness *Letters*, I, 345-46.
Page 115:   Furness to Mitchell: *ibid.*, I, 234.
            Mrs. Mitchell attends Whitman lecture: *Philadelphia Press*, Apr. 16, 1886.
            Whitman on Mitchell's verse: Traubel, I, 454-55. On the publication of Traubel's book in 1906, this much irritated Weir Mitchell.
                "He [Whitman] thought lightly of me and J.K.M. but says no word of the 15$ a month I paid for more than 2 yrs. to keep him alive nor of the care I gave declining all fees—nor of 100$ I gave him to buy a pony or wagon." S.W.M. *Diary*, Feb. 18, 1906.
                "I thought him self pleased as a god and with no good opinion of any but those who flattered or admired a poetic tramp." *Diary*, Mar. 19, 1906.
            "He is my friend . . .": Traubel, II, 271-72.
Page 116:   Mitchell on Whitman and Thoreau: *Doctor and Patient*, p. 162.
            Mitchell, Whitman, and stout lady: *Dr. North*, p. 14.
            Mitchell tricks Gilder: E. P. Oberholtzer, "Silas Weir Mitchell," *Philadelphia Public Ledger*, Jan. 18, 1914.
Page 117:   Whitman on Langdon's verse: Traubel, II, 182.

Page 117:   finally hatched a genius: S.W.M. to J.K.M., Nov. 13, 1878. Family papers.
Mitchell aids Mills: William B. Cadwalader, "The association of Dr. Mills and Dr. S. Weir Mitchell," Reprinted with changes, from *Archives of Neurology and Psychiatry*, Vol. 28 (Dec. 1932), p. 19.

Page 118:   Westphal's discovery: Cushing, I, p. 269-70.
Mitchell and Lewis: Garrison, *History of Medicine*, p. 645.
International Congress of Medicine: Cadwalader, p. 20.
Mitchell elected president of C. of P. & S.: Burr, p. 395.

Page 119:   Lea on Committee of One Hundred: Dana C. Munro, "Henry Charles Lea," *D. A. B.*, XI, 67-69.
Mitchell helps Lea: Bradley, p. 149.
Lea hesitates to dedicate books: S.W.M. to Charles M. Lea, Nov. 29, 1909, Lea Library, University of Pennsylvania.
Aldrich rejects article: Bradley, p. 280.
no bronze statue in park: S.W.M. to Lea, Mar. 7, 1884, Lea Library.
". . . machine for making money": Bradley, p. 133.
plans for library: Correspondence of S.W.M. and H. C. Lea, Lea Library.

Page 120:   Mitchell gives $5,000: J. Norman Henry, "The College of Physicians of Philadelphia," *Founder's Week Memorial Volume*, Philadelphia, 1909, p. 136.

Page 121:   likes praise from Boston: S.W.M. to O.W.H., Dec. 21, 1874, Houghton Library.
central figure at memorial celebration: *Medical News*, Jan. 8, 1887; quoted by Cushing, p. 278.
Mitchell on Bologna: Burr, p. 204.

Page 122:   Mitchell, Allen, and Lowell: S.W.M. to Sarah Butler Wister, Baden, Aug. 13 (1888). Family papers.
mishap at dinner, etc.: Burr, p. 204-7.

Page 123:   Duchess of Baden: *Autobiography*.
Lowell's illness: note by S.W.M. on a letter from Lowell dated London, July 15, 1888. Houghton Library.

Page 123:   Mrs. Mitchell on Lowell: S.W.M. to Lowell, Sept. 27, 1890. Houghton Library.
Lowell on Mrs. Wister: Lowell to S.W.M., Sept. 29, 1890. Houghton Library.

Page 124:   on salmon fishing: S.W.M. to Col. J. W. Higginson, Jan. 1889. Houghton Library.
working on Dalton: S.W.M. to Billings, Apr. 28, 1889. Billings Papers, New York Public Library.

VII. The Crest of the Wave

Page 125:   progress of medicine: Flexner, A Half Century of American Medicine, p. 13.

Page 126:   five trips abroad: In 1891, 1894, 1895, 1897, and Dec. 1898-June 1899.
Williams on Furness: Elizabeth Dunbar, Talcott Williams, New York, 1936, p. 189.
anecdote on night hostess: ibid., p. 185.

Page 127:   Saturday evenings: Felix Schelling, "S. Weir Mitchell," The General Magazine and Historical Chronicle, University of Pennsylvania, Vol. XXXII, No. 3 (Apr. 1930), p. 331.
Miss Anne Williams: S.W.M. to Sarah Butler Wister, Sunday 23, 1889. Family papers.
Mrs. Talcott Williams: Dunbar, p. 183.

Page 128:   Autocrat of the Dinner Table: Burr, p. 250.
Agnes Irwin: Agnes Repplier, Agnes Irwin, Garden City, 1935, pp. 32-33.

Page 129:   Mitchells leave Newport: Autobiography.
social life at Bar Harbor: Repplier, pp. 10-46.
Characteristics not a novel: S.W.M. to J.L. and J. B. Gilder, Nov. 10, 1890.
". . . not . . . the book of your hint: S.W.M. to Sarah Butler Wister, Newport, Aug. 27 (1892?). Family papers.
". . . I shall not like it": Sarah Butler Wister to S.W.M., Nov. 1, 1892. Family papers.

Page 130:   "the most interesting woman I have ever known": Burr, p. 283.

Page 132:   Van Gaetner incident: Diary, Oct. 7, 1895.
Owen North's statement: Dr. North, pp. 93-94.

There seems to have been a tradition of psychic experiences in the Mitchell family. After the death of Weir's brother Alexander, Dr. J. K. Mitchell and his wife heard mysterious and very distinct footsteps on the stairs. *Autobiography.* See also Mitchell's experience at the time of the death of Phillips Brooks (p. 157 above). Late in life Mitchell wrote to Osler: "We must admit the possibility of mind convers..g with mind across space under certain circumstances." ms letter College of Physicians, n.d.

Page 132:   El Din Attar: letter to S.W.M., Mar. 4 (n.d.) from woman in book department of Wanamaker's, asking about a translation of El Din Attar. The lady had searched publisher's catalogues. Trent Collection.

date of "A Madeira Party": In a letter to S.W.M., July 7, 1892, John Brisbane Walker declined "A Madeira Party" for the *Cosmopolitan* because of the drinking question. Mitchell-Howells letters, University of Pennsylvania Library. However, Mitchell in his *Diary* under Nov. 3, 1895, noted: "Wrote Madeira Party." This probably means "rewrote."

Page 135:   "I never found any one human being...": *When All the Woods Are Green*, p. 92.

"... will want their husbands to have women friends": *ibid.*, p. 208.

Sophy Irwin's correspondence: Trent Collection. Letters quoted: Sept. 18, 1897 and Sept. 4 (n.d.)

Page 136:   bad grammar: Burr, p. 381.

Copy No. 1: Furness *Letters*, I, 350.

Annis Lee Wister on Arthur Wynne and John's child: Letters to S.W.M. (n.d.) Family papers.

wish for death: Sarah Butler Wister to S.W.M., Feb. 6, 1904. Family papers.

Page 137:   "Yes, there is no pleasure...": Annis Lee Wister to S.W.M., Sept. 22, 1906. Family papers.

"If you could only know...": A.L.W. to S.W.M., Dec. 31 (n.d., but before Maria's death) Family papers.

Page 137:   Fielding, Richardson, and Scott: Sarah Butler Wister
to S.W.M., July 29, 1897. Family papers.
Constance Trescot: same, May 15, 1904. Family
papers.
Marion Lea's visit: S.W.M. to S.B.W., 189(2?)
Family papers.

Page 138:   Langdon's ambition: S.B.W. to S.W.M., Sunday,
July 8 (n.d.) Family papers.
visit to "Harvard Annex": Same, July 30, 1888.
used to come at twilight: Same, Sunday, Nov. 20
(n.d.).

Page 139:   "Take Wordsworth . . .": *When All the Woods Are
Green,* p. 88.
writing of *Hugh Wynne: Autobiography.* Quoted,
Burr, p. 234.

Page 142:   Sarah Butler Wister sends advertisement for *The
Quaker Soldier:* S.B.W. to S.W.M. n.d. Family
papers.
Caleb Hazelwood: Mitchell told S. W. Pennypacker
that Hugh's father was the only character drawn
directly from life. S.W.M. to S.W.P., Nov. 4, 1897.
Family papers.

Page 143:   "sadly invisible": Mitchell's report of the incident,
Burr, p. 37. What Mrs. Wister wrote was:
"The chief minor defect of H.W. to my mind is
the coldness or lack of conviction in the love
affairs: one knows that Hugh loves Darthea but
one does not feel it . . ." Sept. 15, 1897.
Nor was her capitulation quite so complete as
Mitchell reported. Thus:
"I . . . see and admit your point about this reticence
wh this story's being written for his children im-
posed upon him in regard to the writer's love
affairs. It entirely meets my objection to the lack
of passion in the book but while this autobiogra-
pher professes devotion & engrossing sentiment wh
colored and shaped his whole life I do not think
one gets the impression or feeling that it was a
permanent influence." Oct. 8, 1897 (Family papers).

Page 144:   comments on *Hugh Wynne:* Burr, pp. 237-39.

Page 145: never meant to tell real story: S.W.M. to Mrs. Virginia Q. McNealus, n.d. Family papers.
". . . the merit is small": Burr, p. 226.
Page 146: asks if young man needs money: S.W.M. to J.S.B., Mar. 18, 1890. Billings Papers, N. Y. Pub. Lib.
Clendening: Review of Burr, *Weir Mitchell*, N. Y. *Herald Tribune*, Nov. 10, 1929.
Lea's gift: S.W.M. — Lea correspondence, Lea Library.
Page 147: cholera epidemic: Talcott Williams, "The Higher Life in Philadelphia," *Outlook*, Vol. 54, July 25, 1896, p. 146.
controversial address: William Malamud, "The History of Psychiatric Theories," *One Hundred Years*, etc., p. 296.
letter to Billings: S.W.M. to J.S.B., Jan. 12, 1894. Billings Papers, N. Y. Public Library.
Billings answer: Jan. 16, 1894, *ibid.*
Page 148: Osler's reply: Cushing, I, p. 293.
Page 149: "Where, we ask . . .": Address before the Fiftieth Annual Meeting of the American Medico-Psychological Association, held in Philadelphia, May 16, 1894, pp. 10-11.
"historic scolding": John C. Whitehorn, "A Century of Psychiatric Research in America," *One Hundred Years*, p. 167.
Page 150: productive research from Freud: *loc. cit.*
"The preachment at Radcliffe . . .": Agnes Irwin to S.W.M., Jan. 14, 1896. Trent Collection.
Page 151: Radcliffe address: S.W.M., "Address to the Students of Radcliffe College," Jan. 17, 1895.
Page 152: Billings: *Autobiography* and *Diary*, Nov. 30, 1894 and Apr. 1, 1895.
"When a man . . .": *Diary*, Oct. 9, 1894.
breaking eggs in a glass: Burr, pp. 231-32.
Osler: Cushing, I, 400.
Page 153: Welch: Garrison, *Billings*, p. 339.
Billings dinner: Cushing, I, 424-25.
snake venoms and antitoxin: Gustav Eckstein, *Noguchi*, New York, 1931, pp. 94-95.

Page 153:   looks up Ditmars: L. N. Wood, *Raymond L. Ditmars*, New York, 1944, p. 95.

Page 154:   effects of drug: *Doctor and Patient*, pp. 96-97.
             freezes ulnar nerve: Garrison, *History of Medicine*, p. 645.
             tries strait-jacket: "Address, Am. Medico-Psychological Assn.," p. 15.

Page 155:   asks for hasheesh: S.W.M. to Brander Matthews, n.d., Columbia University Library.
             William James to Henry James: Henry James, ed., *Letters of William James*, 1920, II, p. 37.
             Mitchell praises essay: S.W.M. to W.J., Feb. 29, 1888. Houghton Library.
             quarrel over spiritualism: Mitchell-James letters n.d., Houghton Library. Also: Burr, pp. 221-22 and *Autobiography*.

Page 156:   controversy with Gilder: R.W.G. to S.W.M., Nov. 9, 1897 (with notation in S.W.M.'s hand). University of Pennsylvania.

Page 157:   *Times* reports death: Burr, p. 263.
             Furness plays joke: Furness *Letters*, I, 314-15.
             bogus quotations: Burr, p. 311.
             odd experience at Brooks's death: *Autobiography*.

Page 158:   on Holmes: *Diary*, Oct. 10, 1894.
Page 159:   "Not since Maria died": *Autobiography* (quoted, Burr, p. 254).
             on wife's illness: S.W.M. to T. B. Aldrich, Apr. 30, 1898. University of Pennsylvania.

Page 160:   description of camp: Garrison, *Billings*, pp. 300-1.
             Cushing on Pepper and Osler: Cushing, *Osler*, I, 478.
             trip to Egypt: S.W.M. to Lea, Oct. 30, 1898.

Page 161:   Mitchell on his poem: Burr, pp. 266 and 270.

VIII. *The Sage*

Page 163:   Mitchell and Noguchi: Gustav Eckstein, pp. 89-105 and Simon Flexner, "Hideo Noguchi," *Annual Report of the Board of Regents of The Smithsonian Institution*, Washington, 1930, pp. 599-600.

Page 165:   "I am moved by the warm heart of the doctor": Eckstein, p. 108.

Page 166: "I used to think of age . . .": letter to C. E. Norton, Dec. 27, 1900, Harvard Autograph Collection, Houghton Library.
"What a fine fellow is Flexner . . .": Cushing, I, 542.
Japanese trip: *Diary*, 1901.

Page 167: Letter to Mrs. Mason: Burr, p. 273.
"Why are my services . . .": *Diary*, Oct. 10, 1901.
on Kipling: letter to Norton, July 14, 1903.
the Byron brasses: *Diary*, Jan. 1 and 3, 1898.

Page 172: Owen Wister on Henry James: Burr, p. 323.

Page 173: Mitchell tries to get Henry James to visit: *ibid.*, pp. 320-21.
"Hy James of the inscrutable and not overpleasing face": *Diary*, Jan. 26, 1905.
Gilder rejects "The Sins of the Fathers": R.W.G. to S.W.M., Oct. 31, 1901. University of Pennsylvania.

Page 174: Rabelaisian remark: *Diary*, Feb. 2, 1895.
theory about milk: Charles W. Burr, "S. Weir Mitchell," p. 338.

Page 175: *Index Medicus:* Cushing, I, 409 and 606.
"Medicine is seen at its best . . .": *ibid.*, I, 459.

Page 176: Cushing on Mitchell: John F. Fulton, *Harvey Cushing*, Springfield, Ill., 1946, p. 228.

Page 177: letter to Norton: Dec. 23, 1901. Houghton Library.

Page 178: reticence of Mills: Charles N. Burr, "Dr. Mills as a Teacher of Mental Diseases," p. 11. Reprinted from *Archives of Neurology and Psychiatry* (Dec. 1932), Vol. 8.

Page 179: Ingersoll's theories: A. J. Ingersoll, *In Health*, New York, 1878 (originally pub. 1877), pp. 19-23.

Page 180: psychoanalysis in America: John C. Whitehorn, "Psychiatric Research," *One Hundred Years of American Psychiatry*, New York, 1944, p. 174.

Page 181: asks Hay for clerk: S.W.M. to John Hay, Oct. 3, 1902. Autograph Letter, N. Y. Library.
"This resulted finally . . .": S.W.M. to C.E.N., Sept. 1, 1903. Houghton Library.

Page 182: People shocked at realistic portrayal of Washington's mother:

Gilder asked ". . . could a man as noble have had
such a mother?" Mitchell told him to look in Ford's
letters of Washington: ". . . you will see what
troubles she brought into that dutiful life . . ."
S.W.M. to R.W.G., June 10 (n.d.), University of
Pennsylvania.

Page 184: discussion with White: S.W.M. to J.W.W., Jan. 26
(n.d.) Family papers.
"We loved Thackeray and Tennyson . . .": Agnes
Repplier, *J. William White, M.D.*, Cambridge, Mass.,
1919, p. 92.

Page 188: Controversy with Gilder: S.W.M.'s note on letter
from R.W.G., May 8, 1903. University of Pennsylvania. See also Burr, pp. 365-66.
M. to Howells on *The Pearl:* Dec. 17, 1905. University
of Pennsylvania.

Page 191: Mitchell on *The Red City:* Burr, p. 318.

Page 192: "I accept the consequences of the sale of my story":
Burr, p. 336.
"But, Doctor, you don't drink champagne . . .":
Tucker, p. 50.
Eczema: If Dr. Spurgeon English is correct in his
recent emphasis of the point that eczema is caused
by an unsatisfied desire to be loved, it would furnish
a clue to a psychoanalytic explanation of Mitchell's
personality. Though he was less overtly demanding
of affection than his sister Elizabeth, his letters to his
parents, brothers, sisters, and sons show a deep need
for affectional relationships. Much as he admired
his father, he seems to have felt a lack of complete
approval from Dr. John. There is an almost ostentatious attempt to commemorate the anniversary of
Dr. John's death. Fifty years later Mitchell refers
to it in a letter to Norton, and he always noted it
in his diary. It is as if he had to prove to himself
his filial regard.
Obviously, too, the extremely warm friendships
with Brooks, Billings, Sarah Butler Wister, and
John Cadwalader grew out of the same deep need
for affection. (See also p. 237 above.)

Even more significant perhaps is his almost pathological longing for praise during the years of his
greatest fame. Thus, although the fan mail poured
in about his novels, patients were almost idolatrous,
and honors came in great numbers, his appetite for
praise became a byword. His notorious vanity was
to a large extent this love of flattery. In his conversation he made remarks which were a fishing for
compliments. (Cf. Sarah Butler Wister's jibe, p. 241
above.) All this would fit into the pattern of a
person in search of love and affection. Possible
causes of this are to be found in his sense of not
measuring up to his father's desires and in the early
loss of his first wife, followed by years of widower-
hood.

Page 193: "This fractional decay . . .": *Diary*, Sept. 22, 1902.
Loss of $32,000: *ibid.*, Mar. 29, 1904. Under July 29,
1901, he estimated his income for the first six months
of the year as about $22,000 plus $12,000 from books.
J. K. Vanderbilt: As far back as Aug. 26, 1895,
Mitchell had noted in his diary: "I shall get a fee for
seeing Mr. V- wh. will be more than my serial book
brings—How odd is that."
Alters will: *Diary*, May 23 and 30, 1904.
Real Estate Trust failure: *Philadelphia Press*, Sept. 12,
1906 et seq.

Page 194: letter to Norton: S.W.M. to C.E.N., Dec. 20, 1906.
letter to Billings: Sept. 20, 1906. N. Y. Public Library
sells stock and puts up $50,000: *Diary*, Sept. 16 and
Oct. 9, 1906.

Page 195: offers of aid from friends: Burr, pp. 330-31.
letter to Billings: Jan. 12, 1904, N. Y. Public Library.

Page 196: on Saint Gaudens: *Autobiography*, quoted Burr, p.
260.

Page 197: Letters to Thomas Lounsbury: Mar. 4 and Mar. 29,
1904, and May 3, 1906. Yale Library.
Letter to Norton: Jan. 1906. Houghton Library.

Page 198: "200 M.D.'s . . .": *Diary*, Mar. 29, 1904.
Carnegie gift: *ibid.*, Nov. 6 and 7, 1906.

Page 198: "Thus ends my 7 year struggle": Jan. 28, 1910.
Association with Earl Grey: Mitchell-Grey letters,
N. Y. Public Library.

Page 199: Mrs. Mitchell writes speech: *Diary*, Jan. 31, 1905.
Presentation speech: Burr, p. 328.
Asks advice of John Hay: S.W.M. to J.H., Feb. 17,
1905. N. Y. Public Library.
Choice between Erlich and Mitchell: Cushing, II,
p. 128.

Page 201: Another interesting paper from 1909 is Mitchell's
"Motor Ataxy from Emotion," *The Journal of Nervous and Mental Diseases*, Vol. 36, No. 5 (May, 1909).
It describes nervous reactions in soldiers as related by
officers. Some of these are like those in *Roland Blake*.
Then there is the case of a man who could not sign
a hotel register in the presence of others.
Part of this paper is undoubtedly autobiographical in
the statement: "As everyone knows, the preëxistence
of a doubt as to a man's ability to do this or that may
seriously affect results. This is seen in old age when a
man, aware of his tremulous hand, becomes disturbingly self-conscious if overlooked by others and has
then an increase of tremor, or perhaps something
more positive, like the ataxic condition I have described."
Tucker comes to Philadelphia: *Diary*, May 1, 1902
and Tucker, p. 48.

Page 202: E. B. Ulrich: interview.

Page 203: Elihu Root: Burr, p. 334.
Dr. William B. Cadwalader: interview.
Dr. S. Weir Newmayer: interview.
Letter to Osler: Cushing, I, 651-52.
Friendship with Norton: S.W.M. to Miss Norton,
Dec. 28, 1908. Houghton Library.
death of the two Mrs. Wisters: Burr, p. 283.

Page 205: letter from Billings: Feb. 14, 1904. Trent Collection.
"I have known two great men": Garrison, *Billings*,
pp. 292-93.
loath to leave Bar Harbor: S.W.M. to J.S.B., Sept. 14
and Oct. 9, 1908. Trent Collection.

Page 206: Comparison of S.W.M. and J.K.M.: Mary Reed Huesman, "Son and Father," ms Family papers.
"This rush of work . . .": *Diary*, Apr. 13, 1907.
visit to Bryn Mawr: *Autobiography*. Two years before he had found ironic amusement in Miss Thomas' statement that Bryn Mawr girls produced one and 6/10 babies per marriage. *Diary*, Oct. 17, 1907.

Page 207: Trip to Harrisburg: *ibid.*, Mar. 24, 1909.

IX. Coda

Page 208: "If labor was a curse to Adam . . .": Burr, p. 349.
speaks to regiment: *ibid.*, p. 350.

Page 209: visit to Washington: *Autobiography*.
at the Orthopaedic: Tom Bentley Throckmorton, "Silas Weir Mitchell," Reprinted from *The Journal of the Iowa State Medical Society*, Feb. 1931.

Page 211: "Every green thing I see . . .": Burr, p. 247.
description of Maine forest: *John Sherwood*, pp. 190-91.

Page 214: "My publishers warned me . . .": S.W.M. to Katharine Hunt, Sept. 27, 1911. Fry Collection.
questions about Harvey: S.W.M. to Osler, Feb. 8, 1910. Trent Collection.
complains about reporter: Burr, p. 372.

Page 215: on Johns Hopkins: S.W.M. to Osler, Dec. 2, 1910. Trent Collection.
"This would be the final triumph . . .": Cushing, II, 258 (Original in Trent Collection).
praises work of Reichert: S.W.M. to J.S.B., Nov. 25, 1910. N. Y. Public Library.
discussion of Jakes: Burr, p. 355.

Page 216: experiments with odors: S.W.M. to Osler, Dec. 6, 1910. Trent Collection.
"I want the House of Lords preserved": Cushing, II, 257-58.

Page 217: "Tell your son . . .": *ibid.*, II, 278.
Page 218: recreation at resort: S.W.M. to Osler, Aug. 3, 1911. Trent Collection.
Dr. Thayer: Burr, p. 384.
depression of spirits, *ibid.*, p. 351.
"It is an abominable thing . . .": Cushing, II, 305.

270 S. WEIR MITCHELL

Page 218: Refuses degree twice: S.W.M. to Osler, Nov. 29,
1911. Trent Collection.
"The terrapins used to wallow . . .": Burr, pp. 351-52.
corrects ms during "nap": William B. Cadwalader, interview.

Page 219: "this last loss . . .": Cushing, II, 362.

Page 220: Osler finds Mitchell in good form: *loc. cit.*
"I was afraid of death . . .": S.W.M. to Mrs. Mason,
May 25, 1912. Family papers.
Begins novel laid aside in 1866: S.W.M. to Howells,
Feb. 2, 1911. University of Pennsylvania.
letters to Century Co.: N. Y. Public Library.

Page 221: spends day at Gettysburg: S.W.M. to Mrs. Mason,
Mar. 25, 1912. Family papers.

Page 223: "The mind is something more than grey matter . . .":
S.W.M. to Osler (n.d.), Copy of letter about Osler's
"Science and Immortality." Typed with emen-
dations in Mitchell's handwriting. College of Physicians Library.
The letter is an unusually frank statement of Mitchell's religious beliefs, e.g.:
". . . I have felt of late years prepared to struggle
successfully with beliefs which were inculcated in
my childhood and which for a long while troubled
me with increasing doubt.
". . . if anything be clear in this world . . . it is that
man is gradually rising in the scale of mental power,
and I think, of general goodness & altruism."
Mitchell expresses a belief that God has revealed
himself through Gautama, Mohammed, and Christ.
Dr. Solis-Cohen: Max L. Margolis to Dr. Solis-Cohen,
Nov. 19, 1913. Trent Collection.

Page 224: taking veronal: S.W.M. to Howells, Nov. 26, 1913.
University of Pennsylvania.
imagines himself at Gettysburg: Repplier, *Agnes
Irwin*, p. 114.

X. *The Man*

Page 225: Braithwaite: W. S. Braithwaite, Review of *Westways*
in *Boston Transcript*, Sept. 10, 1913.

Cf. Griffin Mace (*Bookman*, 38:301, Nov. 1913) "Westways contains a sustained freshness and virility as remarkable as it is persistent."

Page 226: Keen's statement: W. W. Keen, "*Personal Recollections*," p. 647.

Fulton: John F. Fulton, Introduction to *Reflex Paralysis*, New Haven, 1941.

Page 227: Lewis: Nolan D. Lewis, *A Short History of Psychiatric Achievement*, New York, 1941, p. 189.

Carlson: A. J. Carlson "Silas Weir Mitchell," *Science*, Vol. 87, No. 2265 (May 27, 1938), p. 475.

Ingersoll: "Dr. Ingersoll was the first American physician to my knowledge who stressed the sexual factors in neurosis." A. A. Brill, "An American Precursor of Freud," *Bul. N. Y. Acdy. of Med.* XVI (1940), p. 631, quoted by Henry A. Bunker. "Psychoanalytic Literature," *One Hundred Years of American Psychiatry*, New York, 1944, p. 214.

O. W. Holmes also could be considered a pioneer in the main stream of psychoanalytic thinking. Cf. C. P. Oberndorf: "Oliver Wendell Holmes a Precursor of Freud," *Bulletin of the New York Academy of Medicine*, second series, Vol. 17, No. 5, pp. 327-36 (May 1941).

Playfair: In an article in the *Lancet*, Jan. 7, 1888, W. S. Playfair says he introduced the treatment six years before. Cf. also *Fat and Blood*, p. 10.

Page 228: Freud's use of rest treatment: Freud's statement in 1895 in Joseph Bruer and Sigmund Freud, *Studies in Hysteria* (trans. A. A. Brill) *Nervous and Mental Disease Monograph Series*, New York, 1936.

"A woman of thirty-three . . .": *Fat and Blood*, pp. 144-49.

Mother protests: "Obituary, Silas Weir Mitchell, M.D., LL.D.," *British Medical Journal*, Vol. I, 1914. (Jan. 10, 1914), p. 121.

S. W. M. takes psychiatry out of madhouse: ". . . it was the neurologists who . . . first concerned themselves, here as abroad, with the ambulatory sufferer from mental or emotional disorder—who first recognized and dealt with, as mentally ill, patients other than those committed or commitable to public institutions." H. A. Bunker, *op. cit.* pp. 495-96.

Certainly Mitchell's work contradicts Zilboorg's statement: "Before the advent of psychoanalysis, neuroses were neglected in America as much as in Europe." G. Zilboorg and G. W. Henry: *A History of Medical Psychiatry,* New York, 1941, p. 506.

Page 229: "no more psychic origin than a colic": S. W. M. "The Treatment by Rest, Seclusion, etc., in Relation to Psychotherapy," Paper read before the American Neurological Association, Philadelphia, May 21, 1908. ". . . for all the new methods in this direction 'psychopathic analysis' I have hearty intellectual welcome and an open mind. I most gladly read the elaborate and novel studies in psychologic diagnosis, the laboratory aids, the association tests, the mind probing examinations. They are interesting and even fascinating, although at times men do seem to me to reach by wandering ways facts of individual history more simply to be discovered by less cumbersome methods." *ibid.,* p. 12.

Mitchell's own methods of minute observation and intuition often baffled his colleagues. Thus:

"He taught me the important art of elucidating the case histories of patients; the importance of little hints which were often the insignificant out-croppings of a richer vein of facts; the importance and methods of cross-examination to ferret out the truth and above all, the ability to interpret these assembled facts in making a diagnosis.

"He had a wonderful faculty of correlating widely separated facts and experiences, often, it might be, years apart. To him one plus one did not make two, but resulted in three—a *tertiam quid*—a new factor inference.

"Never have I known so original, suggestive, and fertile a mind."

W. W. Keen *Memorial Addresses,* pp. 15-17.

hypnotism: John Kearsley Mitchell, "An Essay upon

Animal Magnetism or Vital Induction," in *Five Essays by John Kearsley Mitchell, M.D.*, ed. by S. Weir Mitchell, Philadelphia, 1859, esp. p. 271.

Many of Dr. J. K. Mitchell's findings are in accord with those of Estabrooks ninety years later. Cf. C. H. Estabrooks, *Hypnotism*, New York, 1945.

Among other things, the elder Mitchell stated, "Mesmerism may, for the above reasons, be employed to relieve temporarily affections of a nervous character, when the usual means fail." p. 271.

Through his experiments he discovered that *"tact and sense of pain are independent faculties and are therefore probably sustained by separate nerves."* p. 181.

Page 229: control of neurotic symptoms: S.W.M. "True and False Palsies of Hysterics," *The Medical News and Abstract*, Feb. 1880, p. 71.

Page 230: Park Guard: S.W.M. ms *Diary*, Jan. 29, 1908.

Page 231: "symptoms of a deeper cause": Guy Hinsdale, "Recollections of Weir Mitchell," *The General Magazine and Historical Chronicle*, Uni. of Pa., Vol. L, No. 4 (Summer 1948), p. 253.

treatment of epileptics: Hinsdale, p. 253.

Page 232: DeSchweinitz anecdote: Burr, p. 180.

lack of religious doubts: Talcott Williams, "Memorial Address."

Page 236: None dare tell all his life: ms *Diary*, Nov. 6, 1904.

Page 237: "Ah dear lady," *ibid.*, Apr. 8, 1900.

Sarah Butler Wister: letter to S.W.M. (n. d.) Family papers.

". . . can hardly see to write": Sarah Butler Wister to S.W.M., Feb. 24, 1898. Family papers.

". . . even of the many I love": S.W.M. to S.B.W., Sunday 23, 1889. Family papers.

Page 238: youth in imagination: *Diary*, Dec. 15, 1908.

three or four distinct people: *ibid.*, Jan. 9, 1909.

Page 239: allowance to grandson: Marion Lea Mitchell to S.W.M., June 28, 1908. Family papers.

obligations: *Diary*, Apr. 11, 1907.

Page 240: risqué play: *ibid.*, Mar. 31, 1894.

Page 241:   *Vanity Fair:* Letter to Mrs. Mason, Sept. 10, 1908.
finishes *Hugh Wynne, Diary,* Sept. 6, 1895.
"joy of this week": *ibid.,* Oct. 7, 1895.
"perpetual incense": S.B.W. to S.W.M., June 19,
1903. Family papers.
visit to Charcot: (It was under Charcot that Freud
studied.) Tom Bentley Throckmorton, "Silas Weir
Mitchell." *Journal of the Iowa State Medical Society,*
Feb. 1931. Reprint, p. 9. Date of meeting: S.W.M.
to Lizzie, August 7, 1873. Family papers.

Index

James, Henry, 88-89, 155, 170, 172-73, 232-34
James, William, 155-56
Jefferson Medical College, 2, 18, 35, 59-60, 215
Jenner, William, 23
John Sherwood, Ironmaster (1911), 52, 211-14
Johns Hopkins University, The, 60, 89, 118, 218

Keen, W. W., 2, 44-45, 48-52, 62, 64, 78, 81, 85, 176, 226, 242, n. 272
Kemble, Fanny, 72-73
Kipling, Rudyard, 167
Koch, Robert, 125, 226

Lea, Henry Charles, 14, 118-20, 146, 203
Leidy, Joseph, 91, 110, 112, 119
Lewis, Morris, 77
Little More Burgundy, A, 144
Lounsbury, Thomas R., 56, 197
Lowell, James Russell, 40, 122-23, 157, 217

McKinley, William, 167
Madeira Party, A (1895), 126, 132-33, 261
Mason, Mrs. Amelia G., 135-36, 161, 167, 178, 220
Matthews, Brander, 155
Meigs, Dr. Charles, 3, n. 245
Meredith, George, 40, 99-100
Mills, Charles K., 78, 85-87, 117-18, 176, 178
Miser, The (1884), 108
Mitchell, Edward (Ned), 8, 47, 55, 108-9

Mitchell, Elizabeth, 6, 22, 27-33, 41-43, 54, 67-69, 135, 158
Mitchell, John Kearsley (father), 2-12, 14, 17-21, 28-32, 34-35, 176-77, 237, n. 273
Mitchell, Mrs. John Kearsley (Sarah Matilda Henry), 4-6, 69
Mitchell, John K. (son), birth, 44; 69-71, 74-76, 77, 115-17, 127, 164, 206, 208, 210, 224
Mitchell, Mrs. John K. (Anne Williams), 127
Mitchell, Langdon, birth, 44; 68, 72, 74, 127, 138, 161, 162, 238-40
Mitchell, Mrs. Langdon (Marion Lea), 137-38, 240
Mitchell, Maria Gouveneur, 152, 158-59, 196
Mitchell, Nathaniel Chapman, 4, 8, 47
Mitchell, Robert Walsh, 8, 41, 43, 55, 68-69
Mitchell, Sarah (Mrs. Neilson), 9, 27-28, 195
Mitchell, Silas Weir, birth, 6; schooling, 12-13; college, 15-17; medical school, 18; study in Paris, 23-29; begins practice, 35 ff.; snake venom, 37-39; marries Mary Elwyn, 41-42; Civil War surgeon, 47 ff.; wife dies, 54; health breaks, 58; rejected as professor, 58-59; begins writing, 61-62; Europe, 70-72; marries Mary Cadwalader, 74; "Rest Cure," 80-86; novelist, 91 ff.; degree from Univ. of Bologna, 121-

278 INDEX

Mitchell, Silas Weir—(*Cont.*)
23; *Hugh Wynne*, 139-45;
Medico-Psychological Society Address, 147-50; experiments on self, 154-55; daughter dies, 158-59; trip to Egypt, 160-62; aids Noguchi, 163-65; trip to Japan, 166-67; trustee of Carnegie Inst., 174-75; numerous publications, 181-87; bank fails, 193-95; F. R. S., 199; last novel, 220-23; death, 224. Estimate: in medicine, 226-27; in psychiatry, 227-31, n. 272; in literature, 232-34; personality, 235-43; psychoanalytic hypothesis of, n. 266-67; religious views, 235-36, n. 270.
Mitchell, Mrs. S. W. (Mary Elwyn), 41-42
Mitchell, Mrs. S. W. (Mary Cadwalader), 74, 115, 152, 159, 177-78, 196, 199, 224, 236-38
Morehouse, George R., 48-54, 62, 64, 78, 85, 226
"Motor Ataxy from Emotion" (1909), n. 268
Mr. Kris-Kringle (1893), v, 145

Noguchi, Hideyo, 64, 109, 163-65, 203, 215, 243
North of Market Street, 87
Norton, Charles Eliot, 163, 177, 182, 194, 195, 203-4, 217

Ode on a Lycian Tomb (1899), v, 160-63, 177, 224, 232

"On the Cryptogamous Origin of . . . Fevers," 2
One Hundred Years of American Psychiatry, 149, 249, 254, 263
Orthopaedic Hospital, 76-77, 87, 117, 164, 206, 209-11
Osler, Sir William, 2, 19, 22, 46, 77, 81, 91, 112-13, 118, 121, 148, 152, 160, 165-66, 175-76, 199-201, 203-4, 213-15, 217-20, 223, 242-43

Paget, James, 23, 152
Parkman, Francis, 65, 90
Pasteur, Louis, 125, 226
Pearl, The (1906), v, 188-90
Pemberton, 142-43
Pepper, William, 2, 22, 60, 110, 112, 121, 160, 176
Philip Vernon (1895), 145
Playfair, William, 227
Powers, Hiram, 31
Psychiatry, 85-86, 178-81, 227-31, 266, n. 271-72

Quaker Soldier, The, 141-43

Real Estate Trust Co. failure, 193-95, 239
"Recollections of the Civil War" (1905), 47
Red City, The (1907), 190-91, 193, 194
Reflex Paralysis (1864), 50-51, 62, 77, 226
Reichert, Edward, 109, 215
"Relation of Pain to Weather" (1877), 80
Repplier, Agnes, 128